SAINT
JOHN PAUL
THE GREAT

His Five Loves

SAINT
JOHN PAUL
THE GREAT

His   Five   Loves

Totus Tuus
—P R E S S—

JASON EVERT

Foreword by Swiss Guard Mario Enzler

Published by Totus Tuus Press and Lighthouse Catholic Media
PO Box 280021
Lakewood, CO 80228

Distributed by Ignatius Press
Cover design by Devin Schadt
Typesetting by Loyola Dataworks
Printed in the United States of America

ISBN 978-0-9913754-0-0 (hardcover)
ISBN 978-0-9913754-1-7 (paperback)
Library of Congress Control Number: 2013958271

For Mary

CONTENTS

PRONUNCIATION GUIDE

Częstochowa (Chens-toe-HOE-vah)
Deskur (DES-koor)
Dziwisz (JEE-vish)
Kraków (KRA-koov)
Mickiewicz (Meets-kee-YAY-vitch)
Norwid (NOR-vid)
Sapieha (Sah-pee-EH-hah)
Słowacki (Swoe-VATS-kee)
Stanisław (Stah-NEES-wahv)
Tyranowski (Teer-an-OV-ski)
Wadowice (Vahd-oh-VEETS-uh)
Wawel (VAH-vel)
Wojtyła (Voy-TEE-wah)
Wujek (VOO-yek)
Wyszyński (Vih-SHIN-skee)

FOREWORD

Serving John Paul II as a Swiss Guard was such a privilege and a grace that I feel duty-bound to talk about it and share my experiences with others.

The Swiss Guard are a symbol of fidelity in the Vatican. For more than 500 years, the sons of Switzerland have served the Church by protecting the pope in good times and in bad. In honor of the one hundred and fifty Guards who sacrificed their lives protecting Pope Julius II from invading barbarians, this military corps continues the noble service as *Defensores libertatis Ecclesia* [Protectors of the freedom of the Church].

Those of us who had daily contact with Saint John Paul the Great were always struck by the richness of his intuitions, the example of his prayerfulness, and his immense humility. I remember clearly the intensity with which he celebrated the Eucharist and how he remained deeply recollected in prayer at the conclusion of Mass. He had an uncommon ability to speak to people, both privately and to a crowd, with a particular magnetism toward young people, many of whom had declared themselves far from the Church.

One particular image of this great and Holy Father will remain forever impressed in my memory: I opened a side door to make a security check only to find him sitting, already vested for Mass in Saint Peter's, in a small room adjacent to Michelangelo's famous Pietà statue, embracing a large crucifix just as a mother holds her baby, giving and receiving true love.

On another occasion, I was serving at the elevator of the Pontifical Apartment, awaiting the Pope's return from a meeting of the Synod of African Bishops. It was not the first time I had served at that post and I was waiting a bit nervously, since the other times the Holy Father had stopped to exchange a few words with me about the weather or what was being served for lunch. That day was different, though.

He arrived, I brought myself to attention with a military salute, and into the elevator he went without so much as a glance in my direction! I was so disappointed! I tried to console myself by thinking about all the things he must have on his mind. All of a sudden the elevator doors opened and the *Santo Padre* came walking toward me, saying, "The Rosary is my favorite prayer, marvelous in its simplicity and profundity. Take this Rosary, Mario, and make good use of it. *Ciao* and *buon appetito*." It is no surprise that many of the Swiss Guards were drawn to our Lady.

Pope Saint John Paul the Great frequently demonstrated to us Guards his gratitude for our service, and never missed the chance to express that thankfulness, sometimes to the point of joking around with us.

One Wednesday I was guarding the entrance to the Paul VI Audience Hall, patiently awaiting the conclusion of the general audience. The doors opened, I jumped to attention, and ... uuufff ... the Pope's butler elbowed me in the stomach, causing me to double over just as the Holy Father walked by me. The Pope stopped, grabbed my arm, and winked at me, saying, "Mario, there's no need to bow."

For those of us nearest to him, more than by his goodness we were struck by his tenacity. In his early life he pursued his high ideals in times of war while facing risks that might have cost him his life, never turning back in the face of obstacles. So, too, as pope he was truly a Holy Father, always drawing near to people, traveling to the ends of the earth, stretching out his hand to men of every race and religion, proposing political solutions in the name of peace.

An expression I heard many times from John Paul was "be more." What I took from this teaching was the rediscovery of the beauty and power of my own charisms, remembering that no gift given is meant for one's self, but is given for the good of the Church and her mission.

Reading *Saint John Paul the Great: His Five Loves* will not only deepen your appreciation for the successor of Peter, but will leave you with a renewed affection for everything he loved as well. My prayer for you is that you will become a spiritual Swiss Guard and share with me the great mission *Pro Ecclesia et Pontefice*—for the Church and the Pope!

Acriter et Fideliter!
[Courage and Fidelity!]
MARIO ENZLER

INTRODUCTION

The first time I saw Pope Saint John Paul the Great, I was twelve years old and sitting in the upper deck of Sun Devil Stadium (of all places), gazing through binoculars at a miniscule white figure on the stage, seemingly miles away. Thankfully, the organizers at Arizona State University were gracious enough to cover up the images of their mascot, "Sparky the Devil," for the Pope's Mass.

I don't recall what the Holy Father said that evening, but thankfully I was blessed to see him in person on more than twenty other occasions and took advantage of those opportunities to absorb his message. Many of these encounters were at a distance, where I stood in a crowd of hundreds of thousands. Some were closer, attending his Wednesday audiences in Rome or holding his hand briefly as he rolled by in the Popemobile. But as the fifteenth World Youth Day approached for the Jubilee year of 2000, I began praying that I'd have the chance to meet with him in Rome, face-to-face. I knew it was a long shot, considering two million others would be in attendance, making it the largest pilgrimage in the history of Europe.

At the time, I was fresh out of college and working in Southern California, while volunteering for a high school youth group in La Jolla. In preparation for our trip overseas, Bishop Robert Brom of San Diego paid us a visit to offer his blessing. That night, he shared with us a story that demonstrates the greatness of Saint John Paul the Great.

Every four years, bishops make a trip to Rome for their *ad limina* visit to see the pope. Such visits formed a significant part of the Holy Father's work each week, enabling him to feel the pulse of the universal Church. In 1983, after his appointment as bishop of Duluth, Bishop Brom made his first *ad limina* trip to see Pope John Paul II.

During their visit, the Holy Father looked into Brom's face and said, "I think we have met before." Confident that the two had never crossed paths, the bishop assured him it was their first meeting. John Paul insisted, "I believe we have," but Brom was equally sure they had not. Several days later, during the same visit, the Pope's secretary, Monsignor Stanisław Dziwisz, approached Bishop Brom and said, "Don't argue with the Pope, he remembers when he met you." "When?" Brom asked. "In November of 1963 outside the Church of the Gesù in Rome." Brom paused for a moment of reflection and recalled that he was in Rome that year, during the second session of the Second Vatican Council. At the time he was a seminarian at the North American College, while John Paul was the auxiliary bishop of Kraków. One day, Brom and several of his fellow seminarians were exiting the Church of the Gesù as Bishop Wojtyła was entering with a group of Polish seminarians. The two met briefly, and subsequently Brom forgot all about the encounter.

After Brom's memory was refreshed, he asked Monsignor Dziwisz, "How can he do that?," to which Dziwisz explained that for John Paul, to meet another person is to encounter God. Years later, in another *ad limina* visit toward the end of the Pope's life, the Holy Father brought up the subject again, asking "How many times have we met, and when was the first time?" to which Brom responded properly. John Paul slapped the desk and with a smile said, "Finally you remember!"

When Brom shared his story with our youth group, it only deepened my desire to meet the Holy Father. I contacted everyone I knew in Rome, hoping to receive an invitation to the Pope's private Mass, and then flew to Italy, not knowing if anything would materialize. Upon arriving at our hotel on the Via della Conziliazione, the main artery that flows into Saint Peter's Square, I informed the front desk that I was expecting an important call from the Vatican. Several days passed as our group enjoyed the festivities of World Youth Day, but no calls came.

Upon returning to the hotel one afternoon, I received a message to call the Vatican. My heart raced. When the sister answered the phone, she said in a somber voice, "Jason, where were you this morning?" My heart sank. She continued, "It was very difficult to do, but I was able to reserve one spot for you this morning in the Pope's private chapel for Mass. When I called your hotel to invite you, they said they did not know who you were. I'm sorry it didn't work out this time." Fumbling for words, I begged her to see if there was any way she could obtain another invitation. She seemed doubtful, but said I should trust in God.

Meanwhile, World Youth Day had come to a close, and it was time for our youth group to pack up and fly home to the States. More often than not, my stubborn temperament gets me into trouble, but sometimes God works wonders through it. So I decided to let the group leave without me. I wanted to stay in Rome until I received my blessing from the Pope, like Jacob in the book of Genesis refusing to release the angel until he had received his blessing. A day passed, and then on the night before the feast of the Queenship of Mary, I received the invitation to attend "Holy Mass with *Santo Padre*" the next morning at Castel Gandolfo. I hardly slept, and took a taxi early in the morning to the hills outside of Rome, where John Paul spent a portion of his summer.

I entered the courtyard of his summer residence and joined about two hundred Polish pilgrims who had also been invited to celebrate the feast day with the Holy Father. When the Mass concluded, John Paul took a seat off to the side in order to greet the visitors. I stood back watching as the pilgrims approached him in groups of fifty, paused to take photos with him, and moved on. I nudged one of the papal aides, asking if I could meet the Pope one-on-one. In his best English, he answered, "It is no possible."

I had come so far, and yet all my hopes were hanging in the balance. I had used up all my connections to get this far, but there was one left and it happened to be her feast day: the Virgin Mary. So I spoke four words to her in the silence of my heart, from the ancient Marian hymn, *Ave Maris Stella*: "Show thyself a Mother." Within moments, she did. Nearly all the pilgrims left, and the Holy Father remained. An usher gave me the nod, and I approached Saint John Paul the Great and bent down on one knee before him, looking into his bluish-gray eyes and holding his arm. I presented to him a book I had written for young people about chastity, and after blessing it, he reached out and traced the Sign of the Cross upon my forehead, saying, "God bless you." I stood up, embraced him, kissed him, and told him on behalf of the youth, "We love you."

Five years later, I returned to Rome with my wife, Crystalina, this time seeking a blessing for our new baby, John Paul, who was ill. Again I exhausted all my connections: faxing the Pope's secretary, organizing a private meeting with a cardinal, e-mailing an archbishop—but to no avail. A priest friend in Rome comforted me, "Don't worry. Just get there early for his Wednesday audience and sit in the front. The Pope can't resist babies." I did as he said, waking up long before dawn to be first in line, standing in the rain, and taking a seat in the front row when the doors opened.

Thousands of other pilgrims from around the world filed into the hall, and soon the audience began. Trusting in the priest's words, I perched my child upon the railing in front of me, with a less-than-inconspicuous sign under him that read: "My name is John Paul," with a bright red arrow pointing up at the bait. Sure enough, when the audience ended, one of the papal assistants descended from the dais and approached us. Looking at us while gesturing toward the Pope, he said, "*Il bambino e la solo madre.*" I don't know much Italian, but I thought that sounded a lot like "The baby and only the mother." He confirmed my translation, at which point I attempted to explain to him that I was rather close to the two of them, and thought it would probably be best if I accompanied them to meet the pontiff. His answer? "*Il bambino e la solo madre.*" With that, the railing was opened and Crystalina and John Paul were led up the steps to receive the Pope's blessing, just as I had years earlier. As you are about to read, John Paul had a special love for the young, for mothers, and for those who are suffering.

~

Hundreds of books have been written about the Holy Father, examining him from the perspectives of theology, philosophy, and history. In his definitive biography, *Witness to Hope*, he mentioned to George Weigel that many of these attempts have fallen short because "They try to understand me from outside. But I can only be understood from inside." His words are similar to those of the French novelist Arsene Houssaye, who wrote, "Tell me what you love, and I will tell you who you are." Although there are countless ways to study Saint John Paul the Great, the most direct route is by entering the man's heart. After all, love is the ultimate measure of any person. One week before his election to the papacy, he affirmed this, saying, "And our Lord, conversing with Peter at the beginning of the first pontificate asked about nothing except love: 'Do you love me?' This is the only question through which we are to examine every pontificate and every human life."

Therefore, the aim of this work is to paint a portrait of the Holy Father by examining his five loves. Because of the size of his heart, I will grant that it's impossible to place a finite number on such things. After all, he surely would have counted Poland, unborn children, his Jewish friends, and many others among his loves. But although the present list of five is limited and subjective, it's not arbitrary.

Over the past twenty years, I have studied closely the thought and mission of the late Holy Father. During my travels to speak to more than a million Catholics on six continents, I have had many conversations with those who knew him well. During these discussions, I heard countless remarkable stories about him that have never been published. I often thought, "For the sake of the Church, these need to be printed some day," but the years drew on and the project remained only a hope. With the announcement of the Holy Father's canonization in April 2014, I knew it was time.

It is likely that John Paul was seen by more people than anyone in human history. As a result, I knew there would be no shortage of stories to tell. The challenge was sorting fact from fiction and taking measures to weed out the papal urban legends, of which there are plenty. I began hunting down the primary sources of the stories I had heard over the years and conducting interviews with cardinals, bishops, and priests, as well as with those who had studied under the Pope or camped with him during his days in Poland. I devoured every papal biography I could find, reading tens of thousands of pages. Mining through a mountain of papal resources, I looked for the gems. This book is a collection of those jewels, presented as a treasure chest of the saint's life.

By no means is this book intended to be an exhaustive summary. What was true of Christ could just as well have been said about his vicar: that there were many other things that he did, and "were every one of them to be written, I suppose that the world itself could not contain the books that would be written" (Jn 21:25).

Unfortunately, there are extraordinary stories I did not include in the book because I was unable to locate the primary sources to substantiate them. Regardless of how inspiring they may have been, I knew it wouldn't bring any honor to John Paul to disseminate legends about him. At the beginning of his book *Saints Are Not Sad*, Frank Sheed noted, "many a saint has suffered more from his biographer than from his persecutors. The fathers stone the prophets, and the sons build the monuments: and often the monuments ought to be stoned too." To erect a "monument" worthy of Saint John Paul the Great, I have made every effort to verify the details that are presented in the following pages. I owe a special debt of thanks to

George Weigel for fact-checking my work and offering several helpful corrections and recommendations.

The first part of this book presents a succinct biography of the man Karol Wojtyła. Before delving into his five loves, it is imperative to understand the furnace of human suffering in which he was forged. After all, one cannot understand his love for life without knowing how deeply he had been submerged into the culture of death. The second part of this book is its heart, examining what I believe to be the five greatest loves of the Holy Father: young people, human love, the Blessed Sacrament, the Virgin Mary, and the Cross. My prayer is not merely that you will grow in appreciation for this great saint by reflecting upon what captivated him, but that similar loves will be enkindled within your own heart.

—Jason Evert

PART I

FROM WADOWICE
TO THE VATICAN

1

LOLEK

On the evening of May 18, 1920, parishioners of the Church of the Presentation of the Blessed Virgin Mary gathered to sing evening prayer. Across the street, thirty-six-year-old Emilia Wojtyła was in labor at home and noticed the sound of hymns in honor of the Virgin Mary emanating from the church. She asked her midwife to open the window in order for the songs to be heard. Amidst the sacred music, she delivered a son, Karol Józef.

Fittingly, the future pope lived on Koscielna [Church] Street, in the small industrial town of Wadowice, thirty miles from Kraków. Karol and his older brother, Edmund, lived with their parents in a humble apartment with two bedrooms and a kitchen that the family rented from a Jewish man who owned the glassware store downstairs. As the years passed, he likely would often have heard the sound of Karol and his father, Karol, Sr., playing indoor soccer with an improvised ball made of rags tied together.

Karol, or "Lolek," as his friends called him, was an excellent student and attended a public elementary school where at least a third of his classmates were Jewish. Although anti-Semitism had infected much of Poland, Karol seemed immune to the vice. During soccer games, it was easiest to divide the teams between Catholics and Jews, but Karol had no qualms about being the goalkeeper for the Jews when they needed an extra teammate. The young woman who lived next door to him recalled, "There was only one family who never showed any racial hostility toward us, and that was Lolek and his dad."

Because Emilia's health had been poor for years, Karol, Sr., whose health was also in decline, requested an early retirement from the military in order to remain home to care for her. The family lived on his modest pension and Emilia's occasional work as a seamstress. When Karol was only eight years old, he returned from school one afternoon and learned that his mother had passed away (from kidney failure and heart disease). A neighbor wrapped him in her arms in an attempt to console him, telling the young child that his mother was now in heaven.

The day after her funeral, Karol, Sr., took his two sons on a pilgrimage to a vast outdoor shrine, reminding them that the Virgin Mary would look after them until the day they could be reunited with their mother in heaven. John Paul recalled how his father found solace in God:

> After my mother's death, his life became one of constant prayer. Sometimes I would wake up during the night and find my father on his knees, just as I would always see him kneeling in the parish church. We never spoke about a vocation to the priesthood, but *his example was in a way my first seminary*, a kind of domestic seminary.

Following the example of his father, Karol found consolation in prayer. But he also found solace in his friendship with his brother. Although Edmund was fourteen years older than Karol, the two were very close. Papal biographers Carl Bernstein and Marco Politi wrote:

The two of them could be seen dribbling a soccer ball between them through the streets of the town in the summer, or he would carry Lolek on his shoulders through the fields by the Skawa River. He took Karol on his first long hikes in the mountains, sharing his passion for nature and outdoor exercise; he taught him to ski. For Lolek, Mundek [Edmund] was a refuge from depression.

This refuge wasn't to last long, because three years after his mother's passing, tragedy again struck the Wojtyła family. At the age of twenty-six, Edmund, a doctor at a nearby hospital, contracted scarlet fever from a sick young woman under his care. His father and brother rushed to the hospital when he fell ill, but because his fatal condition was so contagious, he was quarantined and they were forced to remain outside his area while he passed away. They had no choice but to accept what Edmund had said on an earlier date, when he was in perfect health: "True prayer is waiting for God to come when and how He wants to."

Karol often told his friends how deeply he was impacted by the image of his father standing by Edmund's coffin, repeating, "Thy will be done!" Karol remarked, "The violence of the blows which had struck him had opened up immense spiritual depths in him; his grief found its outlet in prayer."

Karol, Sr., and his eleven-year-old son were now alone. To cope with the emptiness of their apartment, they pushed their beds together and slept in the same room. Every morning, the two attended Mass before school, and again prayed together in the evening, often reading the Bible. Despite the weight of his personal suffering, Karol excelled in grammar school, became the valedictorian of his high school, and hoped to attend the Jagiellonian University in Kraków to study Polish language and literature. His father knew his son had a bright academic future, and so they moved to the larger city and took up residence in the basement of a home owned by Emilia's two sisters.

Soon after the Wojtyłas moved to Kraków, a cloistered nun passed away at a nearby convent. Her name was Maria Faustina Kowalska. While Lolek was growing up in Wadowice, she had begun receiving visions and messages from Jesus. In one, he appeared with his hands held out toward mankind's suffering, with red and white rays emanating from his heart, representing the blood and water that flowed from his heart as he hung upon the cross. While Karol was in high school, she also received a prayer known as the Chaplet of Divine Mercy. Then, a year before she died in 1938, she wrote in her *Diary*, "As I was praying for Poland, I heard the words: I bear a special love for Poland, and if she will be obedient to My will, I will exalt her in might and holiness. From her will come forth the spark that will prepare the world for My final coming."

Unaware of the private revelations unfolding nearby, Karol thrived in Kraków during his first year of college and participated in a number of theatrical productions. He had discovered theater at the age of fourteen, and became a talented poet, actor, and director. Those who knew him were impressed not only by his dramatic abilities, but also by his staggering intellect. On one occasion, one of his fellow cast members in a play became unavailable forty-eight hours before the production was to begin. The cast feared that the show would need to be canceled as a result. But Karol volunteered to play both roles, as he had already memorized everyone's lines during rehearsals.

The Nazi Invasion

On the morning of September 1, 1939, one could hear the thud of German warplanes dropping bombs on railroad yards and industrial targets around Kraków. Karol was nineteen years old and had finished only one year of studies at the university. Because it was the first Friday of the month, he went to the historic Wawel Cathedral for confession and Mass, as usual. The church was a monument of Polish patriotism, literature, and religion, housing the tombs of kings, saints, poets, and other leaders who had shaped the nation. As a symbol of the ultimate victory of good over evil, the bells of the cathedral were forged from cannons that had been captured by a Polish king during a battle four hundred years earlier.

When Karol arrived, the church was empty with the exception of one priest. Many years later, as pope, he recalled, "I would serve the Mass during the bombardments, between the bursts of antiaircraft artillery." The priest also remembered standing "at the altar of Christ Crucified, amid the howl of sirens and the blasts of explosions." Upon exiting the cathedral, Karol witnessed the bombs falling from the sky and realized how close the shells were landing. He rushed past burning buildings to his basement apartment at 10 Tyniecka Street, where he and his father embraced one another as their radio blared Nazi propaganda about the impending German invasion from the west.

A university classmate appeared at their door, begging Karol to help him pull a cart with his family's belongings as they attempted to escape to the east. A Polish journalist reported, "They hadn't gone half a mile when a German fighter plane broke away from the trail of the bombers, turned back, and began to machine-gun everything that moved in the streets. The two boys managed to take refuge in a large building, but they were frightened to death." Karol returned to his father, and the two decided to flee on foot, since railways would be too dangerous, as the trains were easy targets for the Nazi planes.

Meanwhile, far north of Kraków, a Polish officer peered through his binoculars as a teacher ushered a group of small children into the woods for shelter. "Suddenly, there was the roar of an aeroplane," the officer later wrote. "The pilot circled round, descending to a height of fifty metres. As he dropped his bombs and fired his machine guns, the children scattered like sparrows. The aeroplane disappeared as quickly as it had come, but on the field some crumpled and lifeless bundles of bright clothing remained. The nature of the new war was already clear."

In Kraków, the Wojtyłas joined a mass exodus of Poles, who were towing as many belongings as they could. Soon, the crowds heard the faint sound of *Stukas* (German dive-bombers) approaching, and Karol dragged his sixty-year-old father against the side of a cliff to shield and rescue him. When the explosions ended and the smoke cleared, the carnage was unspeakable. Those who were left had no choice but to press on, after burying what bodies they could. For part of the journey, the father and son were able to hitch a ride on a platform truck; they spent the nights sleeping in fields and farmhouses. By the end of the expedition, the refugees had trekked one hundred and twenty miles.

An echo of these personal experiences can be heard in John Paul's papal teachings decades later. In his message for a World Day of Prayer for Peace, he spoke about how war does not solve social or political problems, but causes more of them and creates poverty. He added, "Young people see their hopes for the future shattered . . . [victims of war] are forced to flee and become refugees who have no possessions beyond what they can carry with them."

Soon after the Germans invaded Poland from the west, Russia dispatched troops from the east. Stalin didn't trust the Nazis, and wanted to keep the Germans away from his border. Upon learning of the impending Soviet invasion, and without anywhere to hide, the exhausted pair of refugees traveled back to Kraków, hoping to find lodging and safety. Thankfully, their apartment had not been destroyed, and so father and son moved back into the home. However, everything outside had changed. German military leaders ran the city, Nazi flags were unfurled, curfews were enforced, the cathedral was closed, and all Poles were declared slaves of the German Reich. In an effort to wipe away any trace of Polish culture, schools were locked and libraries were destroyed. In Warsaw, German troops shot children for target practice if any of them attempted to sneak out at night in search of food. Entire families were murdered, and the bodies of some parents and children were arranged in the form of swastikas.

In order to prevent them from influencing the masses, German authorities gathered together all the professors at the Jagiellonian University, supposedly to discuss future education programs, then deported approximately one hundred and eighty of them to a concentration camp. Polish men were tolerated as long as they could be enslaved as workers, while many of the women were used in brothels for the German officers. However, the Reich saw no use for the Jews, gathering them into ghettos, starving them to death, and exterminating them en masse. One of Karol's friends was engaged to a young woman who had taken a job in a Nazi medical research institute searching for new vaccines. He told Karol that the Germans "hire young girls to breed lice. They put little cages on the girls' thighs, and the lice drink the blood." In return for feeding their blood to the lice, the girls were given a triple ration of food.

Adolf Hitler's secretary dutifully recorded the instructions the Führer gave to Hans Frank, the governor general of Poland: "The Poles are especially born for low labor. There can be no question of improvement for them. It is necessary to keep the standard of life low in Poland and it must not be permitted to rise." As for the priests, "they will preach what we want them to preach. If any priest acts differently, we shall make short work of him. The task of the priest is to keep the Poles quiet, stupid, and dull-witted." He added, "The Slavs are to work for us. In so far as we don't need them, they may die. . . . The fertility of the Slavs is undesirable. They may use contraceptives or practice abortion—the more the better. Education is dangerous. It is enough if they can count up to 100 . . . Every educated person is a future enemy."

For this reason, Hitler requested that all men capable of leadership in Poland be "liquidated." Thanks to the providence of God, they missed one.

Labor of Love

At four o'clock each morning, Karol rose to stand in line in the frigid temperatures to purchase a small portion of black bread. Because the Nazis did not honor the full benefits paid to Polish army veterans, the Wojtyłas received only a portion of Karol, Sr.'s usual pension. With the university closed and Karol's life upended, he found a job as a store messenger so he could care for his aging father. But to avoid being killed or deported to Germany to perform forced labor, he needed an official "work card" to prove he was "socially useful," meaning that he was useful to the war effort. Therefore, he began working at a quarry with some of his university classmates. Later, in 1942, the card would save his life when the Gestapo arrested him with a number of other men at a café in downtown Kraków. Most of the others were sent to the Auschwitz concentration camp, where twenty-five of them were executed by a firing squad at the "Wall of Death." Karol, however, was released because of his work card.

His worksite was two miles from home, and he made the half-hour trek each morning in his wooden shoes. The temperature during the bitter Polish winters sometimes dropped to 30 degrees below zero Celsius, making it necessary for Karol to coat his face with petroleum jelly in order to avoid suffering frostbite while working outside for eight hours at a time. At the job, he descended into the 60- to 90-foot hole to begin his shift laying rails and hauling crushed limestone. In his poem "The Quarry," he recalled his calloused and split-open hands, "drooping with the hammer's weight," "boots ankle deep in mud," and his tired eyes.

Because of the constant use of explosives, the work was dangerous. In the same poem, he recounted how he witnessed the death of a coworker from a dynamite blast:

> They laid him down, his back on a sheet of gravel.
> The wife came, worn out with worry; his son returned
>   from school. . . .
> The stones on the move again: a wagon bruising the
>   flowers.
> Again the electric current cuts deep into the walls.

But the man has taken with him the world's inner
   structure,
where the greater the anger, the higher the explosion
   of love.

This last sentence echoes a profound theme referenced
earlier in the poem, where Wojtyła declared, "Look, how
love feeds on this well-grounded anger." In the midst of
the hardship, sorrow, and injustice, he found the strength
to transform his righteous rage into a fiery, divine love.
Lest one assume that saints have a superhuman capacity
to absorb suffering, one must keep in mind that this
transformation was a long process for him. In fact, only
three months after the Nazi invasion, Karol told a friend
that he was keeping busy with his studies, his work, and
his prayer, but admitted, "At times I feel great oppression,
depression, despair, evil. At other times, as if I were seeing
the dawn, the aurora, a great light."

In the evenings, Lolek continued his literature studies in
secret, in the living rooms of professors who were willing to
defy the Nazis. Because the supervisors at the quarry were
Poles, and were therefore empathetic, the students were
spared from the heaviest work. In the spring, Karol was
reassigned to become an assistant to the rock blaster. His
new job was to place the cartridges and fuses in position,
and then hurry to a safe location. A coworker recalled,
"After a while, an explosion would rip large blocks away
from the rock face. When the dust settled, a rhythmic
sound of hammers could be heard again."

The man who supervised the detonations occasionally
remarked, "Karol, you should be a priest. You have a good
voice and will sing well." At the time, he was a devout
young man, but the priesthood wasn't on his mind. In

fact, he later told a French historian that while he was in high school, he "rather decisively rejected" the idea. Not only did he dismiss the vocational suggestion, it's likely that he didn't concur with the assessment of his singing abilities either. Later on, as pope, John Paul was speaking about the importance of music and mentioned Saint Augustine's quote that he who sings prays twice. A friend asked him, "Were you a good singer, Holy Father?" John Paul answered, "When *I* sang, it was more like I was praying only *once*."

Although Karol wasn't interested in joining the seminary, his spiritual life was reaching new depths. He often attended Mass at Saint Stanisław Kostka Church, and it was there that he met Jan Tyranowski, a layman gifted with a rich and mystical prayer life. He was not a gifted teacher or speaker, but he spent about four hours each morning in meditation. As a result, Wojtyła said he was able to "accomplish everything through the kind of gravity that his internal life possessed." His apostolate was what every ministry ought to be: an extension of one's contemplation. Jan often told Karol of a maxim he'd heard in a priest's homily at his parish: "It's not difficult to be a saint."

Jan was an unmarried tailor and the founder of a prayer group called the Living Rosary. Each young member of his prayer group was entrusted to pray a mystery of the Rosary daily, and was committed to spiritual reading and other prayers. Karol joined the group, and Tyranowski soon introduced him to the writings of the Carmelite mystics Saint John of the Cross and Saint Teresa of Avila. A priest in Wadowice had already introduced Karol to Carmelite spirituality, but Tyranowski's companionship and example drew him deeper into the writings of these spiritual giants. It was also Tyranowski who first recommended that Karol read Saint Louis de Montfort's spiritual classic, *True Devotion to Mary*, which Karol later described as "a decisive turning-point in my life."

Karol wasn't the only future Polish saint that God was forging during the Nazi occupation. In February 1941, a Franciscan priest named Maximilian Kolbe was arrested at his friary, imprisoned, and then transferred to Auschwitz. Five months later, when a fellow prisoner escaped from his barracks, the SS guards assembled the prisoners and selected ten to be executed in a starvation bunker. When Francis Gajowniczek was selected, he cried out in anguish for the wife and children he would leave behind. Upon hearing his distress, Father Kolbe stepped forward and asked the Nazi guard if he could take the man's place. The request was accepted, and Father Kolbe spent the next two weeks praying with and encouraging his fellow inmates as each of them died, before he was executed with three others by an injection of carbolic acid. His body was incinerated the next day, on the feast of Mary's Assumption into heaven. In October 1982, Pope John Paul II canonized him a saint, declaring him to be a "martyr of love."

Like Saint Maximilian Kolbe, Karol Wojtyła's interior life sustained him in hope through the dark night of the Nazi occupation. When the Germans arrested Kolbe on February 17, it was the last time he would ever see the Franciscan brothers and fathers who had become his family. The very next day, Wojtyła was also orphaned. After returning home from another long day of work at the quarry, he walked into his father's room to bring him medicine, noticed that he was resting in an unusual posture, and attempted to lift him. When he felt his father's cold hands, Karol held his dead body and wept.

His whole family was now gone, and he was tormented by the fact that he was absent at the moment each of them had died. After running to fetch a priest to give his father the last rites, he spent the night in prayer by the bedside, watching over the body of his father and saying to friends, "I'm all alone. . . . At twenty I've already lost all the people I've loved!" Karol had also had a sister, but one he never knew; Olga died as an infant before he was born. Three of his four grandparents had also passed away before he was born, and his only remaining grandparent died when Karol was only three. His friends, classmates, and priests were also disappearing because of the war, suffering execution or imprisonment in concentration camps. One can only imagine the depth of loneliness that engulfed him.

After the death of Karol, Sr., Lolek moved in with another family, who recalled, "He went to Mass every day, he prayed a lot in his room, and he lay prostrate." What he wrote about his own father also became true for him: the pain he encountered "had opened up immense spiritual depths in him." Whereas the faith of some might have drowned under such waves of unrelenting suffering, Karol's aloneness became a means to his holiness.

In October 1942, after a year of working in the quarry, Karol was transferred to the Solvay chemical plant. He worked in the boiler system of the water purification department, often carrying buckets of lime or other chemicals on a yoke. His coworkers recalled how he knelt in the middle of the workplace each day to pray the Angelus. He enjoyed the night shift the most because it afforded him a greater window of silence, allowing him more time for reading or for praying the Liturgy of the Hours on his knees. One coworker recalled, "In the boiler room there were stairs leading up to the tanks; there amid the posts and pipes was a good spot for praying. It was the spot in the corner under the tank. Nobody bothered him there." While some coworkers had respect for his piety, others did not. One recounted, "There were those who would pelt him during his prayers with oakum or other jetsam, trying to interrupt him."

After his night shifts, he'd walk in denim overalls and wooden shoes on his bare feet to an early morning Mass in order to seek God's help to carry on another day. Because weekends were not times of rest, he likely worked for hundreds of consecutive days without interruption. Sometimes he surrendered what little rest he had: When a coworker's wife delivered a baby, he volunteered to take over the man's night shift even though he had already worked all day. He continued doing this so that the husband could be home with the mother and child until the wife regained her strength. This experience of manual labor led him to remark many years later, "I was a laborer for 4 years, and for me those 4 years of work are worth more than two doctorate degrees!"

Because his factory was located only a few hundred yards away from the monastery of Łagiewniki, he often visited the convent chapel and the grave of Sister Faustina, whose popularity had grown as her message of Divine Mercy began to spread. However, because of a poor translation of her *Diary*, the book was placed on the Church's Index of Forbidden Books in 1959, and the ban was not lifted for nearly twenty years. Once the faulty translation issues were resolved, the ban was lifted, and within six months Karol Wojtyła was elected pope.

In 1981, while speaking in Italy, he remarked about her message of Divine Mercy, "Right from the beginning of my ministry in Saint Peter's See in Rome I consider this message my special task. Providence has assigned it to me in the present situation of man, the Church and the world." During a visit to Poland in 1997, he proclaimed:

There is nothing that man needs more than Divine Mercy. . . . And it is a message that is clear and understandable for everyone. Anyone can come here, look at this image of the merciful Jesus, his heart radiating grace, and hear in the depths of his own soul what Blessed Faustina heard: "Fear nothing; I am with you always." And if this person responds with a sincere heart: "Jesus, I trust in you," he will find comfort in all his anxieties and fears. . . . On the threshold of the third millennium I come to entrust to him once more my Petrine ministry: "Jesus, I trust in you!" . . . The message of Divine Mercy has always been near and dear to me. It was an inexhaustible source of hope for the Polish people during World War II.

Three years after giving this message, Pope John Paul II raised her to the altars of the Church as the first saint of the new millennium, and asked, "How could I have imagined that one day I would beatify her and canonize her?" At a banquet after the canonization ceremony, he turned to someone representing those who worked for her cause of canonization and said, "I just wanted to tell you, today is the happiest day of my life."

During his homily earlier that day, he again emphasized the importance of the message of Divine Mercy:

In fact, it was between the First and Second World Wars that Christ entrusted his message of mercy to her. Those who remember, who were witnesses and participants in the events of those years and the horrible sufferings they caused for millions of people, know well how necessary was the message of mercy. . . . This consoling message is addressed above all to those who, afflicted by a particularly harsh trial or crushed by the weight of the sins they committed, have lost all confidence in life and are tempted to give in to despair. To them the gentle face of Christ is offered; those rays from his heart touch them and shine upon them, warm them, show them the way and fill them with hope. How many souls have been consoled by the prayer *"Jesus, I trust in you."*

He then declared that the first Sunday after Easter would henceforth be called "Divine Mercy Sunday," because it was on that day that Christ appeared to the apostles and granted them the power to forgive sins. But, as John Paul noted, "Before speaking these words, Jesus shows his hands and his side. He points, that is, to the wounds of the Passion, especially the wound in his heart, the source from which flows the great wave of mercy poured out on humanity." Karol's faith in God's mercy—as a limit placed upon evil —sustained his spirits during the Nazi occupation.

God Prepares His Arrow

Along with his faith, the theater became a wellspring and an expression of hope for Wojtyła. Together with a number of friends, Karol defied the Germans and formed an underground theatrical organization called the Rhapsodic Theater. Because the Nazis forbade such secret societies, the clandestine group met in various basements, apartments, and houses, risking deportation and death if they were caught.

In order to emphasize the delivery of the spoken word, the dramas were enacted by candlelight, using minimalist scenery and decoration. One of Wojtyła's friends explained:

> The main idea is to pronounce every vowel and every word with the greatest possible precision, not slurring or swallowing anything but at the same time not exaggerating, so that the general effect is attractive and natural. . . . We also try to read whole sentences giving full weight to the punctuation—commas, full stops, exclamation marks—so as to convey everything that the text contains and make it fully intelligible.

It's natural to wonder why anyone would risk death in order to perform plays during a world war. At best, it would seem to be a dangerous method of distracting oneself from the unchangeable and painful realities of life. But for Poles, their dramas were an expression of their destiny. To comprehend this, one must understand Polish history. For more than a thousand years, Poland had been torn asunder by its stronger neighboring nations. Century after bloody century, its borders were shifted and redrawn and its culture suppressed. Time and time again, the nation was trampled, occupied, and then resurrected. At many moments in its history, Poland existed only as a culture and an idea, while its political identity was being repressed and overrun by various tyrants.

During these repeated seasons of suffering, epic ballads of Polish heroism and resilience were written. Tales of woeful exile and gallant uprisings became national treasures of literature and poetry. Polish writers such as Adam Mickiewicz and Juliusz Słowacki proclaimed that there was a greater, cosmic plan behind the ebb and flow of their elusive freedom. They believed that Poland was destined to play a messianic role among the nations of Europe, redeeming others through their suffering. As a result, Polish theater became more of an occasion for contemplation than a mere opportunity for entertainment. The soul of Poland was religion, art, learning, poetry, and theater—without contrived borders separating them. Poland could not afford to forget its past because it was a window to its future and its destiny. John Paul later said that the thoughts of his favorite poet, Cyprian Norwid, "sustained our hope in God, and in times of injustice and contempt . . . they helped us to stand tall and live in dignity."

Because of the depth of Polish cultural roots, Nazi governor general Hans Frank said, "the Polish nation should be transformed into an intellectual desert." In this desert, the Rhapsodic Theater became an oasis. It was a source of life, identity, and hope. It existed as a resistance movement, fighting not only to preserve culture, but to use culture itself as a weapon. As a famous Polish actor once told Wojtyła, "An actor is not a clown, but an activist fulfilling a mission." Through polemics of fear and coercion, Nazis sought to eradicate Polish culture, while Wojtyła and the others sustained it through their courage and freedom. In fact, the first production of the Rhapsodic Theater was "King Spirit," which retells the martyrdom of a bishop of Kraków, Saint Stanisław, at the hands of a wicked king. The death of the saint didn't destroy the faith of the Church, but instead ignited its fervor.

The members of the Rhapsodic Theater likewise transformed the suffering inflicted by the Nazi occupation into a powerful reminder of their identity and their mission. The most poignant example of this was when Karol was reciting an epic Polish poem, "Sir Thaddeus," which had been written during a previous era of Polish enslavement.

While he was speaking the lines of a warrior who became a monk, the booming voice of Nazi propaganda blared from a loudspeaker outside the window. Without flinching, Karol continued his monologue, like a light that shines in the darkness, although "the darkness has not overcome it" (Jn 1:5).

The famous Russian novelist Fyodor Dostoyevsky once wrote that beauty will save the world. Through the Rhapsodic Theater, Karol Wojtyła and his compatriots were attempting to do just this. As one of his friends remarked, "The performers were like a priesthood, guarding and imparting the deepest truths of life; it was their task and their opportunity to regenerate the world by a display of artistic beauty." John Paul later wrote of Norwid that he "persistently reminds us that without heroism humanity degrades itself, loses its identity, and, rejecting God, it betrays itself . . . Woe to societies in which the priestly character of the human person is lost."

Lolek's love for drama and the arts left an indelible mark on his philosophical and theological thought. He considered the joys and tragedies of human life—and history itself—to be something that was being played out under the direction of God, whose plan often surpassed human understanding. The most prominent themes of Polish literature and drama later found their way into many of John Paul's papal teachings, including political and religious freedom, the dignity of labor, the human person, courage under persecution, sacrificial love, and redemptive suffering.

Not only did these themes pervade the messages he delivered as pope, Cardinal Paul Poupard noted that "His experiences from the Rhapsodic Theater, which was deprived of the traditional means of theatrical expression, and where everything was concentrated on the word, as he told me, turned out to be very significant. I think his being an actor in this theater imparted a special key and hallmark to his papal teaching." Indeed, those who watched the Holy Father preach noted that he was gifted in terms of his improvisational skills, purposeful inflections, stage presence, confidence, and memory. Cardinal Andrzej Deskur concurred, saying, "Everything the Holy Father endured in his life, prepared him for what he had to be. Just as an arrow is readied for the shot from the bow, God prepares the proper people, He prepares his arrows. . . ."

2

FATHER KAROL

Despite his love for theater, Karol gradually began to realize that acting was not his vocation. Others, however, seemed to realize this before he did. He told André Frossard, "Towards the end of my years at the lycée [secondary school], the people around me thought that I would choose the priesthood. As for me, I did not give it a thought." But after the death of his father, his path slowly became clearer as he became progressively detached from his earlier plans.

A number of factors influenced his decision. For one, he said that the heroism of his fellow Poles during the war helped him to define his own vocation. Because they laid down their young lives to sacrifice everything in an effort to liberate Poland, their sacrifice was a reflection of the essence of the priesthood. He also greatly admired the example of Adam Chmielowski, a Polish painter who left behind the arts in order to pursue his priestly vocation. He became a Franciscan to serve the poor, took the name Brother Albert, and was later canonized by Pope John Paul II.

In a book John Paul wrote to commemorate the fiftieth anniversary of his priestly ordination, he added:

All I can say is that the tragedy of the war had its effect on my gradual choice of a vocation. . . . But the process was not merely negative. At the same time a light was beginning to shine ever more brightly in the back of my mind: *the Lord wants me to become a priest.* One day I saw this with great clarity: it was like an interior illumination which brought with it the joy and certainty of a new vocation. And this awareness filled me with great inner peace.

However, the decision didn't resonate with his friends at the Rhapsodic Theater. When he told them that he wanted to become a Carmelite monk, one asked him, "Do you think you can solve everything by locking yourself up in a monastery?" Several of the others tried to dissuade him, and one even engaged in an all-night debate with him over the matter. He asked, "What are you doing? Do you want to waste your talent?" By becoming a priest, Karol wasn't hiding from the problems of the world, but choosing to enter fully into the great battle between good and evil.

Despite the protestations of his peers, at the age of twenty-two he walked up to the doors of Wawel Cathedral in 1942 and told the rector of the seminary, "I want to be a priest." Archbishop Adam Stefan Sapieha accepted him, remembering the day he first met Karol when he was in high school: Because the young boy was the school's top student, he was chosen by his religion teacher to give a welcome address to the archbishop in Latin. After the presentation, Sapieha asked the teacher what Karol would be studying at the university. He told him, "He will study Polish language and letters." Sapieha responded, "A pity it is not theology."

Sapieha was well loved by the Poles, having fearlessly opposed the German Reich. When Hans Frank came to the archbishop's residence, Sapieha served the governor general a dinner in the formal dining room consisting of stale black bread, beetroot jam, and faux coffee made from grain. This was the diet given to the Poles—who were expected to live on nine hundred calories per day. Sapieha told the Nazi leader he didn't want to risk the arrest of any of his servants, by having them try to assemble a more elaborate meal. Wojtyła greatly admired his courage, and when he eventually became pope, wore a gold cross around his neck that was an exact replica of Sapieha's.

The Clandestine Seminarian

Karol was accepted into the seminary, but was warned that no one could know of it. It was too dangerous. The Nazis didn't want more priests, and they forbade the Church to accept new candidates. Many who were found studying for the priesthood were either executed or deported to concentration camps. Numerous priests were also removed, including nearly all the priests at Karol's parish, most of whom later died in Dachau. One was beaten and then drowned to death in feces because he refused to grind a Rosary into the ground with his foot. In fact, by the end of the Nazi occupation, one third of the Polish clergy had been murdered. More than three thousand were imprisoned in concentration camps, and because nearly half of them were interned at Dachau, it became the largest monastery in the world.

The ever-present threat of deportation and death was an inescapable reality for Karol. Because Kraków was less than thirty miles from Auschwitz, one of his friends noted, "The stench of Auschwitz was in his nostrils" and would never be forgotten. One papal biographer remarked:

Lolek became a secret seminarian during the occupation's darkest hours, when the four powerful crematoria at Auschwitz-Birkenau were incinerating as many as two thousand bodies a day, nearly all of them Jews evacuated from Polish ghettos and shipped in from all parts of occupied Europe. The sickly sweet smell of burning human flesh and bones drifted for miles through the countryside surrounding the camp.

Despite the risk involved, Wojtyła knew that he had been called. Although the Germans ordered all seminaries to be closed, Archbishop Sapieha created a secret seminary in his own palace, and Karol began making visits there to study. While continuing to work at the Solvay chemical plant, Karol also studied through the theology department of the Jagiellonian University, which had become another underground organization. The defiant teachers met with students in churches, houses, and convents in order to avoid being caught. At times, his coworkers allowed him to rest or to study on the job. One of his friends from school, Juliusz Kydryński, recalled, "In spite of his great friendliness and his eagerness to contribute in our academic life, one could feel that Karol was much more sincere and a little bit withdrawn, as if he were constantly considering problems which surpassed us."

At about three in the afternoon of February 29, 1944, Karol was walking along the road from the Solvay plant when a military truck struck him, tossing his body to the ground. A woman witnessed the accident and ran to find him unconscious and bleeding from his head. He was rushed to a nearby hospital, regained consciousness eighteen hours later, spent nearly two weeks in the hospital, and needed several months to recover from his injuries. Despite the suffering, he considered the fact that he survived to be a sign that he had made the right decision to become a priest. In fact, his hospital room overlooked the grounds of the Carmelite monastery. His friend remarked upon visiting him, "Didn't you want to enter the Carmelites? Well, look, they brought you here!"

His life was again spared when the SS troops stormed through Kraków on "Black Sunday," arresting more than 8,000 males and sending many of them to prison camps. Hans Frank ordered the massive roundup in the wake of the uprising in Warsaw that resulted in the death of 200,000 Poles. As the Nazis stormed through his house, Karol hid in the basement praying. He heard the footsteps of the soldiers pass the door of the basement, but they never opened it. Many years later, as pope, he reminisced, "Sometimes I would ask myself: so many young people of my own age are losing their lives, *why not me?* Today I know that it was not mere chance. Amid the overwhelming evil of the war, everything in my own personal life was tending towards the good of my vocation."

After the troops left, a priest from the archbishop's palace arrived, having been sent by Sapieha to bring Karol to safety. In order to protect them, the archbishop summoned all the seminarians who were studying in secret. Karol and the priest weaved across town through alleys and streets, dodging the swarms of military patrols, with the aid of an elderly woman who scouted ahead for soldiers. Once inside the archbishop's residence, Karol was immediately dressed as a priest, along with several other seminarians, so that any German officers would not arrest them for being seminarians or civilians. Karol's days and nights at the Solvay chemical plant were over, and now he was "free" to study while essentially living under house arrest.

On several occasions, Karol expressed to Archbishop Sapieha his hopes of entering the Carmelites, to live a life of contemplative prayer. Sapieha refused. He acknowledged, "I have given permission a hundred times for all kinds of candidates who wanted to join the monastery," and had only denied it once before. But in Wojtyła's case, he repeatedly denied the requests, mentioning to others, "we have only a few priests and Wojtyła is badly needed in the diocese. . . . And later he will be needed by the whole Church."

A Trade of Tyrants

Foreign military forces were weakening the Nazi regime throughout Europe, and Poland was sensing that the days of its German occupation were coming to an end. On an evening in mid-January 1945, Karol was praying with the other seminarians in the chapel of the archbishop's residence when all the windows burst as the retreating Germans blew up a nearby bridge. Archbishop Sapieha ushered the priests and seminarians to the basement, where he continued praying the Rosary with them, amid the sounds of guns and tanks. The men huddled in the dark, frozen room until after midnight, when they heard a knock at the gate. Russian soldiers were checking for Nazis—and hoping to find some food and vodka in the process.

The next morning, the city streets were flooded with Poles celebrating their liberation. Everyone's jubilation was soon tempered by the realization that six million friends and family members would never be seen again, and also by the fact that the Poles had swapped one tyrannical government for another.

Karol and the other seminarians began cleaning up the broken glass in the archbishop's residence, then walked

outside for the first time in six months to see which friends
and family members were still living. Nearly one fifth of
Poland's population had been murdered. Upon arriving
at the devastated Dębnicki Bridge, Karol and a fellow
seminarian walked down the bank and across the frozen
Vistula River, passing by corpses of soldiers who had been
hurled down to the ice by the explosion the night before.

A few days later, Karol and his classmates visited the
Theological Seminary, which had been occupied by Nazi
guards. The building was in a horrid state. Karol's fellow
seminarian Mieczyslaw Malinski recalls:

> . . . the central heating had failed some time ago; wa-
> ter had frozen in all the pipes, and the inmates had
> had to keep warm by lighting open fires in the rooms.
> The state of the lavatories was appalling, with piles of
> frozen excrement which had to be chopped up and
> carted away. Karol and I and a few other students
> volunteered to do this. The stench was dreadful, and
> we found the only way to keep from vomiting was to
> breathe through the mouth. It was quite a long job, as
> there were three lavatories on each floor.

One papal biographer remarked, it was "hardly a symbolic way to celebrate victory and liberty, but not bad for
a future successor to St. Peter."

The communists were quick to take authority over the
country, and began oppressing the Church by confiscating
land, eliminating religious education from schools, heav-
ily taxing (or bulldozing) religious properties, limiting the
amount of paper the Church could use for publications,
censoring homilies, closing youth groups, and subjecting
seminarians to military service or forced labor. When the
Church didn't agree to allow the government to appoint

and dismiss priests and bishops, eight bishops and a thousand priests and nuns were imprisoned. By 1955, the number of imprisoned priests had reached two thousand.

Rather than resorting to genocide to extinguish Polish identity, the communists sought to use the weapon of time, attempting to suffocate the faith of Poland by promoting a materialistic and atheistic culture, while making the faith more difficult to practice and learn. It was a systematic program of anti-evangelization. As some Poles said, "The Germans will take our body, and the Soviets will take our soul."

G. K. Chesterton once said that the family is a cell of resistance to oppression. Unfortunately, this was one point of Catholic theology that the communists agreed with. To undermine Polish culture, communists struck at its heart—the family. Work and school schedules were organized so that parents had minimal contact with each other and with their children. Birth control and abortion were encouraged, state-sponsored sex education was implemented in schools, and apartments were built to accommodate only small families.

Priestly Life

On November 1, 1946, with a modest number of friends and family present, Karol Wojtyła was ordained to the priesthood at the age of twenty-six, in Cardinal Sapieha's private chapel. During the Nazi occupation, he had often attended morning Mass in the same chapel, with a friend and fellow seminarian, Jerzy Zachuta. In his book *Gift and Mystery*, John Paul recalled:

> One day he did not appear. After Mass I stopped by his house in Ludwinów (near Dębnicki) and learned that

he had been taken away by the Gestapo during the night. Immediately afterwards, his name appeared on the list of Poles who were to be shot. Being ordained in that very chapel which has seen us together so many times, I could not help but remember this brother in the priestly vocation, whom Christ had united in a different way to the mystery of his Death and Resurrection.

He celebrated his first Masses the next day, at Wawel Cathedral. Because it was the feast of All Souls, priests could offer three Masses for the benefit of the faithful, which he offered for his deceased family members: one at Saint Leonard's Chapel and two at the Shrine of Saint Stanisław.

Two weeks after his ordination and by the order of Sapieha, he boarded a train to Italy, leaving Poland for the first time. In Rome, he entered a two-year doctoral program at the Angelicum, studying philosophy and moral theology. Upon completion of his studies, he wrote a 280-page dissertation in Latin, entitled *The Doctrine of Faith According to St. John of the Cross*. He passed his examinations with high marks, but could not receive his degree until his dissertation was published. Since he couldn't afford the printing, he needed to wait until he returned home to Kraków for the Jagiellonian University to confer on him his doctoral degree in Sacred Theology.

After his return from Rome, Father Karol was appointed to serve as the assistant pastor at the Assumption of Our Lady, a country parish in Niegowić, on the outskirts of Kraków. The backwater town lacked electricity, running water, and sewers, but the young priest didn't mind the humble assignment. Upon arriving, he knelt down and kissed the ground, a gesture he learned from reading the life of Saint John Vianney. It didn't take long for the parishioners to realize what a gift they had been given in him. The young priest often spent the night before the Blessed Sacrament, and his parishioners sometimes spied on him, watching him in prayer, lying prostrate on the cold floor.

In order to make personal visits to the families in his parish, he often traveled long distances. Years later, he recalled the treks over beaten paths in the snow:

> But snow will cling to your cassock, then it will thaw out indoors, and freeze again outside, forming a heavy bell round your legs, which gets heavier and heavier . . . By evening, you could hardly drag your legs, but you have to go on, because you know that people wait for you, that they wait all year long for this meeting.

Wojtyła was given charge of five elementary schools and helped the parishioners to start a Living Rosary group, a drama group, and a flourishing parish committee. Because he was so active in building up the parish, communist spies were sent to undermine his efforts. He had already been on their radar since his days in the seminary under Archbishop Sapieha. But now that he was exerting a greater influence on the people, the secret police decided it was time to act. They abducted and beat a young man who was helping to type Father Karol's doctoral thesis, because he refused to divulge information that the Soviets could use against Wojtyła's youth group. Father Karol assured him that he didn't need to hide anything, and comforted him, saying, "Don't worry, Stanisław, they'll finish themselves off . . ."

Many years later, this same friend visited Karol and was astonished to see so many communist books by Marx and

Lenin in his library. He kidded, "What! Did you convert to a different ideology?" "My dear Stanisław," Wojtyła replied, "if you want to understand the enemy, you have to know what he has written!"

Father Karol opposed communism for a number of reasons, including its ideology of viewing its citizens as a means to their ends. More accurately, he wasn't *against* something, but rather was *for* the rights of man. He knew that people do not exist for the good of the state. Rather, the state should exist in order to serve the people. This wasn't about making the government more religious, but about making it more worthy of the human person. In Wojtyła's mind, injustices such as violence and the suppression of human rights are lies spoken against the truth of humanity. When the laws of a state are not based upon the truth of the dignity of the human person, inhuman conditions and acts inevitably follow. This is especially true under a system such as communism, which sees man as a purely material being. In any civilization, the death of God precedes the death of man. When a state imposes a godless ideology upon its citizens, there is the danger, as John Paul warned, of "cutting man off from his own depths."

Wojtyła understood the danger of communist thought—as well as its weaknesses—because he knew the philosophy of Marxism better than the communist leaders themselves! Just before he was elected pope, Cardinal Wojtyła walked into the papal conclave with a Marxist philosophical journal in hand. A cardinal chided him, "Isn't it a bit sacrilegious to bring Marxist literature into the Sistine Chapel?" With a smile, he answered, "My conscience is clear."

His strategy obviously worked, as the Russian president Mikhail Gorbachev later confessed, "I did not destroy Communism, John Paul II did." He added, "Without this

Pope, it would be impossible to understand what happened in Europe at the end of the 1980s." John Paul believed that its collapse was inevitable because of its own errors and socioeconomic weakness, but acknowledged that it would be naïve to reduce the matter to these factors alone. When credit for the collapse of the Iron Curtain was given to him, he said, "It was the Providence of God. The one who did it all was the Madonna." Unfortunately for Father Karol and the rest of Poland, communism reigned and tottered for several decades before it crumbled.

After he spent eight months in Niegowić, Cardinal Sapieha reassigned him to Saint Florian's parish, an upscale church in the heart of Kraków that was bustling with college students, families, and intellectuals. During his stay there, he taught high school theology, led retreats, provided pastoral care to the college students, and prepared couples for marriage. Sapieha knew he needed someone to raise up young leadership within the Church, and Father Karol was just the man for the job.

But after two short years at Saint Florian's, Wojtyła was directed to take a two-year academic leave in order to pursue a second doctorate. By writing a habilitation thesis, he would be qualified to teach at the university level. He soon obtained a doctorate in ethics, entitling his thesis *An Evaluation of the Possibility of Constructing a Christian Ethics on the Basis of the System of Max Scheler* (a German phenomenologist). His habilitation thesis was the last one granted before the communists closed the theology department at the Jagiellonian University after five hundred and fifty years of its existence, in an attempt to divide faith and reason.

After obtaining his second doctorate, he taught theology at the Jagiellonian University for two years before its closure, secretly taught in the banned seminary in Kraków, lectured at the Catholic University of Lublin, and became the chair of its ethics department—while still in his mid-thirties! He also donated his salary to pay for the tuition of poor students. It was no secret that Father Karol was a gifted intellectual, as demonstrated in his book on phenomenology, *Person and Act*. The text was so philosophically dense that some of his students joked that they'd need to read *Person and Act* as a punishment in purgatory! One priest even suggested to Wojtyła that it should be "translated first from Polish into Polish, to make it easier to understand for the reader—including me."

Despite his capacity to philosophize on a world-class level, he knew how to connect with a young audience. Young adults piled into his classrooms to hear his lectures and lined the walls and windowsills to hear his thoughts on life, love, and everything in between. One of his students at the University of Lublin took a summer course on systematic theology, and Wojtyła was one among several lecturers. He remembered that Wojtyła would show up on Monday morning, but would leave before noon to go canoeing with other young people, taking the transcripts of the professors' lectures with him. The other teachers would then present their lectures for several days. Then, on Thursday afternoon, he'd return for the closing and give a one-hour summary. The student remarked, "Everybody got a lot more [in that hour] than from all those three days. He was fascinating, how concise was his mind, and the ability to express difficult thoughts in an understandable way. His writing was rather more difficult to absorb and digest, but his talks were fascinating."

His lectures were not alluring merely because of his intellectual abilities, but because they had been marinated in contemplation. After he lectured at the Częstochowa Seminary, the rector recalled, "One thing struck me: Rev. Prof. Wojtyła spent the breaks between lectures in the Seminary Chapel and not in our Seminary refectory where the professor priests would come for coffee or tea."

3

WUJEK

As a parish priest, bishop, and even cardinal, Karol Wojtyła led groups of young people into the wilderness to hike, kayak, and camp. Such trips were forbidden by the communists, who suppressed all youth associations and saw large gatherings of laity as suspicious antigovernment activities. In order to conceal his identity as a priest, Father Karol dressed like a layman and the young people called him *Wujek* (uncle). One of them explained, "So it was always Uncle—instead of Reverend Professor, your Excellency, then, your Eminence. Instead of Bishop or Cardinal it was simply, 'Uncle' or even 'Unc.'"

While hiking to a campsite or paddling across a lake in a two-man kayak, the youths absorbed his wisdom and insight. Sometimes during the hikes he would drift to the back of the group to spend a few hours in contemplative prayer. One of the hikers, Kazimierz Braun, said, "We even had a saying: 'Uncle went on the mountain.' Of course, he did not go 'on the mountain,' but rather to any solitary, secluded, quiet place. He prayed the Rosary and the Chaplet of Divine Mercy. We had a feeling that he is praying all the time."

Each day, he celebrated Mass with them in the woods or by the lakeside, sometimes using an overturned canoe as an altar, with two paddles lashed together to form a cross.

On one occasion as cardinal, he celebrated Mass during a torrential rain on a mountain summit with seven hundred faithful. However, his camping excursions were much more intimate. At night, they gathered around the campfire to sing and to read aloud various books, including C. S. Lewis' classic *The Screwtape Letters*. Braun reminisced:

> The cardinal's shirt and dress pants were as sweaty and dusty as everyone else's. And what about those retreat meditations and question periods held in the calm of night, broken only by the sound of the dry branches crackling in the campfire? It was the same thing in the classrooms, on the pulpit, at the altar. He was never distant. He never set himself apart, put up barriers, flaunted or paraded himself. He was always present.

He added, "A campfire had always for its ending a religious song which was the final prayer of the day."

These clandestine excursions began during his days at the humble parish in Niegowić and continued until he was elected pope in 1978. The Catholic newspaper in Kraków, *Tygodnik Powszechny*, reported Wojtyła saying, "I have two responsibilities to youth: canoeing and skiing." He even competed in an international kayak race in 1955, but his vessel sank at the finish line. He reported, "Only the breviary did not get wet!"

Bishop Wojtyła

While on a summer canoeing excursion with young friends in 1958, he was asked to report immediately to Cardinal Stefan Wyszyński in Warsaw. Pope Pius XII had responded to a request from the bishop of Kraków to make Father Karol an auxiliary bishop—making him the youngest member of the Polish episcopate. He recalled:

> So I set off, first in the canoe over the waves of the river, and then in a truck laden with sacks of flour, until I got to Olsztynek. The train for Warsaw left late at night. I had brought my sleeping bag with me, thinking that I might be able to catch a few winks in the station and ask someone to wake me when it was time to board the train. There was no need for that in any event, because I didn't sleep.

Upon arriving, he questioned the bishop's decision because of his age, asking, "Your Eminence, I am too young; I'm only thirty-eight." Wyszyński responded, "That is a weakness which can soon be remedied. Please do not oppose the will of the Holy Father." Without any further hesitation, Wojtyła asked, "Where do I sign?"

Before returning to his friends in the woods, he first needed to take a night train to Kraków, to give his archbishop the news of his assignment. Because the train was not scheduled to depart for several hours, he made a visit to a nearby chapel. Father Jan Zieja recalls that evening in 1958, when Wojtyła knocked on the door of the convent, looking to spend some time in prayer. A nun led him to the chapel and he was left alone. Zieja recalls:

> When he did not emerge for some time, they looked in on him. He lay prostrate on the ground. The sister stepped back, filled with respect. . . . After another while, the sister looked into the chapel again. The priest still lay prostrate. But the hour was late. The sister went up to him and shyly asked, "Perhaps Father

would be so kind to come to supper?"—The stranger responded: My train to Kraków isn't until after midnight. Allow me to stay here. I have much to discuss with the Lord.

Eight hours after his prayer began, he departed at 11:30 to catch his train.

When he arrived in Kraków, he delivered the news to Archbishop Eugeniusz Baziak, who led Wojtyła to a waiting room where other priests were sitting, and wisecracked to them, "*Habemus Papam!*" [We have a Pope!]. Father Karol asked if he could return to his companions in the wilderness, but the archbishop initially denied the request. Later, he pressed, "Who will say Mass for them? It will be a privation." Dismissing him with a smile, the archbishop said, "Go on, then. But please come back in time for your consecration!" On September 28, 1958, in the same Gothic cathedral where he served Mass while hearing the Nazi bombardment nearly two decades earlier, he was consecrated a bishop at the tomb of Saint Stanisław.

Seven years later, Wojtyła was selected as the archbishop of Kraków. At the time, the Polish government and the Church were battling over whether state approval was needed to elect bishops. The communists conceded that they would not impose a candidate, but they demanded the authority to reject them if they so desired. When the time came for Cardinal Wyszyński to propose a candidate to become the new archbishop of Kraków, the communists' Department of Religious Denominations rejected six or seven names over the course of eighteen months. The communist leader who was blocking the candidates said, "I'm waiting for Wojtyła and I'll continue to veto names until I get him." In one of the most ironic twists in Church history, Wyszyński was informed that the communists had chosen Karol Wojtyła! A leader of the Communist party in Kraków even boasted that he successfully blocked the top half dozen candidates.

The authorities assumed that Wojtyła would be easier to control, and they hoped to pit him against the older Wyszyński. They may also have viewed him as more of a young intellectual poet and theologian than a stubborn political adversary. In what was perhaps the greatest miscalculation in the history of communism, they decided, "Wojtyła was the best and the only choice . . ." Their providential mistake is reminiscent of Proverbs 21:1, which reads: "The king's heart is a stream of water in the hand of the LORD; he turns it wherever he will."

Spying on a Saint

While Bishop Wojtyła was busy studying communist thought, the Soviets were busy studying him. Before long, they began to consider him "an especially dangerous ideological adversary." Their intelligence service set up a special unit devoted to uninterrupted surveillance of him. For the next two decades, even when he was permitted to travel out of the country for events such as the Second Vatican Council, he was being watched. The earliest information gathered by the secret police about him dates back to his days in the seminary, and by the time he was elected pope, the Soviets had compiled eighteen cartons of reports. His phone line was tapped, his letters read, and every homily recorded, with every sentence examined. The government obsessed over every detail of his life, wanting to know how often he went to the dentist, who polished his shoes, and who purchased his underwear!

Although most of the information gathered isn't particularly illuminating, the reports to Moscow also noted that he often spent between six to eight hours per day in prayer and meditation. When he was a cardinal, a friend recalled him saying, "The more deeply people develop within themselves in their interior life, the more prone they are to silence . . . Every great work, all holiness, is born in silence and recollection. . . . Only falsehood wraps itself in a flood of words. Truth is brief."

The Soviet stalking didn't end after the papal conclave. In fact, during the first five years of his pontificate, the majority of Polish diplomats in Rome were actually communist spies. Even some priests—including an organizer of Pope John Paul II's first trip to Poland—were working for the communists. Many of these clergymen had been threatened, extorted, or corrupted in order to serve as moles to infiltrate Catholic organizations and undermine the Church. The secret intelligence service even attempted to recruit John Paul's closest aides and companions, but to no avail. To prevent him from coming to one city in Poland, the communists sent bags full of forged letters to the bishop of that diocese, pretending they were from Catholics, saying, "We don't want the Pope." It didn't work.

In *The End and the Beginning*, George Weigel describes these antics in detail, reporting that the communists even tried to "reveal" that the Pope had a Polish lover! The secret agents forged the handwritten diary of a deceased woman, claiming she had had a secret relationship with Cardinal Wojtyła. The strategy was to plant the diary in another priest's house, and then have the authorities "discover" it during a police raid. Unfortunately for the Soviets, after successfully planting the diary, the leader of the operation went to a bar with his comrades to celebrate and then became intoxicated and crashed his car on the way home. He was so inebriated that he bragged to the police about being a spy and divulged all the details of the ruse! The diary was uncovered and the plot was foiled.

John Paul was well aware of their tactics, as he had been dealing with such harassment for decades. As a bishop in Poland, whenever he left home the secret police tailed his vehicle. Cardinal Stanisław Dziwisz, who was his assistant from the time he was archbishop, explained:

> They were always there, always on duty, watching from the other side of Franciszkańska Street. And as soon as the archbishop's car left the building, the agents would glide along behind in their sinister black vehicles. In fact, he used to wave at them or even bless them as he was about to leave. He used to call them "my guardian angels."

According to his secretary, on one occasion his driver "came up with a maneuver worthy of 007" because the archbishop needed to have a secret meeting. He accelerated and swerved into a line of other cars, affording Wojtyła the chance to sneak out of the car and into another, while the spies continued to chase after the chauffeur. Such maneuvers were necessary for him, even as a cardinal, just to go kayaking with young people.

But the communists weren't content with external observations. Therefore, the entire archbishop's residence, from the bedroom to the dining room, was bugged with listening devices. The communists were rather clumsy about it, pretending to show up as random technicians who needed to work on the phone lines or electrical system. It became somewhat of a joke, as Wojtyła made sure to speak loudly when he wanted them to know something, but reserved important conversations for the nearby woods or trips to the mountains.

Holy Defiance

Dealing with Wojtyła was much more than the communists had bargained for. One official bemoaned, "when he wrote to the authorities, it took sweat to respond with adequate arguments." One of his biographers noted, "As a negotiator, he was particularly difficult to deal with, since he knew the philosophical underpinnings of Marxism better than did many of the party officials who were sent out to tame him." When the communist prime minister of Poland, General Wojciech Jaruzelski, first met Pope John Paul II in 1983, he admitted, "I was aware that my legs were trembling and my knees knocking together . . ."

He became a persistent thorn in the side of the government, and didn't hesitate to enter the Communist Party headquarters to protest their plans to take over the Kraków seminary. Their purported power wasn't a source of intimidation for him. As he later told a White House correspondent, "The career of every person on earth began in a diaper, even though today he may be wearing the uniform of a military general or the ribbons of an ambassador. And his career will probably come to an end again in a diaper, except perhaps a slightly larger one."

Clashes between Bishop Wojtyła and the communist authorities became a regular affair. When one of his priests couldn't afford the heavy taxes that had been imposed upon him, Wojtyła told him to report to prison and "pay the penalty." When he arrived in jail, Wojtyła went to his church and announced to the thousands of parishioners that he'd be filling in for their priest because the communists had imprisoned him. The priest was quickly released. On other occasions, Wojtyła was unable to prevail. When he petitioned the authorities to allow a procession with the Blessed Sacrament, they refused, on the grounds that it would cause "impediments to transportation"—despite the fact that nonreligious processions apparently did not.

In celebration of a millennium of Polish history, Cardinal Wyszyński decided to organize a "Great Novena," focusing on recatechizing the nation and undermining communist propaganda in the process. The nine-year program leading up to Poland's thousandth anniversary also included a cross-country procession with the sacred image of Our Lady of Częstochowa (also known as Our Lady of Jasna Góra, the Black Madonna, and the Patroness and Queen of Poland). According to legend, the holy icon was painted by Saint Luke the Evangelist on a wooden plank from the Holy Family's table, and was passed down through Saint Helen and Constantine, then transported to the Ukraine, eventually finding its way to Częstochowa, Poland. The image is a national symbol of faith, patriotism, and endurance, having survived numerous persecutions and wars. The face of the Virgin, which darkened over the centuries, bears two gouges on the cheek caused by a Hussite swordsman when the monastery was plundered in the fifteenth century. No religious art in Poland better exemplifies the history of Poland and its struggle for freedom from tyranny. The devotion that Poles have for their Queen is comparable to the love and affection that the people of Mexico bear for the sacred image of Our Lady of Guadalupe.

In an effort to energize the faithful and reconsecrate the nation to Mary, the procession of a replica of the holy image began its journey to every parish in the nation. Authorities soon "arrested" the image and imprisoned it, so to speak, back at Jasna Góra. To bring an end to the public demonstrations, the communists decided to prohibit processions of religious images altogether. But the Polish Church continued the procession . . . with an empty frame. After all, the object of the Church's devotion is not an image, but rather the person of Mary. Crowds swelled, and the hollow frame became its own icon, rich in its own symbolism of the unjust persecution imposed by the government.

The procession took years to complete, and concluded with Mass at the Shrine of Częstochowa. Pope Paul VI was invited, but the communists refused to grant him a travel visa. In keeping with his irrepressible spirit, Wojtyła simply placed an empty throne adjacent to the altar, as a reminder to the faithful of the government's denial of religious freedom.

When Wojtyła asked the government for permission to build new churches (about thirty per year), they refused. When permission was granted, it was for the rebuilding of burned churches or the expansion of small chapels, not for the creation of new ones. He mentioned that if they could build three each year, they would have enough . . . in twenty years. However, Cardinal Wojtyła noted in 1975 that only six percent of their requests were granted. In an act of faithful defiance, he proceeded to celebrate Masses on the vacant lots where he wanted the churches to be built. In his eyes, the Church was already present, and it would just be a matter of time before the authorities would have to concede the point. In the rain and snow, thousands attended these outdoor Masses. This sometimes caused the communist leaders to fold, because they preferred that the churches be built so that the crowds wouldn't be so visible to others. The sight of a bishop and his soggy flock celebrating

Mass under umbrellas in a vacant lot made the government look petulant.

The most notable of these occurrences was in Nowa Huta, which was an industrial town built by the regime as the model city of socialist ideals. It was supposed to be a "workers' paradise," with a solely materialistic vision of humanity and therefore no place for religion. Rows upon rows of apartment buildings were constructed like filing cabinets. If any of the workers wanted to attend Mass, they would have to walk more than two hours to find a church.

When the Soviets refused Wojtyła's request to build anything larger than a tiny chapel for the twenty thousand parishioners, he and the Poles planted a cross in the ground and began celebrating the liturgy in the open air. Midnight Mass on Christmas was celebrated in this way every year, under the stars, often in subzero temperatures. After years of gridlock, the communists caved in and granted permission . . . but then proceeded to delay building permits, interfere with the acquisition of construction materials, and impose every conceivable roadblock to slow the completion of the structure. By the time it was complete a decade later, Archbishop Wojtyła had become a cardinal, and proudly consecrated the structure. Fittingly, the church was constructed to resemble Noah's Ark, as a bastion of hope in a flood of darkness.

4

CARDINAL WOJTYŁA

While the church in Nowa Huta was being constructed, workers at a shipyard in Gdansk, in northern Poland, went on strike when the government raised food prices. Army troops were called in to quell the riots, killing dozens of civilians. Several years later, more riots ensued as the Polish workers began to unite under the leadership of Lech Wałesa in order to demand their rights under the government. The Solidarity movement was born from these uprisings and went on to play a significant role in the downfall of the Soviet Union. Cardinal Wojtyła defended the rights of the workers and was outspoken in his support of the labor unions. He knew that communism wouldn't last, and that the government feared the Church far more than anyone in the Church feared the communists. He knew the gates of hell would not prevail against the Church, while the communist empire had been built upon sand.

Meanwhile, because Wojtyła had impressed the other bishops to such a degree with his faith and intellect during the Second Vatican Council a decade earlier, Pope Paul VI invited him to return to Rome to lead the Lenten spiritual exercises for those in the Vatican. French theologian Father Yves Congar recalled, "Wojtyła made an excellent impression. He has a dominant personality. There is a kind of excitement, magnetic force, prophetic power in him, irresistible and full of peace."

Because he had only three weeks to prepare for the monumental responsibility of preaching to Paul VI and the Papal Household (and translating the twenty-two sermons into Italian), he moved temporarily into a convent to prepare without distractions. The Cardinal woke up each day, early as usual, and wrote until noon. He'd then go skiing for the afternoon and resume writing in the evening.

When asked on one occasion if it was unbecoming for a cardinal to ski, he answered, "It is unbecoming for a cardinal to ski badly." Upon meeting the Italian cardinals, he expressed his surprise that none of them were skiers, and pointed out that in Poland, forty percent of the cardinals ski. When an Italian prelate noted that there were only two cardinals in Poland, he replied, "Oh yes, but in Poland, Cardinal Wyszyński counts for sixty percent."

After he finished his preparations for the sermons, Wojtyła traveled to Rome and offered a retreat with a collection of messages that was later published under the title *A Sign of Contradiction*. The concept was a fitting one, considering the hailstorm of criticism that had befallen Pope Paul VI as a result of his courageous and prophetic encyclical *Humanae Vitae*, issued nearly a decade earlier.

God Lifts Up the Lowly

Despite Wojtyła's rapid ascent within the hierarchy—and becoming the youngest member of the College of Cardinals at the age of forty-seven—his lifestyle remained unchanged. He had always been a simple man. Coworkers at the Solvay chemical plant recalled that he would sometimes arrive at work without his coat or sweater because he met someone while walking to work who needed it more than he did. On one occasion, he arrived shaking from the frigid walk, after having given his coat to an elderly man who was slightly intoxicated and close to freezing. As a parish priest in Poland, someone gave him the gift of a pillow and quilt. He passed it on to a poor woman who had been the victim of a robbery, and returned to his habit of sleeping on his bare bed. Nuns at his church noticed he wasn't dressed warmly enough for the bitter Polish winter, so they knitted him a thick woolen sweater. Within a week, it was gone, because he had given it to the poor. On one occasion, he was late for Mass because he needed the sacristan to loan him shoes for the service because he gave his own away!

Even as bishop, he wore the same pair of shoes until the soles had fallen off. He refused to buy a new pair until a cobbler insisted that they were beyond repair. As bishop, those who were in charge of his wardrobe noticed that his personal clothes were tattered, but he refused to replace them. His Polish housekeeper remarked that his undershirts resembled work rags, with holes in them. When holes appeared in his clothes, he requested that they be patched up instead of discarded. His housekeeper noted, "he refuses to wear new clothing; he always gives it away." She discovered a way to trick the bishop, however, and would buy him new clothes and then soil and wash them repeatedly, so they didn't look new. However, when things began to pile up, he asked her, "Go into my bedroom and clean out my personal belongings. I own too many things. Leave the more worn articles for me and give the better ones to the poor." Once, when he was the auxiliary bishop of Kraków, a poor man came to his residence in search of clothing. Wojtyła instructed the housekeeper to take whatever she wished from his closet and give it to the man. Even as pope, his assistants discovered that his underwear had holes in them. He insisted that they be mended, while the new ones that were purchased for him should be given to the poor.

He lived simply, and was unaccustomed to the wealth of America when he visited the United States in 1976. During the trip, Cardinal Wojtyła was driving with a Polish friend, John Szostak. While commuting down I-95, John asked if he would be willing to stop by his apartment to bless the residence and greet his wife and two small children. Wojtyła welcomed the invitation. However, because cell phones hadn't been invented yet, Szostak was unable to inform his spouse that the Cardinal would be stopping by, and took a gamble that the house—not to mention his wife's hair, wardrobe, makeup, and offspring—would be in order. It goes without saying that most wives would request the excommunication of their husbands for pulling such a stunt.

When Szostak opened the door of his apartment, the family was absent and the domicile was in a state of disaster. Cardinal Wojtyła nearly tripped over a Batmobile toy, but laughed and assured the father, "This disarray is a sign of a happy household." The mother was missing because she picked the wrong day to take a well-deserved break from the chaos, retreating to McDonald's with the children. Although the Cardinal wasn't shocked by the mess, he was astonished at the number of toys American children owned, and couldn't believe two children could have so many things, saying, "For a whole nursery, yes . . ."

Back in Kraków and eventually in Rome, he owned almost nothing but books. In the Vatican, his apartment consisted of a bedroom and a tiny study with a desk and a chair. His secretary, Dziwisz, said he practiced the virtue of poverty to a heroic degree, and seemed to do it without effort. Even the communist spies who were observing him noted, "He is not particularly interested in material things." A friend admitted that if you saw him walking down the street in Kraków, you could mistake him for a tramp! Even when he received considerable wealth, he gave it away. When millions of copies of *Crossing the Threshold of Hope* were sold, he took the first royalty payments and used them to rebuild churches that had been decimated in the former Yugoslavia. When his assistant secretary was asked if there was anything that the Pope didn't like, he replied that he didn't like new shoes, and would wear the old ones as long as possible.

Such a spirit of lowliness was a sign that Cardinal Wojtyła would be the right man for God to raise up to the highest office in the Church. Unfortunately, when it came time to purchase a ticket to travel to the papal conclave in October 1978, he realized he didn't have enough money in his wallet and needed to borrow the cash from a visiting friend.

Papal Premonitions

Karol Wojtyła's humility wasn't the only sign that God had prepared him for greatness. Although he didn't seem to think that he would become pope, many others predicted that his time had come.

More than a century before his election as pope, the famous Polish poet Juliusz Słowacki foretold such an event. He believed that the "exalted mission which is due to us, the oldest among the Slavs, [is] . . . The Papacy," which, "like the kingdom of God, is not outside us but within." He wrote a poem the same year, in which he stated:

Amid discord God strikes
At a bell immense,
For the Slavic Pope,
Open is the Throne . . .
Like God, He will bravely face the sword,
For Him world is dust . . .
So behold, here comes the Slavic Pope,
A brother of the people.

Thirteen years later, in May 1862, Saint John Bosco had a prophetic dream of the Church as a large ship at sea, navigating through treacherous waves and being attacked by smaller enemy vessels. The pope was guiding the boat toward two tall columns that rose out of the sea in the distance. Atop one was a statue of the Virgin Mary, and above the other was the Eucharist. At the base of the pillars were chains with anchors, to which ships could be attached for their safety. Meanwhile, the enemies of the Church did all they could to damage the ship with guns, books, and incendiary materials. Despite taking on damage, the large vessel sailed toward its goal, but the pope died. However, as soon as he passed away, another pope immediately took his place and anchored the boat to the two columns, just before the surface of the sea was embroiled in chaos and the smaller ships collided with each other and sank.

Admittedly, it's not an obvious prophecy that could only be fulfilled by John Paul. However, it is difficult to read Bosco's dream without noticing the parallels between the modern attacks on the Church and John Paul's persistent efforts to guide the faithful into the new millennium under the protection of the Virgin Mary, with a renewed focus on the Eucharist as the source and summit of the Christian life.

Less than a century after Saint John Bosco experienced this premonition, Father Karol decided while studying in Italy that he would spend his Easter vacation in the small town of San Giovanni Rotondo, in order to see the famous mystic and stigmatist, Padre Pio. The reputation of this saintly Capuchin friar had spread across Europe, and thousands flocked to confess to him and listen to him preach. During Wojtyła's pilgrimage, he was also able to receive the sacrament of reconciliation from Padre Pio.

Some biographers report that Padre Pio told him not only that he would become pope, but that his papacy would end in bloodshed, and that explains why John Paul was so industrious as a pope—not knowing how much time he had left to serve the Church.

There is no question that John Paul had an extraordinary work ethic. He worked between sixteen and twenty hours per day, and found television and radio to be "a waste of time." When kindergartners told him they often watched him on television, he replied, "I must say that I watch very little. But this gives me some consolation. If you see it, this is enough for me. I am dispensed!" Even while on vacation, he was known to spend an hour and a half each day reading. Cardinal Franciszek Macharski remarked that on vacation, "If he wasn't praying or studying, he had the feeling he was wasting his time." This was not a matter of being a workaholic, but rather, as he said to a friend, "One must arrange one's life, so that everything praises God." Before becoming pope, he said to a group of young people, "Dedicate your time and effort, even your rest, to this Gospel. Do not be afraid that this is lost time, that you will not rest. This is exactly when you will rest the most, because man must rest with his whole being, both physical and spiritual, so that he may rest in truth and return having found himself."

Perhaps his tireless work ethic came from his military father or from his mentor, Jan Tyranowski, whose motto was, "Every moment has to be put to use." Whether for work or relaxation, not a minute was wasted. So although his work ethic is undeniable, the evidence that Padre Pio predicted his elevation to the papacy and the shedding of his blood is inconclusive. If the legend is true, John Paul considered it a private matter.

What is clear is that Wojtyła left San Giovanni Rotondo with a deep respect for the sanctity of Padre Pio. Years later, after Father Karol became a bishop, one of his friends was dying of cancer. The woman, Wanda Półtawska, was a wife and mother of four children. During the Nazi occupation, she had been sent to the Ravensbrück concentration camp, where she was subjected to five years of inhuman medical experiments at the hands of Hitler's scientists. Now, she was dying from the effects of the torture.

Without delay, Bishop Wojtyła wrote a letter to Padre Pio, requesting his intercession. The secretary of state at the Vatican, Angelo Battisti, personally delivered it to the Capuchin mystic. Padre Pio asked him to read the letter aloud. Battisti recalled: "He had his head down and, as always, was praying. I opened the envelope and read him the letter. He listened in silence. When I finished reading the few lines, he continued to remain silent. He raised his head and, looking at me with his penetrating eyes, said, 'Angiolino, that request cannot be denied.'"

Wanda was instantly healed before her surgery that week, and Bishop Wojtyła wrote a letter of thanksgiving back to Padre Pio. After the letter was read to him, he instructed Battisti, "Angelino, keep those letters because one day they will be important."

Sixteen years later, at the moment Pope Paul VI died, the alarm clock by the Pope's bedside (which he had purchased in Poland) began to ring, although it had not been set to go off. With the death of the pontiff, one hundred eleven cardinals were summoned to Rome, and they entered the conclave to select the new pope. After a few ballots, white smoke billowed from the small chimney above the Sistine Chapel. On the feast of Our Lady of Jasna Góra, the cardinals selected Cardinal Albino Luciani of Venice.

Upon being asked by the Camerlengo if he would accept, Luciani replied, "May God forgive you for what you have done!" After accepting, he was asked the name he would take as pope. He answered, "John Paul the first." When he announced his name, Cardinal Wojtyła thought to himself, "'How well he has chosen!' None of the popes before him had double names, but he wanted in this name to recall his two predecessors John and Paul, the two who opened a new epoch in the history of the Church." However, during the first week of his pontificate, a Church historian informed Pope John Paul I that such a title ("the first") is not granted until a second is elected. He answered, "My name is John Paul the first. I will be here only a short time. The second is coming." In saying this, he not only foretold that his successor's installation would be imminent, but even predicted his name: John Paul II.

At the first papal audience of John Paul I, a group of Mexican journalists in attendance gave him a copy of a plane ticket, telling him they looked forward to his visit to Mexico in 1979. He accepted the gift, then turned to his secretary and said, "Keep that." He walked away and told his secretary, "I will never travel outside of Rome. I will never travel to Puebla. Keep this, and give it to my successor. He will go to Puebla."

A few days before his death, John Paul I told his secretary of state, "Another man better than I could have been chosen. Paul VI already pointed out his successor: He was sitting just in front of me in the Sistine Chapel . . . He will come, because I will go." According to the seating chart of the first conclave of 1978, Cardinal Wojtyła was assigned to that seat.

Some say that John Paul I's assurance in this matter was the result of a visit he made to Fatima in the spring of 1977 as the patriarch of Venice. A rumor had circulated that Sister Lucia, one of the three visionaries to whom the Virgin Mary appeared sixty years earlier, told him that he would reign briefly as pope and would be followed by the Cardinal of Kraków. Although the two did meet and converse, substantiating this legend is difficult. If it were true, it could easily explain why John Paul I felt such a deep premonition that his papacy would be short.

5

HABEMUS PAPAM!

In October 1978, the time had come for all the above-mentioned prophecies, predictions, and premonitions to materialize. Although he sometimes dismissed the possibility of it, Karol Wojtyła may have sensed that he was destined to serve the Church as pope. In Poland, when his driver announced to him at breakfast the news of the passing of John Paul I only thirty-three days into his pontificate, Wojtyła dropped his spoon onto his plate and was overwhelmed with emotion (and a migraine). He retreated to his chapel for several hours, where he prayed prostrate on the floor with his arms outstretched in the form of a cross. Father Andrew Swietochowski, who studied theology and ethics under Cardinal Wojtyła at the Catholic University of Lublin, reported that Wojtyła spent most of the night praying in Wawel Cathedral before departing the next day for the conclave. As Wojtyła was leaving for Rome, his driver wished him a safe and timely trip back to Poland. The Cardinal replied in a serious tone, "One never knows."

At the conclave, he and the other cardinals were each assigned a small cell that would serve as their home until the new pope was elected. Wojtyła was given Cell 91. When the cardinals proceeded into the Sistine Chapel, they assembled before Michelangelo's masterpiece, *The Last*

Judgement. The majestic surroundings offered them a silent homily regarding the gravity of their decision, calling them to look to the one who God points out. Especially because of the early death of John Paul I, there was an added sense of prayerful seriousness. Many surely wondered, "What is God saying to us?"

When the balloting began, two Italian cardinals were deadlocked. Sensing that an alternative needed to be chosen to resolve the stalemate, the votes in favor of Cardinal Wojtyła began to mount. One of the cardinals recalled, "When the number of votes for him approached one half [of what was needed] he cast away his pencil and sat up straight. He was red in the face. Then he was holding his head in his hands."

Years later, John Paul remarked:

I think that the conclave's vote that day surprised many people besides me! But what God commands, which may seem humanly impossible, he gives us the means to carry out. That is the secret to every vocation. Every vocation changes our plans, disclosing a new one, and it is astonishing to see how much inner help God gives us.

When the choice was made, Wojtyła accepted his fate and his mission. He was escorted to the left and under *The Last Judgement* into the *camera lacrimatoria* [the room of tears], before donning his papal vestments. Just as John Paul I took his name in honor of the two pontiffs who preceded him, John XXIII and Paul VI, Cardinal Wojtyła did the same to honor his predecessors and unite himself to their mission to implement the directives of the Second Vatican Council.

White smoke appeared from the chimney above, and the crowds who had assembled in Saint Peter's Square erupted. After the new pope was escorted to the central loggia of the basilica, overlooking the multitudes, Cardinal Pericle Felici announced, *Habemus Papam!* The crowds rejoiced, but were perplexed when they heard the name "Cardinalem Wojtyła." "Voy-tee-wa?" they wondered. Many who heard the unexpected name guessed he was from Africa or Asia. After all, it had been 455 years since a non-Italian had been pope.

Upon approaching the microphone, Pope John Paul II immediately broke from protocol. Instead of only offering the usual traditional Latin blessing, he began speaking to them in Italian, and immediately won them over, saying that the cardinals have called him from a faraway country, adding, "I do not know whether I can explain myself well in your . . . *our* Italian language. If I make a mistake, you will correct me."

In Poland, pandemonium ensued. Church bells began ringing throughout the nation, and people poured out of their homes and celebrated in the streets and flooded the churches. Father Franciszek Florczyk, who was a seminarian in Kraków at the time, said that he and the other ecstatic seminarians hastened to Wawel Cathedral to rejoice, singing the *Te Deum* to offer thanks and praise to God.

Meanwhile, the Soviets were as dumbstruck and dour as the Poles were elated. There were rumors of an angry call from within the Kremlin to the authorities in Poland, demanding to know how they could have allowed him to become a cardinal in the first place. But it was too late. In a futile effort to dampen the jubilation, the communist-controlled press ordered that no papal photograph should be larger than one column in the newspaper, and no headline could be wider than two. But it was a *fait accompli*.

Open Wide the Doors to Christ

Although the Polish government had previously blocked the Church from having sufficient access to the media, they acquiesced and allowed John Paul's installation Mass to become the first one ever televised, permitting three hours of coverage. John Paul learned of this, and made sure the Mass lasted exactly three hours. Because Poland and Italy are in the same time zone, the ten o'clock ceremony on the morning of Sunday, October 22, took place when most Poles usually attended their own Sunday services. But the nation wanted only to bask in the glow of their television sets and see their beloved bishop dressed in white for the first time. As a result, the churches were virtually abandoned. One journalist remarked, "Amazing John Paul II. On the first day of his reign, he managed to empty the churches of Poland—and on a Sunday at the hour of High Mass. Strange irony of fate, to bring about what thirty-three years of a totalitarian regime, of persecution and of police harassment had failed to achieve."

Some communists felt a sense of relief when he left Kraków to become the pope, hoping that he'd shift his focus away from them and toward the world at large. But such empty hopes imploded immediately. During the inauguration Mass, John Paul established the theme for his entire pontificate, proclaiming, "Be not afraid! Open wide the doors to Christ. To his saving power open the boundaries of states, economic and political systems, the vast fields of culture, civilization, and development."

The first item on his international agenda, however, was not Poland. Rather, he chose to accept the invitation that his predecessor had been unable to fulfill, to visit Mexico and the Dominican Republic. The Roman Curia was opposed to the visit for safety reasons, and understandably so. The Mexican government was so anti-Catholic and overrun by Masons that public displays of religion were banned. Even priests and nuns were forbidden to wear their clerics and habits in public.

Upon the Pope's arrival, the president of the republic, José López Portillo, offered him a chilly reception, greeted him with three sentences, and left. Despite the government's obvious lack of enthusiasm, the people of Mexico were so euphoric that one would have thought the Pope was in Poland! Millions lined the streets and town squares to catch a glimpse of him, waving papal flags and shouting *"Viva el papa!"*

During the trip, the Holy Father visited the miraculous image of the Virgin Mary at the Basilica of Our Lady of Guadalupe. According to Cardinal Justin Rigali:

> It was there at the shrine of Our Lady of Guadalupe, at the feet of the Blessed Mother, that he understood what God was asking him to do, which was to take the gospel to the ends of the earth. . . . He understood that it was to be a very significant part of his pontificate, traveling around the world to proclaim Jesus Christ.

When it was time to leave, as his plane ascended into the clouds, he looked down and saw thousands of flashes of light shimmering from Mexico. The faithful were pointing small mirrors and pieces of glass skyward, sending him off in a unique final gesture of love and thanksgiving. Twenty-three years later, and nearing the end of his pontificate, an ailing John Paul wanted to return to Mexico to make a pilgrimage of thanksgiving to Our Lady of Guadalupe. His aides insisted that he avoid such an unnecessary and arduous overseas trip, in light of his frail health. But his mind was set, and he informed them that he was going, and they could either come with him or not!

At the time, Monsignor Eduardo Chavez was the rector of the Basilica of Our Lady of Guadalupe. Chavez remembers watching John Paul receiving injections of medicine during the trip and struggling mightily to make his way to the basilica. When asked why it was so imperative that he return at the end of his pontificate, John Paul said that this is where everything began. He saw in 1979 that if a state that denied religious freedom could open its doors to Christ, then the same could be done in Europe. Now that Mexico had permitted his presence, how could Poland refuse?

However, no pope had ever set foot in a communist country. At the prospect of John Paul's visit to Poland, Russia was not merely opposed to the trip, but was terrified by the thought of it. The Soviet leader, Leonid Brezhnev, phoned the general secretary in Warsaw, Edward Gierek, to express his consternation that the Church had invited John Paul to visit Poland. Brezhnev recommended that the borders be closed to him. When Gierek explained that this wouldn't be feasible, Brezhnev suggested, "Tell the Pope—he's a wise man—he can declare publicly that he can't come due to an illness." Realizing that he couldn't perpetually postpone the pontiff's visit under the guise of an imaginary, unending sickness, Gierek reiterated that blocking the visit wasn't an option. Brezhnev told him,

"Gomulka was a better communist [than you], because he didn't receive Paul VI in Poland, and nothing awful happened. The Poles have survived the refusal to admit the pope once; they'll survive it a second time."

John Paul sent a message to the Polish Church, saying that he hoped to visit them for two days on the nine-hundredth anniversary of Saint Stanisław's martyrdom. However, the communists declined the request because the political overtones of the feast would be too sugges-tive and volatile. After all, Saint Stanisław was a Polish bishop whose murder was ordered by a corrupt king. The saint was a Polish symbol of religious resistance to unjust tyranny, and the communists didn't want to be equated with his persecutor by allowing John Paul to celebrate his feast on Polish soil. So, instead of coming to visit two cities for two days in May, John Paul was permitted to visit six cities for nine days in June! To accommodate the govern-ment's snub, the Polish bishops decided to declare a month-long feast for Saint Stanisław, and John Paul preached about him at nearly every event.

Although the Holy Father missed the actual feast day of Saint Stanisław, the timing of his visit allowed him to celebrate the feast of Pentecost in Poland. Before a crowd of 300,000, he celebrated Mass in Victory Square, where the communists held their most significant celebrations and rallies. However, they had never seen a crowd of this magnitude. During his homily, John Paul proclaimed: "Christ cannot be kept out of the history of man in any part of the globe, at any longitude or latitude of geography. The exclusion of Christ from the history of man is an act against man." His homily was punctuated by song and applause, with one ovation lasting fourteen minutes! In perhaps the most significant moment of the trip, John Paul thundered a prayer to invoke an outpouring of the Holy Spirit: "Send down Your Spirit! Send down Your Spirit! And renew the face of the Earth! Of this land!" He later explained that we must "call down from heaven that peace which human efforts alone cannot effect." His prayers were answered. Some have said that although the birth and baptism of Poland happened a thousand years ago, the nine days of John Paul's visit were its confirmation.

The government scrambled to assuage the damage. Although the regime typically forbade the Church to use the media, they permitted some of the papal events to be televised, in hopes that fewer people would show up. The plan was a catastrophe, as one third of the entire nation's population showed up to see him in person, while the rest watched on television. The communist-controlled media did all they could to restrict the camera angles to minimize the visuals of the size of the crowds. They were ordered not to show young people, but rather to focus on the religious, handicapped, and elderly. They rarely showed the Pope himself, and used tight close-up shots of him in order to conceal the multitudes that had gathered. One person remarked, "someone said afterwards that the Polish communist television coverage of this was like coverage of a soccer game when you showed everything except the ball." No one was fooled. In fact, the distorted video coverage only revealed the state's vulnerability and fear.

Whereas other nations preserved John Paul's Popemobiles as mementos of his visits, following his pilgrimage to Poland, the Communist Party dismantled his car in a vain effort to erase the memory of his trip. The cross that had been erected for the Papal Mass was torn down by ten o'clock that same night. However, the Poles began to bring flowers each day to the spot where the cross had been, arranging them in the shape of a cross. The government would have the floral decoration removed, and it would appear again the next day. Not knowing how to curb the people's pious enthusiasm, the entire area was walled off and the communists said the cobblestones needed to be "repaired." Indeed, the time had come for much more than the cobblestones of Poland to be repaired.

George Weigel summarized the visit well:

> That was the turning point, even if *The New York Times'* editorial for the day after the Pope left opined that, however inspiring the Pope had been, his visit would make no difference whatsoever to the politics of east central Europe. Which, I suppose, tells us something else: that *The New York Times* maintained a spotless record of getting John Paul II absolutely, spectacularly wrong for more than a quarter-century.

When the Holy Father returned to Poland in 1983, the authorities demanded to preview his speeches and requested that several changes be made to soften the tone. John Paul rejected their proposal and said, "if I am not allowed to say what I want in my own homeland, then I have nothing to do here and I am going back to Rome." They had no choice but to back down. Less than ten years later, communism had fallen and World Youth Day was celebrated in Częstochowa. Hundreds of thousands came from Russia, Belarus, and the Baltic States, gathering beneath the cross in a former Soviet bloc country. One pilgrim remarked, "That day was like a miracle . . . some were still wearing the gray-green uniforms of the Red Army but all of them went to prostrate themselves before the Icon of the Black Madonna, and former enemies, that day, became friends beneath the World Youth Day Cross."

6

POPE JOHN PAUL II

Those who knew Saint John Paul the Great often remarked that besides his constant prayerfulness, he was also exceedingly prolific, personal, and even playful. One can begin to trace a portrait of the Holy Father by examining these qualities of his personality.

Prolific

Pope John Paul II's pontificate was the third longest in history, lasting nearly twenty-seven years. Only two popes (Saint Peter and Saint Pius IX) served longer. However, the Holy Father did not merely view himself as the successor of Saint Peter but also as the heir of Saint Paul, the missionary. Over the course of John Paul's papacy, a half billion people saw him in person, which is arguably more than anyone in human history. He traveled 775,000 miles to spread the gospel, which is more than three times the distance from the earth to the moon. He made 146 trips within Italy and 104 abroad to 129 nations to deliver more than 3,000 speeches! On many of these pilgrimages, he'd visit more than a dozen cities at a time. His life was an expression of his conviction that the priest ought to be a "generous and tireless evangelizer."

For his visit to Ireland and America in 1979, one journalist chronicled, "he had travelled ten thousand miles in nine days, seen ten million people, slept an average of four-and-a-half hours per night and delivered seventy-two discourses." His longest trip was to Asia in 1986, where he traversed 32,615 miles in thirteen days. And he did most of this after the age at which most people retire! He said, "We can't wait for the faithful to show up in St. Peter's Square; we have to go to them." Some within the Vatican joked, "What is the difference between God and John Paul II? God is in all places, but the Pope has already been there."

When asked why his travel schedule was so intense, the Holy Father replied, "The more difficult the life of people, families, societies, the world is, the more it is necessary to create in their mind an image of the Good Shepherd, who 'lays down his life for the sheep.'" He added, "The more ready you are to give yourselves to God and to others, the more you will discover the authentic meaning of life."

As the bishop of Kraków, he made personal visits to his parishes on Sundays. Upon being elected the bishop of Rome, he continued the practice, visiting 320 of the 336 parishes in Rome (or inviting them to visit him, when he was too weak to travel). He did this because he realized that it was easier for one person to come to a parish than for an entire parish to come to one bishop. These encounters afforded him the opportunity to converse with everyday parishioners, as he did as a parish priest in Poland. In his mind, it wasn't only important for the faithful to hear him, but for him to hear them as well. During his parish visits, he always made time for the youth. While visiting one of his churches in Rome, a teenage boy playfully informed him of a soccer score: "Italy two, Poland zero, Your Holiness."

Commenting on John Paul's rigorous daily schedule, a reporter once asked him, "Holy Father, when do you get some free time?" He answered with a smile, saying, "All my time is free!" Another pointed out, "Holy Father, some people say that you are traveling too much." He confirmed the allegation: "Yes, I am convinced that I am traveling too much. But sometimes it is necessary to do something of what is too much." Despite his old age—and much to the dismay of his handlers—he refused to change his schedule. One of his Swiss Guards exclaimed to a crowd of college students, "There were a hundred and fifteen of us, but we could not keep up with this guy."

His assistant secretary described him as a "volcano of energy," and those who traveled with him were astonished at the amount of stamina they needed just to document his activity. On his way to Alaska, his airplane crossed the International Date Line, gaining a day. Mischievously, he looked to his exhausted team of aides and journalists, and said, "Now we must decide what to do with the extra day we have been given." Then during his brief stopover in Alaska, he donned a wolverine parka and rode a dogsled across the snow. Those who organized his travel schedule knew he was prone to such spontaneity, as could be seen when he received a handwritten letter in Rome from a farmer in Iowa, inviting him to come visit the heartland of America. The Pope accepted, and inserted a visit to Des Moines as part of a hectic American pilgrimage that had originally been scheduled for New York, Washington, D.C., and other major metropolitan cities.

However, papal pilgrimages weren't always friendly encounters with the faithful. In 1983, during his visit to Nicaragua, he scolded clergy for their involvement in liberation theology, mingling their religious vocations with political and military activism. During the Holy Father's Mass, members of the Marxist Sandinista National Liberation

Front attempted to drown out the Pope's Mass with revolutionary slogans shouted over megaphones, and lowered the volume on his microphone from backstage. He reverently paused with closed eyes and folded hands, looked up, and shouted, *"Silence!"* In Chile, he gave children their First Holy Communion at the same Mass at which protestors burned tires and soldiers launched tear gas. The fumes made it difficult to breathe, but he refused to surrender the liturgy to its opponents.

During each of these trips, the Holy Father often prepared dozens of unique speeches. Upon returning to Rome (and often in transit), he'd write apostolic letters, encyclicals, and a host of other documents. In the first nine months of his pontificate, he wrote nearly 500 speeches! The Vatican Press publishes an annual volume of these papal discourses. John Paul averaged more than 3,000 pages every year, and the written text of his 15,000-plus discourses and documents take up nearly a dozen linear feet of shelf space! According to the postulator of his cause for canonization, Sławomir Oder, if you were to compile everything he wrote during his pontificate, it would be approximately the length of twenty Bibles.

However, what he wrote paled in comparison to what he read. He was such a prolific reader that his staff referred to his room as a library with a bed in it. In Kraków, his driver, Józef Mucha, installed a table and reading lamp in the backseat of the car so that he could study and write while in transit. What is fascinating, though, isn't the amount of time he spent reading, but that he was capable of absorbing information from two sources simultaneously. His secretary recalled, "On his holidays he read something sophisticated, while somebody next to him read [aloud] something lighter. He had that gift of split concentration. That wasn't a myth."

Several of his close associates noticed that he could have a full conversation with someone while reading. Other times, he'd read his mail while presiding over formal discussions, or write a speech while an instructor taught him a new language! He mentioned that he would sometimes get tired at meetings if he weren't able to work on something else simultaneously.

Even during the proceedings of the Second Vatican Council, Cardinal Albino Luciani (Pope John Paul I) recalled that Wojtyła "never stopped writing." However, he wasn't taking notes on the Council speeches. He was absorbing the content of the presentations while working on his poetry and other yet-to-be-published books. Even during the conclave that elected Pope John Paul I, Cardinal Wojtyła was writing what the world would soon know as the Theology of the Body. This was not a division of his attention, but rather evidence that his concentration could be multiplied.

John Paul's intelligence was evident during his first homily as pope—in which he spoke eleven languages! Not surprisingly, Archbishop Derek Worlock of Liverpool described him as "the greatest intellect I have ever met." John Paul's breadth of knowledge was formed in part by the vast number of conferences and meetings he hosted as a bishop and cardinal. Each week, he would meet with scientists, attorneys, doctors, actors, engineers, and other professionals, listening and contributing to their presentations on topics ranging from "the division between physics and the philosophy of nature" to ethics, nursing, and marital counseling.

Thanks be to God, John Paul offered his intellect to serve the Church. In order to offer the faithful examples of the universal call to holiness, he canonized 482 new saints and beatified 1,338, and had files with all their biographies in his bedroom, which he often read for inspiration. Since the time when the canonization process was formalized in 1588, all previous popes combined had canonized only 302 saints. John Paul averaged one canonization every three weeks!

The Holy Father knew that the world had seen an unprecedented amount of evil in the twentieth century, and it was therefore essential to demonstrate that grace prevails where sin abounds. According to a special commission that was established by the Church to catalogue martyrs, of the estimated forty million martyrs in the history of Christianity, perhaps twenty-seven million of them were murdered in the twentieth century. Therefore, more Christians died for their faith in the last century than in all previous centuries combined. However, John Paul knew that it wasn't enough to denounce the tyrannies and persecutions that afflicted the saints. What mattered more is that their heroic virtue would be manifested to the faithful.

But John Paul wasn't interested in merely focusing on the saints. He also shone a piercing light upon the sinners of the Church as well, asking forgiveness on behalf of the Church "for the weaknesses of so many of her sons and daughters who sullied her face." In order to purify the identity and mission of the Church as it entered the new millennium, it was necessary to focus on its history with humility.

Cardinal Wyszyński predicted at the outset of John Paul's pontificate that God was calling him to lead the Church into the third millennium. As he guided the Church to the threshold of this goal, he explained that, "preparing for the *Year 2000 has become as it were a hermeneutical key of my Pontificate.*" In his first encyclical, *Redemptor*

Hominis, he declared that the Church was in a season of a new Advent. What this meant for John Paul was that he was being called by God to usher in a springtime of evangelization in order to build up a civilization of love. He believed from the outset of his pontificate that this task was not merely the responsibility of the priests. In the spirit of Vatican II, John Paul sought to promote the Church's identity as the people of God, inviting the laity to take a more active role in spreading the gospel.

John Paul's zeal for souls extended far beyond Catholicism, as can be seen by his heroic efforts of ecumenism toward Judaism, Islam, Eastern Orthodoxy, and Protestantism. He was the first pope to set foot in a mosque, the first in the modern era to enter a Roman synagogue, and the first to visit Canterbury Cathedral. His respect for religious freedom and his willingness to dialogue with other religions explains why eighty thousand Muslim youth gathered to hear him preach in Morocco, and why more than one hundred of the world's most prominent religious leaders responded to his invitation to join him in Assisi to pray for peace.

He not only visited the tombs of Catholic martyrs, but during a trip to Slovakia paused to pray to God before a monument remembering two dozen Protestants who had been killed by Catholics! Despite the objections of some within the Church, he wasn't glossing over the serious doctrinal differences and promoting religious syncretism. Rather, he was making the effort to reconcile with people of good will, at least in the areas of faith that could be mutually agreed upon. Especially in regard to Christian unity, his ecumenical efforts were not, in his words, "a matter of choice but the wish and prayer of Christ."

Beyond the mere absence of discrimination, John Paul was well known for defending people who embraced other creeds. One of his Jewish friends was troubled upon hearing that a Polish church displayed a painting of Jews as ravenous animals attacking Christ as he carried his cross. A monsignor replied to the man, "Oh, that! I know just the painting you mean. It was horrible and disgusting! But didn't you know? Your friend Wojtyła had it removed when he was archbishop."

"Removed it to where?" he inquired. "A museum?"

"Oh, no," the monsignor said. "Better than that. He had it put down in the basement at the monastery, where it would be eaten by rats."

Personal

John Paul's tireless efforts to evangelize were visible to millions. However, many who came to see him were only able to catch a glimpse of his white zucchetto as he passed by in the Popemobile. What many never had the opportunity to discover was his warm personality and heroic patience. One of his friends remarked, "He sort of reminded me of my grandfather—his concern, his solicitude for everyone, the gentleness about him."

Father Raniero Cantalamessa often witnessed these qualities while serving as the preacher to the Papal Household, meaning that he offered retreats to the Pope, cardinals, bishops, and others in the Vatican. He noticed that in the midst of the Holy Father's incessant meetings, he never seemed rushed. Cantalamessa explained:

This is an aspect of the Pope that has impressed me greatly; it would seem he is never in a hurry. Despite everything the Pope has to do and all the problems he has to address, when he is with someone he exists only for that person. Once I was caught in Rome's traffic and, despite the driver's efforts, we arrived a quarter of an hour late for the preaching. To tell the truth, some cardinals were impatient and waiting at the door. The Pope, instead, was tranquil in his chapel, praying the Rosary, showing no sign of impatience for my delay.

The first time he preached in Saint Peter's Basilica, Father Cantalamessa knew he had to speak slowly because of the strong echo. "But by speaking slowly," he recalled, "my preaching lasted ten minutes longer than foreseen." Meanwhile, in the audience, the prefect of the Pontifical Household—who was charged with the planning and carrying out of papal ceremonies—was growing anxious and began glancing at his watch periodically. The next day, John Paul called the prelate and, according to Father Cantalamessa, "told him affably that when someone speaks to us in the Name of God we must not look at our watch."

Even when people spoke to him about nonreligious matters, he exercised tremendous patience. General Wojciech Jaruzelski remarked that he "is a man who knows how to listen calmly even when he disagrees completely with what he hears . . ." His journalist friend, André Frossard, concurred: "He is such a good listener that you even begin to get the impression you are saying something truly interesting."

However, his patience often tried the patience of others. He was chronically late because he'd often spend more time with individuals than anyone had anticipated. One priest who assisted him said, "To him the value of the present person always outweighed the value of where we were going, because we'd get there eventually." As a result, appointments would not infrequently begin two hours later than expected. On one occasion as a cardinal, a lunch was supposed to begin at 1:30, but he arrived late and announced, "The Cardinal arrived for lunch at half past one. It is not true what your watch says."

John Paul viewed each encounter as a divine appointment, and those who conversed with him sensed this. One man remarked, "he spoke to me with his eyes, because he could do that, you know. He could look right into your soul." Another added, "Talking to him gave the impression that he knew what you were saying better than you did yourself. . . . around Wojtyła, it was impossible to lie, because he saw right through you, even if he seemed to be enjoying your fabrications." Still another reminisced, "Despite that killing schedule of his, he never rushes things. He focuses his whole attention on me. He has ears only for me. I'm chosen. Raised up. Unique. The most important one. And yet, in some strange way, others are included." He added that the Pope "had this incredible, mysterious gift: even talking to a crowd, even a crowd of millions, he made each and every member of the crowd feel that it is only him or her to whom he speaks."

The Holy Father's memory was superb, and it was universally reported that he had the capacity to recall unimportant details of conversations that took place years ago. Those close to the Holy Father also noticed that he kept a personal atlas on which he marked every diocese and knew by heart the names of every bishop in the world. Considering that there are more than two thousand dioceses, one marvels at the breadth not only of John Paul's intellect, but more important, his heart. In *Crossing the Threshold of Hope*, he spoke of "a kind of *geography of the Pope's prayer* . . ." This became evident to Cardinal Theodore McCarrick of Washington, D.C., when he told the Holy Father that he recently visited the churches in central Asia. The Pope replied, "Central Asia . . . Yes: Kazakhstan, Turkmenistan, Kyrgyzstan, Tajikistan, and Uzbekistan." McCarrick recalled, "I was so amazed, I said, 'Holy Father, that's very good.' He gave me a look that said, 'Aren't I supposed to be pope for all the world?'"

But it wasn't just the nations, prelates, and dignitaries who received personal attention from the Holy Father. One year during Advent, he left the Papal Apartments in order to visit the Vatican's outdoor Nativity scene. A Roman street cleaner's daughter managed to approach the Holy Father, asking if he would be willing to officiate her wedding. Much to the surprise of Vatican officials, he gladly accepted and celebrated the private Mass two months later in the Vatican.

On yet another occasion, on Christmas Eve of 1986, a Swiss Guard named Andreas Widmer was standing at his post when John Paul exited twenty feet away on his way to the Midnight Mass. The Holy Father didn't recognize the young man, and called out, "You're new! What's your name?" The Pope approached him, noticed his reddened eyes, and immediately perceived what was happening. "This is your first Christmas away from home, isn't it?" The Guard recalled, "I replied in the affirmative, barely holding back tears as I answered. Yet again, he stepped closer, pausing just inches from me this time. Taking my hand with one hand and holding my elbow with the other, he pulled me slightly toward him, looking at me with his deep gray eyes, and said, 'Andreas, I want to thank you for the sacrifice you are making for the Church. I will pray for you during Mass this evening.'" To John

Paul, the person who is working is always more important than the work the person is doing.

Playful

Despite the endless number of meetings and responsibilities that the Holy Father attended to every week, he lived a balanced life. Recreation for John Paul was truly a time for re-creation. Tuesday was his day off, but instead of recharging in the Vatican, once or twice each month he and a few friends would leave to go on daylong excursions. Initially, no one in the Vatican knew about them. In order to sneak out without being noticed by the Swiss Guards, the Holy Father disguised himself by hiding behind a newspaper or wearing a black hooded cloak and riding in the backseat of a priest's car. Later on in his pontificate, he'd escape in a black car with tinted windows, and even the most observant Vatican reporters were unable to keep track of him. Late in his pontificate, when he was confined to a wheelchair, he continued making his secret getaways. He took more than one hundred of these excursions, most of them to Abruzzo, a mountainous region two hours east of Rome.

John Paul had a great love for the mountains, and three years after his assassination attempt, at the age of sixty-four, he could still be found skiing on an 11,000-foot glacier in the Italian Alps. He continued skiing until he was seventy-three, when hip surgery required him to hang up his skis.

During one of his clandestine ski excursions, a young boy noticed the Pope and began shouting "The Pope, the Pope!" The priest accompanying the Holy Father told the youngster, "Don't be silly! . . ."—before they rushed back to their car and bolted to the Vatican. On another occasion, a boy of about eight seemed to be watching the Holy Father, who kept smiling back at him. Eventually, the youngster approached him and asked, "Are you the Pope?" John Paul's reply? "Yes, do you want to ski with me?" The two went up the ski lift and down the mountain a number of times. After one of their runs, the boy yelled to his mother, who was sitting at a chair at the bottom of the slope, "Mom, did you know I'm skiing with the Pope?" The mom simply grinned and shook her head at the boy's overactive imagination. Later in the morning, John Paul decided to pay a visit to the mother, who an eyewitness described as "flabbergasted."

With the exception of corrupt politicians and dissident theologians, John Paul always seemed to put people at ease. Early in his pontificate, while taking a stroll through the Vatican Gardens, he met one of the gardeners. John Paul extended his hand to greet the man. The gardener looked down, embarrassed at his grimy hands, but the Holy Father grabbed them both and pressed them against his white cassock, saying that he didn't mind if they were dirty, because he didn't have to do his own laundry!

At times, bishops were on the receiving end of John Paul's humor. One of his biographers recounted, "One bishop, who had put on weight since he had last seen the Pope, was asked by John Paul, 'Is your diocese growing?' The bishop replied, yes, parishes were expanding. 'So is the bishop,' said the Pope."

During a meal with bishops in America, Theodore Mc-Carrick, then archbishop of Newark, pointed out the elderly, retired leader of the Archdiocese of Philadelphia, Cardinal John Krol, and playfully said to the Pope: "Holy Father, isn't it wonderful that Cardinal Krol looks so well? He's getting younger all the time. Why, he probably could take another diocese now!" The bishops laughed, and then John Paul turned to McCarrick and suggested a new appointment: "Newark!"

His charm was apparent to the thousands of people he invited into his home. At the Papal Apartments, he found solace in company, inviting friends and other guests in a seemingly endless stream of visitors who joined him for meals. Some within the Vatican were perturbed by the traffic, saying that the Papal Apartments had turned into Campo de' Fiori (a vast, outdoor Roman marketplace).

Those who dined often with John Paul couldn't help but notice that he had a sweet tooth. His assistant secretary recalled his fondness for after-dinner treats. He remembered that on one occasion:

> The nuns were not serving the dessert because the Holy Father was thinking about his figure. But he liked sweets so much that quite often he would give the nuns a sign that he wanted a cookie. We all knew that sign. He didn't need to say anything. Not even looking toward the nuns, he would draw a circle on the tablecloth with his index finger. He would draw and draw. And he was mysteriously smiling. It looked very funny. And the nuns had no choice but to bring him a cookie.

John Paul was living proof that the more holy a person becomes, the more human he becomes. As he told the college students in Kraków, "every man who seeks the Kingdom of God finds himself."

Hiking in Poland, 1997.

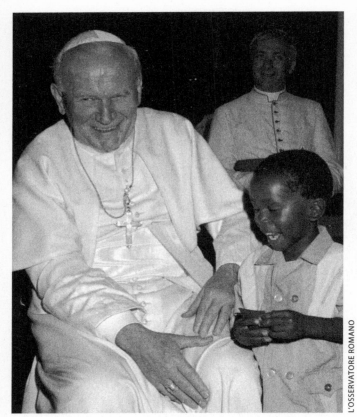

"It is no secret that the Pope loves young people . . . and that he feels immensely happy in your company."

—*John Paul II*

L'OSSERVATORE ROMANO

"Il bambino e la solo madre," Crystalina and John Paul Evert, February 2005. (See page xvii).

Praying in the chapel of the archbishop's residence in Baltimore after discovering the closed chapel, October 1995. (See page 138).

"Were we to disregard the Eucharist, how could we overcome our own deficiency?" —*John Paul II*

Making an unscheduled visit to the chapel of St. Mary's seminary, October 1995. (See page 139).

Praying the Rosary for the attendees of World Youth Day in Denver, August 15, 1993. (See page 91)

W. H. KEELER

"[The Rosary is] our daily meeting which neither I nor Blessed Virgin Mary neglect."

—*John Paul II*

Praying to our Lady on April 12, 1993.

"One hand shot, and another guided the bullet."

—*John Paul II*

The bullet that injured John Paul II inserted into the crown of Our Lady of Fatima (See page 152).

Blessing the sick in Lombardia, Italy, 1992.

"You can do very much by your prayer and your sacrifice, your suffering . . . you can obtain much from Jesus Christ for those who may not need physical help, but who often are in terrible need of spiritual help . . . Your role in the parish is not merely passive." —John Paul II

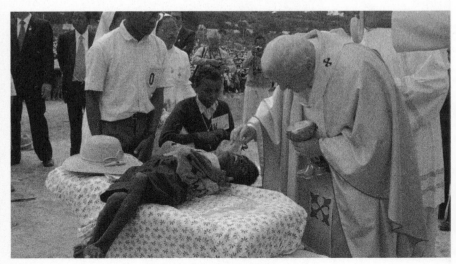

Distributing Communion to the sick in Africa, 1989.

Praying at St. John Lateran Basilica June 19, 2003.

"The papacy brings with it "thorns and crosses that often remain hidden in the secrecy of the heart. But . . . these sufferings are the guarantee of fruitfulness of an apostolate that, with God's help, will produce abundant results." —John Paul II

Hearing confessions, Good Friday, 2002 (See page 189).

MAX ROSSI/REUTERS/CORBIS/ L'OSSERVATORE ROMANO

Praying the Stations of the Cross, Good Friday, 2005 (See page 201).

"Prayer joined to sacrifice constitutes the most powerful force in human history." —John Paul II

The Funeral Mass of the Holy Father, April 8, 2005 (See page 203).

PART II

HIS FIVE LOVES

7

YOUNG PEOPLE

In 1980, on a summer's night in France, 50,000 teenagers gathered to spend the evening with Pope John Paul II at Parc des Princes Stadium—with another 35,000 standing outside. Although they had come to hear the Pope, he had come for the opposite reason; he wanted to listen to them. Regarding his interactions with young people, he said, "I always explain [to] them that what I tell them is not important. What really matters is what you tell me."

Because he wanted to hear about their thoughts and struggles, he arranged for them to have their own microphone during the event. The youth were given the opportunity to present twenty-one questions to the Holy Father, covering a wide range of issues that mattered most to them. During the dialogue, John Paul put down the text for his speech and gave personal answers to their questions, and nearly three hours passed before the exchange came to an end.

Some asked him why the Church's teachings on sexual ethics were so strict. One inquired, "In questions of a sexual nature the Church has a rather intransigent attitude. Are you not afraid, Holy Father, that young people will move further and further away from the Church?"

He replied:

If you think of this question deeply, going right to the heart of the problem, I assure you that you will realize only one thing, which is that in this domain the only demands made by that Church are those bound up with true, that is, responsible, conjugal love. She demands what the dignity of the person and the basic social order require. I do not deny that they are demands. But that is the essential point, that man fulfills himself only to the extent that he knows how to impose demands on himself. In the opposite case "he goes away, sorrowful," as we have just read in the Gospel. Permissiveness does not make men happy. The consumer society does not make men happy. It never has.

The idea that love is "demanding" was a thread woven into the Pope's messages to young people throughout his pontificate. Yet joined to this constant challenge was the assurance that God would never request that which exceeds man's abilities.

All the teens' questions had been posed to him in an orderly manner until one young man interrupted the program and jumped up to the microphone, identifying himself as an atheist. He proceeded to ask the Holy Father a barrage of questions: "I am an atheist. I refuse to accept any belief and any dogmatism. I also mean that I do not combat anyone's faith; but I do not understand faith. . . . Holy Father, in whom do you believe? Why do you believe? What is it that is worth the gift of our life and what manner of being is this God that you adore?"

Before John Paul could discuss the matter with him, he ducked back into the crowd, and the evening's schedule continued. When the event concluded and the Pope returned to Rome, the thought of that young man weighed upon his heart and he regretted that the boy's questions were left unanswered. Like the good shepherd who leaves the ninety-nine sheep in search of the one who is lost, John Paul wrote to the French prelate who presided over the visit, Cardinal François Marty, asking for him to begin a search for the young man—among the 85,000 youth who came to the stadium! Once the prelate managed to locate the boy, John Paul asked the Cardinal to deliver a personal message to him, apologizing that he had left his questions unanswered. The message included an invitation to join the Holy Father in the Vatican for lunch. The Holy See flew the young man to Rome, where he was able to sit with the Pope, sharing his struggles with the idea of believing in God.

The encounter at Parc des Princes Stadium was such a memorable experience for John Paul that whenever he prepared to visit a foreign nation, he always asked "whether they have a Parc des Princes there." It became a catalyst for the idea of World Youth Days, which began six years later in Rome.

The Eternal Teenager

John Paul was always at ease with young people because he had dedicated so much of his pastoral ministry to them from the beginning. He asserted that ministry to the youth was in his blood, and that he never neglected it at any point in his life. During his first parish assignment as a priest, Father Karol began taking students on the camping trips mentioned above. At nighttime, the teens would join hands with him around a campfire, praying and singing popular songs. These experiences were the seed of World Youth Days, which eventually bloomed into outdoor festivals of prayer that inspired more than ten million young souls.

After he was reassigned to St. Florian's, he spent much of his time in the heart of Kraków with the men and women from the local universities. One Polish priest who watched him interact with the college students in Poland remarked that he was "never happier than when working with young people," who considered him "the eternal teenager." He led high school and college retreats, and the attendees regularly sought him out to help them with their personal difficulties or relationship issues. The students recalled that he wouldn't lecture them, but instead listened intently and then led them by asking questions that brought them closer to the answer.

Many of these heart-to-heart colloquies took place in the wilderness, while students hiked beside him or took turns kayaking with him. An instructor at the University of Lublin, who had spent time with "Wujek" on canoeing trips, said, "He lived and breathed these problems. And because young people live and breathe love, he lived and breathed these young people's love."

Even after becoming the Cardinal of Kraków, Wojtyła remained a youth minister at heart. Father Franciszek Florczyk was a high school student in Poland at the time, and hiked with the future pope in the wilderness. He remembered how Wojtyła would often visit the teenagers on their high school retreats, even though there were only between forty and sixty students. The Cardinal would arrive in the morning, but didn't come only to pray with them. He would teach them, dine with them, sing with them, and watch their comedy routines, laughing with them late into the night. Bishop Andrew Wypych assisted at some of the retreats as a seminarian in Kraków, and recalled that the Cardinal would often remain with the young people at the bonfires talking and praying so late that he would not get home until after midnight. More than two decades after these retreats, Father Florczyk visited the Holy Father in the Vatican, and was astonished that John Paul began asking about one teenager after the other by name, inquiring as to how they were doing.

Whether in a classroom, forest, or stadium, he never shied away from challenging young people, and he knew they thrived on the confidence he had in them. He declared to them: "I believe in youth with all my heart and with all the strength of my conviction." He knew that their hearts were made for love and their minds were made for the truth. In *Crossing the Threshold of Hope*, he added:

> . . . young people are always searching for the beauty in love. They want their love to be beautiful. If they give in to weakness, following models of behavior . . . in the depths of their hearts they still desire a beautiful and pure love. This is as true of boys as it is of girls. Ultimately, they know that only God can give them this love. As a result, they are willing to follow Christ, without caring about the sacrifices this may entail.

The Pope was an inspiration for young people, but they were also a wellspring of hope for him. On the day of his papal inauguration, October 22, 1978, he said to the young people gathered in Saint Peter's Square, "You are the hope of the Church and of the world. You are my hope." He added later, "the young are the comfort and the strength of the Pope." There was no doubt about the fact that he had confidence in the youth. The only question was if the youth would hold the hierarchy of the Church in equal esteem. When a young woman told him that she hoped the bishops of Poland would not be disappointed in the young people, he replied that he hoped "the young people of Poland would not be disappointed in their bishops!"

His love for the youth was manifested on virtually every papal pilgrimage. In 1979, during his first visit to Poland as pope, the young people gathered beneath his window and wouldn't let him sleep. Their presence was never a surprise to him, because he would say before the visits, "If someone is interested, I am staying at Franciszkańska Street 3." The modern equivalent of this would be a professional athlete or musician using social media to announce to all his fans what hotel room he'd be staying in during an upcoming event! John Paul wasn't focused on secluding himself, because he wanted to see the people he loved. They sang and prayed in the street below his room in the bishop's residence, waiting for him to join in. He always conceded to their requests for spontaneous dialogues, fellowship, and prayer.

On one occasion, he jumped up to stand on the windowsill, saying that in the past he had been a well-behaved person who would never do such a thing. But now? "What happened to me?" When the youth cried out to him, "Take us with you!," he assured them, "I have taken you with me everywhere I go. Not a day goes by without my feeling your presence near." He sang along with the students a Polish folk song that described a homesick man:

Don't you miss the country you came from,
Don't you miss the mountains, the pastures?
Return to your pastures and valleys and streams.
But the highlander cannot return, because he has been
Called away by the Lord and is on his way to heaven.

When he reminisced about how he missed the Tatra Mountains, the youth cried out to him, "Then stay with us." He answered, "Ah, you're wise now . . . but it's too late.

Where were you on October 16 [the date of his election]? You weren't there to defend me. Just like Poles, to close the barn door when the horse is gone." Laughter erupted, and it was impossible to know who was enjoying the presence of the other more.

On the Pope's next international trip, he celebrated Mass with the young people in Ireland. Father (now Cardinal) Justin Rigali accompanied him on the visit, and recalled that the audience burst into applause no less than forty-two times during the Pope's homily! Toward the end of his message, John Paul declared, "Young people of Ireland, I love you!" Rigali noted, "The applause, according to my watch, was between—believe it or not—between twelve and thirteen minutes. This was the forty-first applause of forty-two."

After the Holy Father's trip, a group of young people from Ireland traveled to Rome to repay his visit. Cardinal Rigali recalled that during their private audience, a young man said, "Holy Father, do you know what you did for the young people of Ireland?" The Pope smiled, patted him on the shoulder, and moved on to the next person and continued down the line, greeting the others. The young man was obviously disappointed that the Pope didn't say anything in reply to his question. However, after greeting a few more young pilgrims, the Pope turned around and returned to the boy and put his hand on his shoulder and said, "And do you know what the young people of Ireland did for the Pope?"

World Youth Days

His reception among young people on every other continent was just as affectionate and exuberant. In Mexico, the youth shouted, *"Juan Pablo Secundo, te quiere todo el mundo!* [John Paul II, the whole world loves you!]" In the Philippines, in what may have been the largest gathering in human history, between five and seven million people celebrated the closing Mass of World Youth Day in 1995.

However, when he chose to hold the eighth World Youth Day in Denver, many—even within the hierarchy of the Church—doubted that American teens would be interested in listening to the seventy-three-year-old successor of Saint Peter. Bishops recommended that the event be hosted in Cleveland, Minneapolis-St. Paul, or Buffalo, but John Paul insisted that the host city be Denver. Pessimists expected as few as 20,000 people to show up, but more than a half million were in attendance, forming the largest gathering of people in the history of Colorado.

As the Pope's helicopter descended upon Mile High Stadium, the teenagers erupted and the roar of their voices was sufficient to create an atmospheric disturbance. George Weigel reported, "The turbulence created by the youngsters' cheers, the pilot later said, was buffeting the aircraft so strongly that it was causing instability." As he landed, a rainbow arched across the sky, as if on cue. Cardinal James Stafford recalled, "Young people were pointing to it [the rainbow] in wonder . . . The Pope wept openly before the thunderous ovations of the universal Church." The Holy Father evoked similar responses from the youth in St. Louis six years later at the Kiel Center, with one journalist describing the sound of the teenagers as "ear-splitting." As usual, they thundered their chants of "John Paul II, we love you!" He then exhorted the young people of America, "Remember: Christ is calling you; the Church needs you; the Pope believes in you and he expects great things of you!"

The warm reception offered to him by American teens further bolstered his hopes for the next generation of the faithful. Just two months after the visit to Colorado, he greeted Cardinal Stafford, "Ah! Denver, *una rivoluzione!* [a revolution!]" Those who had the opportunity to dine with the Holy Father in the Vatican soon noticed that the only photo in his dining room was of him, holding his Rosary and peering out the window of his helicopter at the multitudes of young people awaiting his arrival for the closing Mass. Many years later, he added that the event in Denver "still lives on in my heart as one of the highlights of my pontificate."

In rain or shine, young people flocked to see him at World Youth Days across the globe. His helicopter landed in Toronto in 2002 amidst a torrential downpour of rain. Saturated pilgrims had spent the previous night in the open fields, hunkering down as tornado warnings were issued for the area before the papal Mass. When the Pope arrived, the organizer of World Youth Day, Father Thomas Rosica, apologized to the Holy Father for the poor weather. The Pope smiled, looked at the sky, stretched out his hand in the direction of the dark clouds, and blessed them. "Don't worry," John Paul told him. Mass began, and the rains began to slow. The rays of light peered through the clouds at the moment of the Gospel reading, and as John Paul began his homily, the sky cleared.

The phenomenon of World Youth Days became an enigma for the modern media as they sought to unravel the mystery of why so many teens and young adults were enraptured by the elderly pontiff. *Time* magazine reported:

> His appearances generate an electricity unmatched by anyone else on earth. That explains, for instance, why

in rural Kenyan villages thousands of children, plus many cats and roosters and even hotels, are named John Paul. Charisma is the only conceivable reason why a CD featuring him saying the Rosary—in Latin —against a background of Bach and Handel is currently ascending the charts in Europe.

While some credited "charisma," others assumed his popularity among the youth was just a case of youngsters being starstruck by a celebrity figure. But the reason why millions flocked to him was not because they viewed him as a superstar. No, they came because they wished to see Jesus. The more the world deprives young people of what is true, good, and beautiful, the more earnestly will they yearn for it. The vacuum of modern secularism is actually a fragrant invitation for young people to rediscover the sacred.

John Paul knew this. He knew the events weren't about him, as he explained in *Crossing the Threshold of Hope*:

As a young priest and pastor I came to this way of looking at young people and at youth, and it has remained constant all these years. . . . anywhere the Pope goes, *he seeks out the young and the young seek him out. Actually, in truth, it is not the Pope who is being sought out at all. The one being sought out is Christ*, who knows "that which is in every man" (cf. Jn 2:25), especially in a young person, and who can give true answers to his questions! And even if they are demanding answers, the young are not afraid of them; more to the point, they even await them. This also explains the idea of holding World Youth Days. . . . *No one invented the World Youth Days. It was the young people themselves who created them.*

If it was Christ who the young people were looking for, why were they coming to see the Pope? The answer is simple: Like Jesus, the Pope was uncompromising, authentic, and loving.

Uncompromising

Young people yearn for meaning, truth, love, and freedom, and they get themselves into no small amount of trouble attempting to unravel these mysteries of life. As they stumble to find the answers, they grow weary of a culture that views them as a disappointment. Then along comes Saint John Paul the Great, declaring: "Young people of every continent, do not be afraid to be the saints of the new millennium! Be contemplative, love prayer." And on the occasion of another World Youth Day:

> Dear young people, do not be content with anything less than the highest ideals! Do not let yourselves be dispirited by those who are disillusioned with life and have grown deaf to the deepest and most authentic desires of their heart. You are right to be disappointed with hollow entertainment and passing fads, and with aiming at too little in life.

This was perhaps the first trait of John Paul that the youth discovered upon encountering him: he was uncompromising. Perhaps one bishop put it best when he said that the Holy Father was "happy and demanding." It never occurred to the Pope that he might want to tone it down to draw bigger crowds, or lower the bar so as to avoid putting off teenagers. That was the world's job, not his. If he lowered the standard, he'd miss the chance to invite people to live lives of heroic virtue. Some suggested that young people would be more interested in the Church if the Holy Father would unwind a bit and lighten up about all the moral regulations. But his refusal to do so is precisely what drew people to him. He wasn't alluring *despite* his challenges, but precisely *because* of them. If young people wanted someone to offer them an easy life, insulated by their own subjective moral values, they could have sat in front of a television instead of making an intercontinental pilgrimage and sleeping overnight with a million strangers on a dirt floor.

Young people didn't make the trips to see him because he was simply a good man, but because he was capable of revealing to them their own capacity for goodness. He saw something in the youth that perhaps they didn't even see in themselves. As one attendee of World Youth Day remarked, "He showed us to ourselves." John Paul did this by directing them to the person of Jesus Christ. In his words, "Without the Gospel, man remains a dramatic question with no adequate answer."

The youth wanted answers, and John Paul never vacillated in offering them. He knew young people well enough to understand that they don't want a watered-down version of the faith. They want to be presented with the fullness of a message, and then be given the freedom to accept or reject it. He knew this, and reminded teens in Madison Square Garden that they are "approaching that stage in your life when you must take personal responsibility for your own destiny."

In Canada, he challenged the youth to avoid the trap of seeking out the false consolations of the world: "In times of darkness do not seek an escape," the Pope said. "Have the courage to resist the dealers in deception who make capital of your hunger for happiness and who make you pay dearly for a moment of 'artificial paradise,' a whiff of smoke, a dose of drinking or drugs. What claims to be a shortcut to happiness leads nowhere." The most famous maxim of Marxism was that religion is the opium of the people. One of John Paul's friends noted that he rightly inverted this notion, demonstrating that opium [in its many modern forms] had become the religion of the people.

John Paul knew what the youth wanted because he knew them. He was well aware that young people don't want authority figures pandering to them. One of the young people who had camped with him in Poland noted, "Today, many priests try to be like the kids. We were trying to be like him."

Authentic

Those who gathered to hear him also discovered that he was authentic. Young people have a knack for detecting duplicity and authenticity, and this is one reason John Paul's personality was such a magnet for them. As Pope Paul VI remarked, "Modern man listens more willingly to witnesses than to teachers, and if he does listen to teachers, it is because they are witnesses."

A French journalist observed, "In him the Gospel, the vocation and the person all form one—not a very frequent occurrence—and it is this literally nuclear inner coherence that gives him his radiance." There was no difference between what he believed and what he said, or what he thought and who he was. Young people often sense an unnerving level of disintegration within themselves because their beliefs and behaviors aren't often in harmony. They sense a lack of integration. To many people—both young and old—John Paul was a much-needed examination of their conscience. One author noted, "For every person, an encounter with the successor of Christ was, and it had to be, a challenge, a moment of reflection on one's self and on one's life. It was really as if one stood in front of one's own conscience, in total truth in front of one's self."

John Paul's presence was an invitation for people to evaluate not only their current spiritual state, but also where they would ultimately stand before God. While offering a day of recollection for youth in Poland, he encouraged them to examine their own conscience, "so that God does not surprise us with an examination one day . . . We are often tempted not to enter the depth of our own conscience; let us reject this immediately and proceed into the depth." Although the idea of the final judgment is intimidating, John Paul said, "In his transcendence man goes to meet God, who is infinitely perfect. He halts, so to speak, on the threshold of *judgment*, which is to be understood as a need to see where he stands when finally confronted by absolute and universal truth."

As the Vicar of Christ, he showed the young people that this was not about standing in a courtroom, awaiting a guilty verdict. Rather, it meant putting aside all masks, rumors, façades, and illusions of themselves in order to see themselves as God sees them. One should not fear this, because as he said to the youth in Toronto, *"We are not the sum of our weaknesses and failures*; we are the sum of the Father's love for us and our real capacity to become the image of his Son." In many ways, John Paul was an earthly icon of *the* Holy Father in heaven. As he wrote in his play *Radiation of Fatherhood*, "And in the end . . . everything else will turn out to be unimportant and inessential, except for this: father, child, and love."

Loving

The Holy Father's uncompromising authenticity was alluring, but nothing endeared him to young people as much as their realization of how much he loved them. He told the youth in Asia, "It is no secret that the Pope loves young people like you, and that he feels immensely happy in your company." On one occasion, when American teenagers chanted to him: "John Paul II, we love you!" he replied, "Perhaps he loves you more!" They knew he was right. In a sense, what Saint John the Evangelist said of God the Father was also true of the Pope: "We love, because he first loved us" (1 Jn 4:19).

Perhaps the greatest gift of love that John Paul offered to young people was that he taught them *how* to love. In his first encyclical, the Pope acknowledged that the human person is made for love:

> Man cannot live without love. He remains a being that is incomprehensible for himself, his life is senseless, if love is not revealed to him, if he does not encounter love, if he does not experience it and make it his own, if he does not participate intimately in it. This, as has already been said, is why Christ the Redeemer "fully reveals man to himself."

Young people incessantly search for such love, but he pointed out, "It is not enough simply to want to accept such love. One must know how to give it, and it's often not ready to be received. Many times it is necessary to help it to be formed." In order to form young people in their ability to love, John Paul reminded them that authentic love is pure, and always leads others to the source of love, which is God himself. But instead of merely inviting young people to be abstinent, he called them to *love chastity*, understanding it as a virtue that frees them to love in the image and likeness of God.

When speaking to the youth in Uganda, he offered a succinct explanation of God's plan for human love and sexuality, through the lens of the Theology of the Body:

> *Essential to preparing for marriage is your vocation to chastity.* I know that young people reject hypocrisy. You want to be honest with yourselves and others. A chaste person is honest. When God created us he gave us more than one way to "speak" to each other. *Besides expressing ourselves through speech, we express ourselves through our bodies.* Gestures are like "words" that tell who we are. Sexual actions are "words" that reveal our hearts. *The Lord wants us to use our sexuality according to his plan.* He expects us to "speak" truthfully. Honest sexual "language" requires a commitment to lifelong fidelity. To give your body to another person symbolizes the total gift of yourself to that person. But if you are not married, you are admitting that you might change your mind in the future. Total self-giving would then be absent. *Without the bond of marriage, sexual relations are a lie.* . . . Do not be deceived by the empty words of those who ridicule chastity or your capacity for self-control.

Many thought the Pope was being unrealistic by expecting teenagers to practice chastity. The Pope, meanwhile, thought it was unrealistic to lead teenagers to believe they could find fulfillment outside of the will of God. Although chastity is a demanding virtue, John Paul believed that love could never be separated from struggle and heroic sacrifice. He acknowledged, "Genuine love . . . is demanding.

But its beauty lies precisely in the demands it makes." He added, "These demands . . . are precisely capable of making your love a true love." Through the gradual battle of self-mastery, one becomes free to make a gift of oneself, and therefore capable of love. On the other hand, if a person is mastered by his desires, he resorts to treating the other person as a "loveless object of use." Although growing in purity requires interior struggles against one's weaknesses, John Paul believed that the youth were ready to wage such an interior war for the sake of love. He assured them, *"Happiness is achieved through sacrifice."*

Despite what the critics expected, the youth of the world were enticed by the gravity of the commandment to love. The Holy Father made the challenge realistic, reminding young people that the grace to be pure is not something that arises from a person's willpower. When demands are placed upon a person, he admitted that it is natural to view them as constraints: "Confronted with such demands, one has to say to oneself frankly, 'They are beyond my capacity.' But to say this does not mean that they are *restrictive*. It means: *I appeal to something more than my capacity*." Purity, then, is the fruit of one's union with Christ. As he said at the twelfth World Youth Day, "The more you cling to Jesus, the more capable you will become of being close to one another." Authentic human love is always a participation in divine love.

Although sexual temptation is often seen as the main obstacle to purity, John Paul recognized a more fundamental challenge: the false notion of freedom. Having lived under totalitarian governments for decades, he and the rest of Poland yearned for basic human rights. However, when communism was toppled and freedom was granted, the nation didn't know how to properly use it. John Paul sees this as a problem plaguing much of humanity. He wrote, "[Freedom] cannot simply be possessed! It comes as a gift, but keeping it is a struggle. . . . For freedom you pay with all your being, therefore call that your freedom which allows you, in paying the price, to possess yourself ever anew."

Authentic freedom is not merely the ability to express one's will against the will of others. This is merely the freedom *from* something. A fuller notion of freedom involves a person's freedom *for* something. As he said in his *Letter to Families*, "Freedom cannot be understood as a license to do *absolutely anything*: it means a gift of self. Even more: it means an *interior discipline of the gift*." It is not enough to be free from external constraints; one must also be free from internal constraints that limit one's ability to choose the good. If a person is enslaved by the vices of lust or egoism, he is not free to love. Therefore, one's freedom is best measured by his or her capacity to love.

One of his biographers noted, "Many would regard liberty as the ability to do whatever one wishes; the saints would regard it rather as the additional ability to do what one does not wish, out of charity or self-denial or to please God." This is not ultimately about acting against one's self, but about aspiring for greater things than passing pleasures. According to John Paul, true sexual freedom is not the unfettered license to use and be used. When the unbridled pursuit of sensual desires becomes the measure of one's sexual liberation, he pointed out that "Such a use of freedom might seem at first 'liberating,' but subsequently it always turns out to be enslaving. Moreover, it is normally egotistical and anti-social."

Although the culture calls such sexual expression "free love," it leads to the slavery of lust because it divorces freedom from truth and reduces love to self-gratification. Man has been endowed with an intellect not merely to calculate the greatest possible pleasure that can be achieved, but more importantly to discern what is truly good. He has been endowed with a free will not to do whatever he pleases, but to make a gift of himself in love. For this reason, the Pope told the young people that "their life *has meaning to the extent that it becomes a free gift for others.*"

The Fruit of Love

The fruit of John Paul's love for the youth is already budding in the lives of millions of young people, but it will not reach its full bloom for generations. The reason for this is that the effects of his ministry will only be revealed through the future vocations of those whose lives he touched. When he became the archbishop of Kraków, the seminary was almost empty. By the time he left for Rome, it had nearly five hundred seminarians. His papacy triggered a similar effect, inspiring countless young men and women to give their lives in service to the Church— through both the married and religious vocations. Many of these callings were a direct result of his interaction with the youth.

At the Easter Vigil Mass in Saint Peter's Basilica in 1997, a college student named Michael stood near the back of the dimmed church as the Holy Father entered. As he walked toward the altar, he stopped every ten yards or so to pray, and then would continue walking. Michael remembers:

> From my heart, I "spoke" to him interiorly: "Holy Father, I want to be a priest like you. I want to pour myself out completely." As soon as I finished, he lifted his

bowed head and opened his eyes. He looked right at me. His look seemed to say (pretty clearly): "This is serious, Michael. You have to be quite serious about it." This took me by surprise, but I gathered myself and, as the Pope was bowing his head again and closing his eyes, I firmly repeated what I had "spoken" before. As soon as I finished, the Pope opened his eyes, raised his head, and again looked directly at me. This time his look seemed to say, "Alright, then."

Today, Father Michael Gaitley is the director of the Association of Marian Helpers, leading promotion globally for the message of Divine Mercy. He represents only one of the countless young people who have responded to the Holy Father's call to "be not afraid." Many religious orders today report a new form of "vocations crisis," one in which they can't accommodate all the young people who are seeking to consecrate their lives in service to God. Again and again, John Paul exhorted people to overcome their fears—and not merely the fear of evil or persecution, but also the fear of who God is calling them to become. To fulfill their vocation to either the married or religious life, men and women cannot be afraid "to follow Christ on the royal road of the Cross!"

John Paul sensed that young people were ready to accept his challenge, acknowledging, "The youth that I have met gave me the certitude that our world has a future thanks to them." Without denying the obvious modern challenges that the Church will face in the third millennium, he often spoke of a "new springtime" and "new evangelization" in the Church. By calling young people to become "the saints of the new millennium," John Paul was not overestimating their potential, but inviting them to realize it.

8

HUMAN LOVE

"As a young priest, I learned to love human love." These words, written by Pope John Paul II in *Crossing the Threshold of Hope*, reveal the pure intentions of a man who spent decades of his priesthood and papacy exploring the issues of love and sexuality. While in Kraków, he started the first marriage preparation program in the history of the archdiocese. He also wrote a play called the *The Jeweler's Shop: A Meditation on the Sacrament of Matrimony*, and another entitled *Radiation of Fatherhood*. He spent countless hours counseling engaged and married couples, and often traveled with groups of them into the mountains, discussing God's plan for human love. In fact, according to a pair of his biographers, of the fifty or sixty young men and women who accompanied him on his camping excursions, none of them ever divorced. When one discovers what he was telling them about love, it becomes obvious why.

Love and Responsibility

In the late 1950s, Karol Wojtyła brought a manuscript into the wilderness with college students, giving each of them a portion of it. One of them remembered, "we discussed [it] with him, sitting on the grass, on the lakeshore, and on the edge of the forest." He also shared the text with engaged couples, suggesting they read it as a form of spiritual exercise. In it, he presented a brilliant, challenging, and reverent examination of issues including chastity, sexology, contraception, pornography, sexual frigidity, modesty, lust, and a plethora of other topics that were taboo for anyone to discuss in the 1950s, especially a priest!

The text wasn't something he only discussed among friends, but was based on lectures he delivered at the Catholic University of Lublin. One of his students recalled, "One day, someone finally asked him, 'How come you talk so much about sexuality? There are more important things.' He answered, 'There's nothing wrong with sexuality itself, but the abuse of sexuality is the main obstacle to spirituality.'"

His manuscript was published in 1960 under the title *Love and Responsibility*, and according to John Paul, it was the fruit of many years of close friendships with young couples and university students who "confided the secrets of their hearts" to him. In it, he extolled the beauty of marital love while at the same time gently disabusing young couples of the myth that marriage will bring only happiness and joy.

Because of its content, it was a shock to many. Despite the criticism he knew it would draw from some within the Church, he wasn't afraid to proclaim God's plan for human love or to tackle tough issues. He understood that silence on the topic of sexuality would not serve anyone, especially young people. He knew what the youth were up against: While he was rehabilitating the concept of chastity, communists were promoting abortion and inviting teens to attend youth camps that encouraged promiscuity and sexual experimentation. The government had implemented a strategy to "atheize" the youth by darkening their souls through sin. Meanwhile, he was saving the soul of Poland one couple at a time, by reminding them that the pure in heart will see God (Mt 5:8).

In order to promote purity, he took an unconventional approach: reminding young people that "Sexual drive is a gift from God." However, he maintained that the sexual urge must never be separated from love—the desire to do what is best for the other. He noted that all too often, the concept of love is reduced to emotions and attractions. Such sentimental love often results in disillusionment, whereby the woman eventually discovers that the man's sentiment is merely a screen for his desire to use her. Or, conversely, the man discovers that he was simply a means to an end. When relationships are built on such a foundation, the truth eventually emerges, often within marriage. He explained:

> The essential reason for choosing a person must be personal, not merely sexual. Life will determine the value of a choice and the value and true magnitude of love. It is put to the test most severely when the sensual and emotional reactions themselves grow weaker, and sexual values as such lose their effect. Nothing then remains except the value of the person, and the inner truth about the love of those connected comes to light. If their love is a true gift of self, so that they belong to the other, it will not only survive but grow stronger, and sink deeper roots. Whereas if it was never more than a sort of synchronization of sensual and emotional experiences it will lose its *raison d'être* [reason for existence] and the persons involved in it will suddenly find themselves in a vacuum. We must never forget that only when love between human beings is put to the test can its true value be seen.

To Karol Wojtyła, love is not something that is given to couples or something that "happens" to them. Rather, it is a task, thrown to them by God. The measure of their love is not the intensity of their emotions or attractions, but rather the degree to which they feel responsible for one another. In his words, "When a man and a woman are united by true love, each one takes on the destiny, the future of the other, as his or her own." Thus, only when love is virtuous does it deserve to be called love.

The basic premise that undergirds all of *Love and Responsibility* is that the human person is made in the image and likeness of God, and therefore the only adequate response to another person is love. The opposite of loving is using. Therefore, chastity and modesty should not be viewed as prohibitions, but as virtues that free a person from the selfish attitude of using, thus making him or her capable of love. Because of this, he declared, "only a chaste woman and a chaste man are capable of true love."

An essential insight from Wojtyła's book is that chastity can only be understood in relation to the virtue of love. When people don't understand the connection between the two, they develop a warped idea of purity. Chastity becomes the blind repression of desires for the sake of conforming to externally imposed moral regulations, requiring one to shun the values of the body and sexuality.

That isn't purity. It's prudishness. However, when one views sexuality through the lens of Wojtyła's personalism, the body is no longer the villain. The person's tendency to use is the issue that needs to be healed. The body itself is pure. It is *very good*, but often a person's intentions are not. Therefore, the problem with immodesty is not that it reveals too much, but that it obscures the value of the person. Modesty, then, is not about hiding one's body but about revealing one's worth. It is an invitation to contemplation. It conceals certain areas of the body not because they are bad, but in order to invite others to discover one's full value as a person, thus opening a way toward love. When that invitation is accepted, one can experience nakedness without shame within marriage, where love swallows up shame.

Even within marriage, spouses are not immune from the tendency to use one another. In Wojtyła's candid discussion of the matter, he pointed out that female sexual frigidity often results when the man seeks only his own satisfaction: ". . . it is a result of egoism on the part of the man, who fails to acknowledge the woman's subjective longings in intercourse and the objective laws of the sexual process that takes place in her, and who seeks merely his own satisfaction in a way that is at times even brutal."

Although one does not automatically learn to love from engaging in sexual intercourse, a love that is virtuous will manifest itself within the sexual act. Wojtyła reminds men that because the woman's arousal curve tends to be more gradual and long lasting than a man's, tenderness is required on behalf of the husband both before and after the sexual act—while not ignoring the fact that marital intimacy cannot be reduced to its physical dimension, lest the emotional aspect be overlooked. He adds that a man ought to learn the unique nature of sexual arousal for a woman not for hedonistic intentions, but in order to love her more perfectly. As much as possible, sexual climax should be reached in harmony, and it is virtuous for the man to strive for this goal. He stated, "Hence, there is a need for harmonization, which is impossible without good will, especially in a man, and without a careful observation of a woman."

Love and Responsibility should forever put to rest the worn-out objection, "What could a celibate priest know?" In Karol Wojtyła's insightful commentary on marital intimacy, he displays without defensiveness why those who ridicule the Church as a fraternity of celibate curmudgeons lose all credibility.

The Soul of the Woman

Much of the persuasiveness of John Paul's vision of human love and sexuality flows from his deep appreciation and understanding of the feminine soul. During a pastoral visit with bishops at an old Spanish mission in California, John Paul addressed the fact that many Catholics do not adhere to the Church's teaching on issues of sexual morality or divorce and remarriage. Nonetheless, they assume their behavior is compatible with being a good Catholic and receiving the sacraments. This poses an obvious pastoral challenge for bishops, but the Holy Father declared:

> We must also constantly recall that the teaching of Christ's church, like Christ, himself, is a "sign of contradiction." It has never been easy to accept the Gospel teaching in its entirety, and it never will be. The Church is committed, both in faith and morals, to make her teaching as clear in understanding as possible, presenting it in all the attractiveness of divine truth.

One of the prelates in attendance, Bishop John Michael D'Arcy, was struck by one phrase during the Pope's speech, and brought it up later to the Holy Father. D'Arcy recalled:

> What struck me then and stayed with me, which I presented to the Pope later at the *ad limina* luncheon,

was the term: attractiveness. It was only one word. How do we make it attractive, I asked him. Then he gave me that response that is forever written in my heart. He got very serious, like a philosopher, and said, "It is necessary to understand the soul of the woman. All these things, which are meant to liberate the woman: premarital sex, contraception and abortion, have they liberated her or have they enslaved her?"

It is necessary to understand the soul of the woman. Isn't this what every woman desires, and what every true man strives to accomplish? In one packed sentence that could take a lifetime to assimilate, the Holy Father summed up not only the intrinsic drama of human love, but also the solution to some of the most difficult questions of sexual ethics.

John Paul understood the soul of the woman, even when she struggled to understand herself. In fact, his insights on femininity were often so perceptive that some of his female students in Poland wondered if he hadn't once had a wife or even a fiancée. He was at ease with women not because he ever married one, but because he listened to them, he loved them, and they knew it. One of his biographers observed, "he treated women with absolute ease and a sense of friendliness that held no trace of embarrassment or inappropriate familiarity." One day, he appeared at the window of his Apostolic Palace alongside a young Italian woman, who was to present a message addressed to the youth. John Paul joked to the audience below, "Surely, this is the first woman who speaks from this window."

His comfort level around women stemmed from the many years of interactions he had with them in the theater and in his priestly ministry. He spent thousands of hours in the confessional and had countless conversations with college students and young married couples. As the bishop in Kraków, he also offered an unprecedented amount of help to unwed mothers, which met with criticism from older clergymen who thought such actions could be perceived as a tacit form of approval for illicit behavior. So many women flocked to the home he established for them that the diocese soon ran out of space for the residents. In order to make more room, Wojtyła made a substantial payment from his own income so that another building could be purchased. He saw this not only as a way to assist women in need, but as an opportunity to safeguard numerous children as well. His unconditional love allowed the women who were under his care to feel hopeful for their futures instead of merely ashamed of their pasts.

One can gain a sense of his pastoral style by reading the transcripts of the retreats he led for college students. On one occasion, while speaking to the young women, he recalled the encounter Jesus had with the Samaritan woman. Although she had five husbands and was living with yet another man when she met Christ, Wojtyła remarked:

> There must have been something in this conversation which did not humiliate or mortify her, crushing her, but relieved her. . . . In every Gospel episode involving meetings with women, they find their independence at Christ's side. . . . There are no slaves at Christ's side. The public sinner becomes a promised bride, a sister.

During the same retreat, he reminded the college women, "Men must be taught to love, and to love in a noble way; they must be educated in depth in this truth, that is, in the fact that a woman is a person and not simply an object." While men ought to learn these things from other good men, Wojtyła would sometimes tell the women on his camping trips that they also have the power to ennoble men. He would ask, "Would you like to educate him? . . . Would you like to make a man of him?" Even as he was inviting the women to live lives of virtue, he balanced the scales and called men to do the same. In *Mulieris Dignitatem*, his letter on the dignity of women, he also exhorted the men, saying, "each man must look within himself to see whether she who was entrusted to him as a sister in humanity, as a spouse, has not become in his heart an object of adultery."

In an age where female empowerment often equates to male bashing, masculinizing women, or resenting the gift of motherhood, John Paul sought to empower women by unveiling what he called their "feminine genius." He remarked:

> . . . *contemporary feminism* finds its roots in the absence of true respect for woman. Revealed truth teaches us something different. Respect for woman, amazement at the mystery of womanhood, and finally the nuptial love of God Himself and of Christ . . . In our civilization woman has become, before all else, an object of pleasure. It is very significant, on the other hand, that in the midst of this very situation the authentic *theology of woman* is being reborn. The spiritual beauty, the particular genius, of women is being rediscovered.

Theology of the Body

The last time the Catholic Church had a non-Italian pope, he was troubled by the amount of nudity that Michelangelo depicted in the Sistine Chapel. To remedy the matter, he suggested the entire ceiling be stripped. Thankfully, Pope Adrian VI's papacy ended before his wish was fulfilled. Not long after his death, a papal master of ceremonies remarked that the painting belonged in a brothel or tavern, not a papal chapel. A few popes later, Pope Paul IV complained that it was "a stew of nudes" and sent word to Michelangelo to "make it suitable," to which the artist replied, "let him make the world a suitable place and painting will soon follow suit." A year after Michelangelo's death, more than three dozen loincloths and other coverings were painted over the figures. Saint Blaise was entirely chiseled out of the wall so that his head could be turned away from the nude Saint Catherine of Alexandria, and toward Jesus instead.

More than four hundred years later, John Paul requested that the masterpiece be restored to its original vibrancy and many of the loincloths were able to be removed in the process. When the renovation was complete, John Paul declared the Sistine Chapel to be *the sanctuary of the theology of the human body.*

During a conversation with the Holy Father, one journalist remarked:

And while he is talking, I have a flashback of the feeling I had the day I got my first close view of the newly cleaned frescoes in the Sistine Chapel: when I watched that sort of black tide, rolling back under the skillful hands of the restorers as they carefully sponged off soot and grime, receding from the vaults it had so long obscured and bringing the people Michelangelo had painted back to the light they were made of in the first place. Going up and down the aisles from bay to bay was like looking at Michelangelo's work before

and after a cataract operation. It has the same effect
on people when John Paul II explains Genesis: with all
the accumulation of mud from century after century
of fashionably bored disbelief washed off, that garden
of Eden reappears in its original colors.

In short, what the technicians did to restore Michelangelo's radiant original design, John Paul's Theology of the
Body did to explain God's plan for human sexuality. For
many Catholics, the Church's teachings on human intimacy
have been reduced to a litany of regulations, encrusted under countless misunderstandings. John Paul knew that the
time had come for a fresh re-presentation of sexual ethics, so
that God's glorious plan for human love could be revealed
in its fullness, allowing individuals to see it "in a depth,
simplicity, and beauty hitherto altogether unknown."

Therefore, the Holy Father bequeathed to the Church
the Theology of the Body, which is the popular title given
to approximately one hundred and thirty of his Wednesday
audience messages spanning from 1979 to 1984. While the
Theology of the Body is most well known for its winning
explication of marital love and sexual ethics, the scope of
the messages goes far beyond that. Through the "lens" of
spousal love, the teachings plunge one, as John Paul says,
into "the perspective of the whole gospel, of the whole
teaching, even more, of the whole mission of Christ." The
Theology of the Body is obviously important in regard to
marriage, but is equally essential in understanding what it
means to be human. As he explained to the youth, *God
has a plan for us*—a plan for our lives, for our bodies, for
our souls, for our future. This plan for us is extremely
important—so important that God became man to explain
it to us."

From the time he was a young priest, John Paul's style of teaching sexual ethics was never an imposition or a rebuttal, but rather a proposition and a reminder of what mankind has forgotten. The Theology of the Body is the prime example of this. He does not begin his case with how a person *ought* to behave, but rather with an exploration of who the person *is*. Once a person understands that he is made in the image and likeness of a God who is love, he will know how he ought to live. Sexual morality, then, means rediscovering one's own God-given identity and calling, so that one can be free to love. Although some critics object that the Church tries to roll back morality to the Middle Ages, John Paul was going much further back in history . . . to the beginning.

He began his teaching by reflecting on Jesus' response to the Pharisees who questioned him about divorce and remarriage, reminding them that in the beginning, it was not so. When God created mankind, he declared it to be "very good," yet it was "not good" for man to be alone. The reason for this is that Adam and Eve are made in the image and likeness of God, and God does not exist in solitude. The Trinity is a communion of love: Father, Son, and Holy Spirit. Therefore, although humans image God individually in their rational abilities and immortal souls, they also reveal their likeness to God in their relationships as male and female. Adam and Eve were created for communion, and through their one-flesh union, they became a visible icon of the inner life of God.

Needless to say, this was a dramatic development of Catholic sexual thinking. By proposing this teaching, John Paul was not saying that God is sexual, but rather that our sexuality is heavenly. When we live and love as we ought to, we make visible the invisible reality of God—that He is love.

If this is God's original plan for human love, it becomes obvious why Adam and Eve could be naked without shame. In the beginning, Eve's naked body was an invitation for Adam to love her in a way that reflected the very love of God: a love that is free, total, faithful, and life-giving. Because of the purity of their hearts, they did not view each another as objects to be used, but as persons to be loved. They were peacefully united in this awareness: that their bodies revealed that they were called to make a gift of themselves to the other—and by doing so, to love as God loves. What shame could there be in this?

Nakedness is not the source of shame. Rather, John Paul points out, "Only the nakedness that turns the woman into an 'object' for the man, or vice versa, is a source of shame. The fact that 'they did not feel shame' means that the woman was not an 'object' for the man nor he for her." However, because of original sin, mankind has received the unhappy inheritance of darkened intellects, weakened wills, and disordered appetites. People don't automatically view the human body as an invitation to love, but often see it merely as a temptation to lust. Because of this tendency, some Christians have erred in distaining the body as an obstacle to living a spiritual life.

Despite the wound of original sin, the call to love is still stamped into one's anatomy. John Paul called it the "spousal meaning of the body." To understand what it means to be human, one *must* understand this. The human body "has the power to express the love by which the human person becomes a gift, thus fulfilling the deep meaning of his or her being and existence." Or, as the Second Vatican Council explained, man "cannot fully find himself except through a sincere gift of himself."

Because the body reveals the call to love through a total gift of self, one's holiness as well as one's humanity depends upon the degree to which one accepts this invitation. Most people will answer the call to make a gift of themselves through the married vocation. However, those who choose lives of celibacy "for the sake of the kingdom of heaven," as Jesus said, are not spurning the call. They are embracing it by making a total gift of themselves in service to God.

These insights have profound implications for human sexuality. Whether or not a person wants it to, the sexual act speaks the language of total self-giving. It is the wedding vows made flesh. Although one cannot take away this meaning, one can speak sexual lies through the body. Examples of this include adultery, pornography, contraception, or premarital sex, where one's body seems to make the promise "I am entirely yours," yet this isn't the case in reality. Therefore, the total gift of one's body should only be offered with a total gift of the person.

By inviting individuals to speak the truth with their bodies, John Paul reframed the entire question of sexual ethics. Instead of merely offering believers a litany of sexual regulations, he challenged them to listen within their own hearts for an echo of Eden, where the man intuited the naked body of the woman as an invitation to love her, and vice versa.

This is the ultimate purpose of purity: to liberate a person to rediscover the spousal meaning of the body. Therefore, to love with a pure heart is to rediscover the meaning of life. Purity isn't about censorship, but about illuminating one's vision. It isn't merely about keeping one's sexual desires in check, but about transforming one's desires altogether. Instead of annihilating passions or dousing desires, it sets them ablaze with divine love. Love brings desire to fulfillment by purifying it.

Having control over one's eyes plays an important role in guarding purity. However, having a clean heart does not mean spending the rest of one's life attempting to look away from the human body, but learning how to properly see it. As John Paul says, purity "opens the way toward an ever more perfect discovery of the dignity of the human body." Purity enables one to view the entire person, whereas lust limits one's vision to the sexual values of the body. Because of this, lust robs sex of its depth. It is a reduction that blocks intimacy. Some have defined intimacy as "into-me-see," but how is such closeness possible when one cannot see beneath the skin? Purity is not about seeing less of the body, but about seeing more of the person. This, John Paul says, "creates precisely the fullness of the intimacy of persons."

Because John Paul understood the difference between God-given sexual desire and selfish lust, he explained in one of his Wednesday audiences that a husband should not lust after his wife. To put it mildly, the press had an absolute conniption fit. An Italian paper reported, "Pope John Paul tells us that we cannot even desire our own wives." Another Italian writer mocked John Paul, saying he was making it easier on unfaithful men because they "no longer need that endless round of cover-ups, tricks, juggling of the daily calendar, and the buying of useless and expensive presents for two women at once. Now the Pope says, 'You can have infidelity in your own house.'" Modern man's inability to distinguish sexual desire from lust proved the importance of the Holy Father's teaching.

Lust is the tendency to use another as an object for one's selfish gratification, and a woman's intuition often perceives when such a motive is present in the heart of her partner. It often brings with it a sense of restless vulnerability and resentment on her part. On the other hand, when Eve saw the way Adam originally looked at her with purity of heart, John Paul explained that she experienced "all the peace of the interior gaze." In calling husbands not to lust after their wives, the Pope was encouraging them to bless their brides with the peaceful reassurance that only comes from pure desire. By rejecting lust, John Paul explained that "we acquire the virtue of purity, and this means that we come to an ever greater awareness of the gratuitous beauty of the human body, of masculinity and femininity. This gratuitous beauty becomes a light for our actions."

When one considers the depth of the Pope's thinking on the subject of lust in marriage, it's clear that he wasn't asking husbands to think less of the body or of sexuality. Rather, the husband is called to learn how to see and honor his wife's body and sexuality as the revelation of her dignity and greatness, not as the occasion for selfish indulgence. (This invitation extends to the woman as well, since women often forget what is most valuable about themselves, too.)

Living the Theology of the Body is challenging, but John Paul pointed out in a later writing that with the passage of time, sexual virtue becomes more natural. He explained:

> . . . we feel less and less burdened by the struggle against sin, and we enjoy more and more the divine light which pervades all creation. This is most important, because it allows us to escape from a situation of constant inner exposure to the risk of sin—even though, on this earth, the risk always remains present

to some degree—so as to move with ever greater freedom within the whole of the created world. This same
freedom and simplicity characterizes our relations with
other human beings, including those of the opposite
sex.

In other words, the more deeply one enters into union
with God, the more one begins to see him in his creation.
The Pope continues:

> We can find God in everything, we can commune
> with him in and through all things. Created things
> cease to be a danger for us as once they were, particu-
> larly while we were still at the purgative stage of our
> journey. Creation, and other people in particular, not
> only regain their true light, given to them by God the
> Creator, but, so to speak, they lead us to God himself,
> in the way that he willed to reveal himself to us: as
> Father, Redeemer, and Spouse.

This is the ultimate goal of purity: to see the mystery of
God in and through the body. This idea did not originate
with John Paul. Thousands of years ago, the Old Testament
declared, "For from the greatness and beauty of created
things comes a corresponding perception of their Creator"
(Wis 13:5). Later, in the seventh century, the monk Saint
John Climacus described a bishop who was pure in heart,
saying:

> A certain man, on seeing a beautiful body, thereupon
> glorified the Creator, and from that one look he was
> moved to the love of God and to a fountain of tears.
> And it was wonderful to see how what would have
> been a cause of destruction for one was for another
> the supernatural cause of a crown.

He added that if such a person acts this way consistently, "then he has risen immortal before the general resurrection."

For good reason, George Weigel described the Theology of the Body as a "theological time bomb set to go off, with dramatic consequences, sometime in the third millennium of the Church." Through it, one discovers that modern man's sexual confusion is not caused because the world glorifies sex. Rather, it fails to see the glory. However, when a man and a woman live out God's plan for love in their bodies, they perform what is perhaps the greatest form of evangelization—making visible the invisible love of God.

Criticisms

Not everyone appreciated that the Pope pontificated about sexual morality. Some labeled him an insensitive, out of touch, medieval misogynist. One woman remarked, "His harsh prohibitions, especially regarding abortion in whatever situation, betray a sort of unconscious hatred of the freedom of women." Others bemoaned that his insistence on chastity "may chase even more Catholics away from the Church," giving them no other option but to "responsibly dissent" from the Vatican. They protested his "rigid" ideas and accused him of being "violently opposed" to contraception.

Such opponents have a difficult time explaining how the Pope resorted to violence to promote chastity in marriage or how pro-lifers are misogynists (especially considering that so many of them are women). However, what his opponents never seemed to grasp was that the Pope couldn't "lift the ban on contraception" any more than he could lift the ban on bearing false witness or coveting thy neighbor's wife.

Truth cannot be determined by a majority vote, much less overturned by a veto. Therefore, the Church is not a democratic institution. John Paul explained, "This is not my teaching we are talking about. This is the teaching of the Church, and it is my responsibility to insist that it be obeyed. I cannot change that teaching. I have no *right* to change it!"

Many have labeled the Holy Father a "conservative" because of his stance on sexual ethics. He wasn't offended by such a label, saying that "The Pope is not here to make changes but to conserve what he has received into his charge." However, such political language is futile in defining the Holy Father or his vision of God's plan for human love. As one theologian remarked, "There is nothing conservative in returning to the origins."

Those who read his works realize that he wasn't an opponent of culture, freedom, or modern development. He simply knew that if a culture's "progressive" thought and behavior is leading that society off a cliff, then such "progress" becomes countercultural.

One of the most common criticisms leveled against the Holy Father was that he refused to endorse contraception, even as a strategy to stem the tides of HIV and overpopulation in developing nations. Some ranted that he was responsible for killing millions of people because of his obstinate refusal to promote condoms. After all, the argument goes, shouldn't prostitutes at least be encouraged to use them?

Aside from the fact that prostitutes probably aren't waiting for the Vatican's permission to use contraceptives, is there any merit to these objections? Harvard scientist Edward Green remarked, "20 years into the pandemic there is no evidence that more condoms leads to less AIDS. . . .

Over a lifetime, it is the number of sexual partners [that matter]. Condom levels are found to be non-determining of HIV infection levels." Although some try to paint the Church as the villain of HIV prevention efforts, the *British Medical Journal* reported an interesting pattern that has emerged in Africa: "The greater the percentage of Catholics in any country, the lower the level of HIV. If the Catholic Church is promoting a message about HIV in those countries, it seems to be working."

But what should one make of the claims that the Pope is exacerbating the problem of poverty in overpopulated third-world countries by refusing to endorse contraception as a means of family planning?

John Paul believed that the solution to poverty is not to reduce the number of innocent poor children, but to reduce the number of corrupt rich politicians. The cause of poverty is not the poor. It's war, inhumane political systems, lack of education, and an unjust distribution of resources. Distributing birth control pills in the barrios might reduce the number of children, but it won't improve the living conditions of the living. Although Western nations often try to impose "family planning services" on developing nations, the poor rarely clamor for access to it. They possess enough wisdom to view children as their greatest treasure.

If a couple needs to plan their family, Natural Family Planning is safe and effective, even in developing nations. The *British Medical Journal* reported, "Indeed, a study of 19,843 poor women in India [practicing NFP to delay pregnancy] had a pregnancy rate approaching zero." However, what's more important for the long-term wealth of nations is not that they decrease their population, but that they learn how to create an economic system that can sustain growth while helping families to thrive by enacting just public policies.

Opponents of the Church may view her teaching on contraception as an obstruction to advancing feminine sexual liberation. However, John Paul's insistence on natural means of avoiding conception when necessary raises an interesting set of questions for the modern couple: What if the woman's body is already perfectly made? What if she doesn't need drugs, chemicals, and barriers? What if she simply needs to be understood? If a couple can learn the woman's fertility, consider the outcome: Instead of controlling her body with chemicals and devices in order to conform to their sexual desires, the couple learns to control their sexual desires in order to conform to the perfect way that God has created their bodies. This is authentic sexual liberation.

There's no need to live in opposition to one's fertility. Rather, the proper disposition should be one of gratitude. As he told the college students in Poland, "God who is Father, who is Creator, planted a reflection of his creative strength and power within man. . . . We should sing hymns of praise to God the Creator for this reflection of himself in us—and not only in our souls but also in our bodies."

The Church's stance on contraception does not stem from naïve traditionalism. It comes, in the words of one Vatican reporter, "from a profound analysis of the need to integrate sexuality in an exclusive and permanent relationship open to life in the context of marriage. The wisdom of this view is becoming increasingly clearer." Critics may belittle the Catholic Church now, but as the saying goes, "All truth passes through three stages. First, it is ridiculed. Second, it is violently opposed. Third, it is accepted as being self-evident."

Indeed, the Church's teachings on sexuality are polarizing, as was Christ himself. As John Paul said to the college students while he was a bishop in Kraków, "Christ is found particularly in the field of sexual morality, because it is here that Christ makes demands on men." If people feel estranged by the Church's teachings on sexual morality, who is to blame? Is the Pope alienating people, or are people rejecting the cross and blaming him for its weight? Christ promised he would be a cause of division. This isn't because he lacks the desire to be one with humanity, but because sin drives a wedge between the creation and the Creator.

While some attacked the Pope for being too frank in his discussions about sexual intimacy, others in the media ridiculed him as a prude. While some disagreed with his decision to remove the loincloths from the nudes in the Sistine Chapel, others charged him with censorship because he loathed the scourge of pornography. Some called him a liberal for endorsing Natural Family Planning, while others dismissed him as a troglodyte for failing to embrace the Pill. Without having him in mind, G. K. Chesterton seemed to define him perfectly:

Suppose we heard an unknown man spoken of by many men. Suppose we were puzzled to hear that some men said he was too tall and some too short; some objected to his fatness, some lamented his leanness; some thought him too dark, and some too fair. One explanation (as has been already admitted) would be that he might be an odd shape. But there is another explanation. He might be the right shape. Outrageously tall men might feel him to be short. Very short men might feel him to be tall. Old bucks who are growing stout might consider him insufficiently filled out; old beaux who were growing thin might feel that he expanded beyond the narrow lines of elegance. . . . Perhaps (in short) this extraordinary thing is really the ordinary thing; at least the normal thing, the centre. Perhaps, after all, it is Christianity that is sane and all its critics that are mad—in various ways.

9

THE BLESSED SACRAMENT

Between 5:00 and 5:30 A.M.—and sometimes as early as 4:00—Pope John Paul II would arise each morning, keeping virtually the same schedule he had as the bishop of Kraków. Although he enjoyed watching the sunrise, the main reason for his early start was to make time for prayer. He prayed the Rosary prostrate on the floor or kneeling, followed by his personal prayers, and would then go to the chapel in order to prepare for 7:30 Mass. According to his press secretary, Joaquín Navarro-Valls, his sixty to ninety minutes of private prayer before Mass were the best part of his day.

At the chapel, he would kneel before the Blessed Sacrament at his prie-dieu. The top of his wooden kneeler could be opened, and it was brimming with notes people had given to him, seeking his prayers for all kinds of petitions, including healings, the conversion of family members, or successful pregnancies. Perhaps thirty to forty new petitions were given to him each day, and he would pray specifically over every one. He said that they were kept there and were always present "in my consciousness, even if they cannot be literally repeated every day."

He told one of his biographers, "There was a time when I thought that one had to limit the 'prayer of petition.' That time has passed. The further I advance along the road mapped out for me by Providence, the more I feel the need to have recourse to this kind of prayer." Quite often, those who sent the petitions wrote back in thanksgiving for answered prayers. His assistant secretary noted that most of them expressed gratitude for the gift of parenthood. Not only did he intercede before the tabernacle for these individuals as if they were his most intimate friends, he routinely sought information about the progress of the cases. The liturgy would not begin until he had before him the petitions people had asked him to offer on their behalf.

After going to the sacristy to don his vestments for Mass, he would again kneel or sit for ten to twenty minutes. When visitors arrived to join him for Mass, they would always find him kneeling in prayer. Some said, "he looked like he was speaking with the Invisible." One of the masters of ceremonies added, "it seemed as if the Pope were not present among us." Bishop Andrew Wypych, who was ordained to the diaconate by Cardinal Karol Wojtyła, added, "You could see that he physically was there, but one could sense that he was immersed in the love of the Lord. They were united in talking to each other."

During the celebration of the Eucharist, one observer noticed, "He lingered lovingly over every syllable that recalled the Last Supper as if the words were new to him." Then, after the moment of Consecration, he would genuflect before Christ's presence on the altar with tremendous reverence. Visitors to his private Masses noticed that you could hear the thud of his knee slamming down upon the marble floor when he became too weak to support himself as he genuflected. After Mass, a lengthy time of thanksgiving followed before the Holy Father greeted guests and gave each of them a Rosary.

The Eucharist was the principal reason for his priest-hood. He said, "For me, the Mass constitutes the center of my life and my every day." He added, "nothing means more to me or gives me greater joy than to celebrate Mass each day and to serve God's people in the Church." John Paul didn't merely offer the Mass. He lived it. Like the Eucharist itself, he became an immolation of love—a living sacrifice offered to the Father for the salvation of mankind.

Because of his deep faith in the Real Presence of Christ in the Eucharist, he was adamant with priests and bishops about how the Mass ought to be celebrated. He told a group of American bishops, "This is why it is so important that liturgical law be respected. The priest, who is the servant of the liturgy, not its inventor or producer, has a particular responsibility in this regard, lest he empty liturgy of its true meaning or obscure its sacred character."

Prayer was the rhythm of the Holy Father's life. He made time to pray before and after his meals, and interspersed his Breviary prayers (the Liturgy of the Hours) throughout the day and night, calling it: "very important, *very* important." At six in the morning, at noon, and again at six in the evening, he would stop whatever he was doing to pray the Angelus, just as he had done while working in the chemical plant in Poland. He prayed several Rosaries each day, went to confession every week, and did not let a day pass without receiving Holy Communion. Each Friday (and every day in Lent), he prayed the Stations of the Cross, and preferred to do this in the garden on the roof of the Papal Apartments. During Lent, he would eat one complete meal a day, and always fasted on the eve of our Lady's feast days. He remarked, "If the bishop doesn't set an example by fasting, then who will?" The Holy Father knew that his first duty to the Church was his interior life. He declared, "the shepherd should walk at the head and lay down his life for his sheep. He should be the first when it comes to sacrifice and devotion."

Each night, he looked out his window to Saint Peter's Square and to the whole world, and made the sign of the cross over it, blessing the world goodnight. For many years, he ascended to the roof of the Papal Apartments to offer this nightly blessing. Visitors standing in the square noticed that his light often went off between eleven and one in the morning. One of his biographers noted that he seldom went to bed before midnight. As a priest and bishop, and perhaps as pope, he sometimes slept on the bare floor. In Kraków, his housekeeper knew of this, and noticed that he would crumple his bed sheets to conceal it.

The Old Lion

More remarkable than his daily, weekly, and annual traditions of prayer was his habit of incessant prayer. While walking from place to place inside the Vatican or outside, prayer became as natural and vital to him as his breath. While strolling to his next appointment, Archbishop Mieczysław Mokrzycki said, "he was immersed in prayer for those five minutes. He was then beyond our reach, turned off. There were dozens of moments like that during the day. We knew that we were not supposed to disturb the Holy Father then because he was with God. They were united in an unusual way." He added that John Paul's mysticism was evidenced by the fact that he would "disconnect" himself from his surroundings and appeared oblivious to external distractions. Cardinal Dziwisz noticed that even times of work were "peppered with prayers, with short bursts of prayer." One member of the Curia noted, "No sooner does he pause than he starts praying . . ." Cardinal Christoph Schönborn observed:

The Holy Father looked as though he never stopped praying. I never saw anyone so constantly immersed in union with Christ and God, as though it were a permanent state that led him to submit everything he did unto the Lord's hands. His attentiveness to others, his gestures, words and readings—everything he did was bathed in prayer, like the great mystics.

It could be said that he didn't make time to enter prayer. Rather, he made time for the sake of others to come out of it.

Because he believed that every encounter was providential, he stated, "As soon as I meet people, I pray for them." Those who had the blessing of meeting him in person would not be surprised by this information, based upon how fully present he was to each person he encountered. One of his secretaries affirmed this: "He prayed for everyone he met. He prayed before and after the meeting." This didn't apply only to formal meetings, as he could often be seen praying the Rosary as he waved at crowds from his Popemobile.

However, what's more fascinating than when the Pope prayed or what he prayed, is how he prayed. While hiking atop the Italian Alps, Dziwisz told the guide, "Lino, the Holy Father wants to be alone for a little while in recollection, let's look for a good spot." They noticed a large flat rock and guided him over to it. The guide explained what happened next in his book, *The Secret Life of John Paul II*:

It was then that I witnessed for the first time something I will truly never forget, and that—overcoming my reservations—I am telling here for the first time. I seek to do so accurately and with purity of heart. His head was bowed and he was absorbed in prayer, totally immobile, without even the slightest movement. He was in a sort of trance—or I dare say, ecstasy—which he was modestly hiding from us. In fact, I couldn't see his face or even tell whether his hands were folded or not. Nor if his eyes were open or closed. Instead, I had the very clear sensation that I was observing someone endowed with a spiritual power that was no longer human; someone who no longer belonged to this world, but was living those minutes in complete communion with God, with the saints, and with all the souls of heaven. The unreal sparkle of the snow all around emphasized this impression. A complete silence had descended. Everything was motionless, as if a state of contemplation had taken hold of every element of nature. . . . He never moved so much as a millimeter, his muscles were motionless like everything else around him. Then, the strangest thing occurred. The Pope, after [the] tiniest imperceptible movement, revived and then slowly got up, and when we looked at our watches, realized that almost an hour had gone by.

Such episodes of deep prayer were commonplace, according to those who spent time with the Holy Father. In 1995, when John Paul visited the Sacred Heart Cathedral (now Basilica) in Newark, he made a visit to the Blessed Sacrament before departing. When he knelt at the prie-dieu, Cardinal McCarrick remembered:

It was my hope, my intention to kneel a little behind
him. I couldn't. I couldn't. As soon as he knelt, it was
like a sacred space, like a tent was around him, and
I moved away. I moved three or four yards back and
stood by one of the stone pillars of the cathedral. Because you had to leave space there. . . . He went into
the deepest prayer. . . . I've rarely seen anyone in that
state of such deep prayerfulness. He wasn't with us
any more. He was with the Lord. He knelt and then
in ten seconds he was gone. It was so holy, I moved
back. And he was there, for about maybe seven or
eight minutes, lost in total prayer.

Then, Monsignor Dziwisz took his elbow and he gently
got up, turned around with a great smile, waved to the
people, and walked on.

Cardinal Justin Rigali recalled a similar incident that
took place in Canada when the Pope was kneeling in prayer
before the Blessed Sacrament, prior to the beginning of a
ceremony. The master of ceremonies decided it was time
for the Holy Father to wrap it up and suddenly said, "The
Pope will now rise . . ." Rigali recalled what happened
next:

Well, the Pope didn't rise. He just stayed put. And
the poor man [the master of ceremonies], whatever got
into him, it went from bad to worse: So he waited
a couple of minutes, and then he made the second
announcement: "The Pope will now rise." Incredible.
And the Pope didn't rise. So then he just knelt down
and stayed quiet. When the Pope was ready, then he
rose and went on.

Sometimes when John Paul emerged from such inter-
ludes of deep prayer, he didn't seem refreshed, but was

instead preoccupied and burdened with the weight of information that others were not privy to. On one such occasion in the wilderness, a witness reported that he appeared to be "shaken to the core" and immediately requested that he descend from the mountain to return to his lodging. Within hours, the Iraqi army invaded Kuwait, and the Gulf War began.

The stirrings of John Paul's deep interior life often manifested themselves exteriorly. Father Maciej Zięba noticed, "When he prayed, it was physical. He sighed deeply and made grunting sounds like a lion. Some of us called him the old lion. This was a mark of respect, the way you respect the king of the realm." Countless visitors to his private chapel witnessed his unforgettable prayerful groaning as he knelt before the tabernacle. The Holy Father explained:

> In order to understand profoundly the meaning of prayer, one should meditate for a long time on the following passage from the Letter to the Romans: "For creation awaits with eager expectation the revelation of the children of God; for creation was made subject to futility, not of its own accord but because of the one who subjected it, in hope that creation itself would be set free from slavery to corruption and share in the glorious freedom of the children of God. We know that all creation is groaning in labor pains even until now; and not only that, but we ourselves, who have the first fruits of the Spirit, we also groan within ourselves as we wait for adoption, the redemption of our bodies. For in hope we were saved" (Rom 8:19–24). And here again we come across the apostle's words: "The Spirit too comes to the aid of our weakness; for we do not know how to pray as we ought, but

the Spirit himself intercedes with inexpressible groan-
ings" (cf. Rom 8:26).

From his childhood, his father instilled in Karol a strong
devotion to the Holy Spirit. He recalled his father telling
him, "You don't pray to the Holy Spirit enough. You ought
to pray to him." Karol, Sr., gave him a prayer book on the
Holy Spirit, which he used throughout his life, and also
taught him the following prayer and instructed him to
recite it daily:

> Holy Spirit, I ask you for the gift of Wisdom to better
> know You and Your divine perfections, for the gift
> of Understanding to clearly discern the spirit of the
> mysteries of the holy faith, for the gift of Counsel that
> I may live according to the principles of this faith,
> for the gift of Knowledge that I may look for counsel
> in You and that I may always find it in You, for the
> gift of Fortitude that no fear or earthly preoccupations
> would ever separate me from You, for the gift of Piety
> that I may always serve Your Majesty with a filial love,
> for the gift of the Fear of the Lord that I may dread
> sin, which offends You, O my God.

He kept this prayer on a handwritten note, and prayed
it every day for the gifts of the Holy Spirit, offering a
Hail Mary and an Our Father for each of the seven gifts.
He said this prayer resulted a half century later in his
encyclical on the Holy Spirit, *Dominum et Vivificantem*.
His father's witness may have given birth to an encyclical,
but its greatest effects took place within the Holy Father's
soul. As Saint Louis de Montfort explained, "the greatest
things on earth are done interiorly in the hearts of faithful
souls." The Pope's relationship with the Holy Spirit was
summed up best when he was asked, "How does the Pope

pray?" He answered, "You would have to ask the Holy Spirit!"

Eucharistic Amazement

Although John Paul loved communing with God in the wilderness, it was clear that his favorite place to pray was before the Blessed Sacrament. Witnesses report that he spent hours at a time—and sometimes the entire night— prostrate on the marble floor before the tabernacle, with his arms outstretched in the shape of the cross. One witness remarked that this union with our Lord in the Eucharist allowed him "not merely to speak to Christ, but actually to converse with him." As a bishop, he told college students that for each person, the reality of the Eucharist means "we have two people in one another's presence: Our Lord and me."

Cardinal Dziwisz reported that you could sometimes hear him talking aloud with God, having a dialogue. The Holy Father believed that authentic prayer is when a person desires to be as attentive to God as he is to us; when one yearns to hear God's voice, just as God yearns to hear each person. In *Crossing the Threshold of Hope*, he wrote, "Man achieves the *fullness of prayer* not when he expresses himself, but *when he lets God be most fully present in prayer*."

When a tabernacle wasn't available, John Paul would make do. One of his aides found him kneeling at a sink in a washroom because there was no other private place to prepare for Mass at the Pordenone Fair. Another witness walked into a utility closet at the Pope's summer residence and inadvertently found him "rapt in prayer."

The Holy Father often spent hours at a time writing before the Blessed Sacrament. He explained:

I have always been convinced that the chapel is a place of special inspiration. What a privilege to be able to live and work in the shadow of His Presence. . . . It is not always necessary to enter physically into the chapel in order to enter spiritually into the presence of the Blessed Sacrament. I have always sensed that Christ was the real owner of my episcopal residence, and that we bishops were just short-term tenants. That's how it was in Franciszkańska Street for almost twenty years, and that's how it is here in the Vatican.

In his chapel in Kraków, the kneeler was more of a prayer desk, with a desktop large enough so that he could write while kneeling or sitting before the Eucharist. A lamp was installed nearby so he could work at any time of night as well. As pope, he spent time in adoration before every Wednesday audience, and always made a short visit before and after every meal. He also spent long amounts of time before the Blessed Sacrament before and after his pilgrimages. Marathons of prayer were not unusual for him. One papal photographer recalled, "I remember that in Vilnius he prayed for six hours in a row . . ."

To John Paul, it is not enough for Catholics to receive the Eucharist. One also must contemplate it. He said that when one ponders the love that is present in the tabernacle:

. . . love is ignited within us, love is renewed within us. Therefore, these are not hours spent in idleness, when we isolate ourselves from our work, but these are moments, hours, when we undertake something that constitutes the deepest meaning of all of our work. For no matter how numerous our activities, our ministries, however numerous our concerns, our exertions —if there is no love, everything becomes meaningless.

When we devote our time to ponder the mystery of love, to allow it to radiate in our hearts, we are preparing ourselves in the best possible way for any kind of service, for any activity, for any charitable work.

His life of contemplation was the wellspring of his thoughts, words, and actions. As he said, "all activities should be rooted in prayer as though in a spiritual soil." His job was not to advance his own opinions and agendas, but to transmit to the world the fruit of his own interior life. One of his aides noted that he made "all of his major decisions . . . on his knees before the Blessed Sacrament." The Pope warned others, "In the absence of a deep inner life, a priest will imperceptibly turn into an office clerk, and his apostolate will turn into a parish office routine, just solving daily problems." He knew well the primacy of "be-ing" over "do-ing," as can be seen when he prayed: "Help us, Jesus, to understand that in order 'to do' in your Church, also in the field of the new evangelization that is so urgently needed, we must first learn 'to be,' that is, to stay with you, in your sweet company, in adoration."

John Paul's extravagant love for Christ in the Eucharist sometimes became problematic for his handlers. In fact, the prefect of the Papal Household often warned the organizers of papal events to make sure not to allow the Pope to pass within view of a place where the Eucharist was reserved. Otherwise, he'd surely enter the chapel for prolonged periods of time and the entire schedule would be thrown off.

In 1995, Father Michael White was invited to organize the Pope's visit to Baltimore on behalf of the archdiocese. Prior to the Holy Father's arrival, the chief organizer for papal pilgrimages, Father Roberto Tucci, SJ, came to

Maryland to scout out the venues and make the necessary arrangements for John Paul's trip. When he arrived at the archbishop's residence, he noticed that one of the doors in the hallway the Pope would pass through opened into a chapel with the Blessed Sacrament.

He instructed Father White, "Keep that door closed so he doesn't know there's a chapel in there." Upon the Pope's arrival, the door was closed, and John Paul took some time to eat and rest at the residence. When it was time to leave, he walked down the hall, which was lined with doors leading into various rooms, passed by the door of the chapel, then suddenly stopped. He looked back at the door, then looked over at Father Tucci, and without saying a word, wagged his finger at him and shook his head.

Father White recalled:

> He's never been in this place before, never set eyes on the place, and there was nothing about the door that distinguished it in any way as a chapel. It was just one more door in a corridor of doors. But he turned right back around, he opened that door up, and he went into the chapel and he prayed.

According to Father White, the Holy Father remained in prayer long enough to "do some damage" to the schedule, then left the residence to head to his appointment.

The Holy Father ended his visit to Baltimore at St. Mary's Seminary in Roland Park. A helicopter was staged on the front lawn of the seminary to take him to the airport, where he was to meet with the vice president of the United States. A crowd of enthusiastic future priests gathered on the steps to wave at the Pope when he arrived, but John Paul's handlers were clear about the schedule: There was no time for him to make a visit. The seminary had been begging for months to be included in the Holy Father's schedule, but time would not allow it.

However, after seeing the young men, John Paul pulled Father Tucci aside and informed him in Italian that he wanted to see the seminary—much to the amazement of that community when they were hurriedly informed. Once there, Father White was astonished that the Pope instinctively knew where to go:

> He walked in the door, and this was completely un-planned and unscripted at this point. The Secret Service hadn't even done a complete sweep of the building because this wasn't part of the deal. And he just walked into that building and walked right to the chapel, like he knew where it was. It was just remarkable.

After spending a generous amount of time before the Eucharist, briefly viewing the facility, and greeting the future priests—with evident joy and absolutely no sense of urgency—he proceeded to his meeting at BWI Airport, where he had kept Vice President Gore and the entire entourage for the departure ceremony waiting!

The Pope's spiritual priorities were proof that he believed the Eucharist was the greatest treasure the Church possesses. Because of its inestimable value, he felt it was his mission to "rekindle this Eucharistic 'amazement'" in the hearts of the faithful. To help Christians understand the reality of Christ's presence in the Blessed Sacrament, he appealed to the human experience of love. During a homily in Brazil, he asked:

> How many times in our lives have we seen two peo-ple separated who love each other? During the ugly

and bitter war, in my youth, I saw young people leave
without hope of return, parents torn from their homes,
not knowing if they would one day find their loved
ones. Upon leaving, a gesture, a picture, or an object
passes from hand to hand in a certain way in order to
prolong presence in absence. And nothing more. Human love is capable only of these symbols.

Motivated by an even greater love, when the hour had
come for Christ to part with his disciples, he had the
power to leave his Church with more than a gesture. In
his absence, he left his presence. John Paul explained:

> Thus, to say farewell, the Lord Jesus Christ, perfect
> God and perfect man, did not leave his friends a symbol, but the reality of himself. . . . Under the species
> of bread and wine, He is really present, with his Body
> and his Blood, his Soul and Divinity.

For John Paul, the question is not whether Jesus is
truly present in the Blessed Sacrament, but rather whether
Catholics are truly present to God in their midst! For
this reason, he spoke of adoration as "an important daily
practice" that one should not omit in the course of the day.
He declared:

> The Eucharist is the secret of my day. It gives strength
> and meaning to all my activities of service to the
> Church and to the whole world. . . . Let Jesus in the
> Blessed Sacrament speak to your hearts. It is he who
> is the true answer of life that you seek. He stays here
> with us: he is God with us. Seek him without tiring,
> welcome him without reserve, love him without interruption: today, tomorrow, forever.

If a person is unable to visit or receive the Eucharist, John Paul recommended that he or she make a spiritual communion, taking a moment to invite Jesus into one's heart.

For John Paul, the key to rekindling Eucharistic love is to look to Mary, who was the first "tabernacle" in history. In his encyclical on the Eucharist, he explained, "And is not the enraptured gaze of Mary as she contemplated the face of the newborn Christ and cradled him in her arms that unparalleled model of love which should inspire us every time we receive Eucharistic communion?"

Today, John Paul's tomb rests in the most fitting of locations: in the heart of the Church in Saint Peter's Basilica, between the Chapel of the Pietà and the Chapel of the Blessed Sacrament. Even in death, he reminds the faithful of what he said in life: "Were we to disregard the Eucharist, how could we overcome our own deficiency?"

10

THE VIRGIN MARY

On May 10, 1981, Pope John Paul II celebrated Good Shepherd Sunday while preaching at a parish in Rome. During his homily, he reminded the faithful, "The image of 'shepherd' is opposed to that of 'hireling' (*mercenario*) and serves to highlight all the deep concern of Jesus for his flock, who we are, to the point of giving himself completely for our salvation: 'The good shepherd lays down his life for the sheep' (Jn 10:11)." Little did the Holy Father know that in three days he would nearly do the same.

Two days after this homily, he examined the facilities of the Vatican medical center and met with its staff members. After the visit, a physician asked John Paul if he would bless their new ambulance. The Holy Father did so with holy water and said, "I also bless the first person who will use this ambulance." John Paul became the recipient of his own blessing, because he was the first patient to need it.

May 13 was a typical Wednesday in the Vatican. As was his custom, John Paul invited guests for lunch, hosting the renowned French geneticist Jérôme Lejeune and his wife to discuss Natural Family Planning and other pro-life matters. After the usual course of afternoon meetings and prayer, he descended to Saint Peter's Square to participate in his weekly Wednesday audience with the faithful. He was approaching the halfway mark of his lectures on the Theology of the Body.

He climbed aboard the Popemobile and crisscrossed through Saint Peter's Square, kissing babies and blessing the 20,000 pilgrims who had gathered to see him. At 5:17 P.M., moments after blessing a two-year-old girl and handing her back to her elated parents, blasts from a 9mm semiautomatic pistol rang out. Pigeons throughout the square scattered skyward as John Paul fell backward into the arms of his secretary, Monsignor Dziwisz. One bullet fractured two bones in his left index finger and passed through his abdomen before exiting through his sacrum and coming to rest in the Popemobile. Another bullet grazed his right arm, and two American women in the crowd were injured.

His assailant, Mehmet Ali Agça, was a trained twenty-three-year-old Turkish gunman who had been incarcerated for murdering a journalist. Three days before the Pope's visit to Turkey in 1979, Agça escaped from an Istanbul prison and sent a letter to the Turkish newspaper *Milliyet*, stating that if the papal visit is not canceled, "I will without doubt kill the Pope-Chief. This is the sole motive for my escape from prison."

Although the Istanbul daily paper printed the letter on its front page, John Paul moved ahead with his plans and safely made his apostolic pilgrimage. However, Agça was determined to follow through on his threat. He arrived in Rome two years later, on May 9, and stayed at the Pensione Isa hotel, a fifteen-minute walk from the Vatican. Over the next few days, he examined Saint Peter's Square and developed his strategy for murdering the pontiff. After the assassination attempt, police searched his room and discovered a note that declared, "I have killed the Pope."

After the gunshots were fired, the Popemobile fled the scene and John Paul was transferred into the familiar ambulance. Dziwisz climbed beside him and could hear him praying, "*O Maria, Madonna! Maria, Madonna!* [O Mary, my Mother]." In Saint Peter's Square, as the faithful were praying for his survival, a group of Polish pilgrims took an icon of Our Lady of Częstochowa and placed it beside the empty seat that the Holy Father would have sat upon during his audience. A gust of wind blew it over, and a bystander noticed the inscription on the back of the image, which had been written days or weeks earlier: "May Our Lady protect the Holy Father from Evil."

The ambulance sped through the streets of Rome, honking desperately because the siren had failed shortly after leaving the Vatican. The Pope was losing a great deal of blood, but managed to stay conscious until his arrival at the Gemelli Hospital. Because he was now in critical condition and unconscious, he was given last rites and surgery was performed. Thankfully, a surgical room had been prepared and most of the staff was already in place because an Italian soccer player had been scheduled for an operation— which could now afford to wait.

The surgeon, Professor Francesco Crucitti, rushed from across town and began the operation. He discovered severe internal bleeding due to a perforated colon and five wounds to the intestines. After making the initial incision, he noted, "I saw blood everywhere. There were some six pints of blood in the abdomen." Considering that the average adult male only has ten pints of blood, the medical team feared the worst, later admitting that they did not believe the Pope would survive. John Paul, however, said that after he was shot, he had a premonition that the wound would not be fatal.

After sponging up the blood, the doctors noticed that the path of the bullet missed the aorta by millimeters, which would have meant certain death. After a blood transfusion and five hours of surgery, the Holy Father's condition stabilized. He woke up early the next morning with a broken tooth, a result of the hasty administration of anesthesia. He took a brief rest, and then upon awaking again, wanted to ask something but was wearing a mask. Dziwisz lifted it, and because John Paul thought it was still the previous day, asked if they had recited Compline (night prayer) yet.

As if the assassination attempt wasn't a sufficient cross for the Holy Father to bear, four days later, on the eve of his birthday, Italy voted decisively against a pro-life proposal that would have restricted abortion. Then on May 28, Cardinal Wyszyński passed away. John Paul remained hospitalized at Gemelli for three weeks before returning to the Vatican. However, two weeks after his homecoming, his condition worsened and he returned to the hospital to receive treatment for a cytomegalovirus infection that had been caused by a tainted blood transfusion. For the next fifty-six days, he lived at Gemelli under the watchful care of a team of zealous physicians.

John Paul was eager to return to the Vatican, but remained in good spirits about needing to negotiate with those who wanted to make medical decisions on his behalf. Across the hall from his room was a meeting space where the doctors would convene to discuss his treatment. He playfully referred to the gathering as "the Sanhedrin." He would inquire, "What did the Sanhedrin say to-day?"

In time, his infection cleared, but a second surgery was required to repair the colostomy that had been performed because of the damage the bullet inflicted on his digestive system. The doctors wanted to postpone the operation until October, but he insisted that he was well enough to endure it. He met with them and gave them an impromptu half-hour speech about the proper relationship between a patient and his caregivers. During it, he gently reminded them that the patient must never be viewed as an object of treatment, but rather as the subject of his illness. He also reiterated the importance and necessity of dialogue between physicians and their patients. Whatever he said must have worked, because he set the date for his operation for August 5 (the feast of Our Lady of the Snows) and he was back home in the Vatican on the fourteenth, in time for the feast of Mary's Assumption the following day.

The Secret of Fatima

During his sabbatical in the hospital, he began to reflect upon the timing of the attempt upon his life. May 13 was also the feast of Our Lady of Fatima, which commemorates the first time that the three children from Fatima, Portugal, saw a vision of the Virgin Mary in 1917. John Paul realized that he was shot on the anniversary of the very same month, day, and hour that those apparitions began. A year later, he made a pilgrimage to Fatima and said, "As soon as I regained consciousness after the attack in St. Peter's Square, my thoughts turned to this shrine and I wanted to express here my gratitude to our Heavenly Mother for having saved my life. . . . there are no mere coincidences in the designs of Divine Providence."

During the visions in 1917, our Lady urged the three children—Lucia, Jacinta, and Francesco—to pray the Rosary every day for peace, and asked them, "Will you offer yourselves to God, and bear all the sufferings He sends you?

In atonement for all the sins that offend Him? And for the conversion of sinners?" The theme of the messages was simple: prayer, penance, and conversion. During one of the visions, the children were given a secret, consisting of three parts.

The first part was a vision of hell, in which the children saw a sea of fire. Sister Lucia described the apparition:

> Plunged in this fire were demons and souls in human form, like transparent burning embers, all blackened or burnished bronze, floating about in the conflagration, now raised into the air by the flames that issued from within themselves together with great clouds of smoke, now falling back on every side like sparks in a huge fire, without weight or equilibrium, and amid shrieks and groans of pain and despair, which horrified us and made us tremble with fear. The demons could be distinguished by their terrifying and repulsive likeness to frightful and unknown animals, all black and transparent. This vision lasted but an instant. How can we ever be grateful enough to our kind heavenly Mother, who had already prepared us by promising, in the first Apparition, to take us to heaven. Otherwise, I think we would have died of fear and terror.

Horrified, the children looked to the Virgin Mary, who told them in the second part of the secret that God wished to establish devotion to the Immaculate Heart of Mary in order to preserve souls from such torment. She added that World War I would end, but that if people do not cease offending God, a more terrible war would begin during the pontificate of Pius XI. In saying this, Mary not only accurately predicted the beginning of World War II, but also foretold the name of the pope. She also requested that Russia be consecrated to her Immaculate Heart, and that on the First Saturday of every month, Communions of reparation be offered in atonement for the sins of the world. She added:

> If my wishes are fulfilled, Russia will be converted and there will be peace; if not, then Russia will spread her errors throughout the world, bringing new wars and persecution of the Church; the good will be martyred and the Holy Father will have much to suffer; certain nations will be annihilated. But in the end my Immaculate Heart will triumph. The Holy Father will consecrate Russia to me, and she will be converted, and the world will enjoy a period of peace.

On March 25, 1984, following Mass in Saint Peter's Square—before the actual statue of Our Lady of Fatima that had been flown in from Portugal for the occasion—John Paul offered a prayer to consecrate the world to the Immaculate Heart of Mary. According to John Paul, such an entrustment means drawing near to Christ as the source of mercy, through his Mother's intercession.

Some objected that he didn't perform the consecration according to the wishes of the Virgin Mary. Sister Lucia was asked her opinion, and she said, "The Holy Father did everything he could, so Jesus is content. However, not all the bishops are united with him. The consecration is valid but has not reached its fullness." In 1989, she confirmed, "Yes it has been done just as Our Lady asked, on 25 March 1984." The secretary of the Congregation for the Doctrine of the Faith added, "Hence any further discussion or request is without basis."

Although the first two parts of the secret were made

public, the third was not. Lucia described the third part in a letter given to Pope Pius XII in 1944, leaving to his discretion when it would be told, but adding that she did not wish it to be revealed at least until 1960. John XXIII was pope at that time, and neither he nor his successors revealed the secret. As a result, rumors and speculation abounded as to what it could be, and why the popes were keeping it to themselves.

Following the assassination attempt, John Paul asked to read the third part of the secret of Fatima for the first time. Two envelopes were brought to him from the secret archive of the Holy Office: one containing the original letter in Portuguese that Lucia had given to her bishop, and the other containing an Italian translation. On June 26, 2000, the text was made public during a press conference in the Vatican. It was only one page long, and read:

After the two parts which I have already explained, at the left of Our Lady and a little above, we saw an Angel with a flaming sword in his left hand; flashing, it gave out flames that looked as though they would set the world on fire; but they died out in contact with the splendour that Our Lady radiated towards him from her right hand: pointing to the earth with his right hand, the Angel cried out in a loud voice: "*Penance, Penance, Penance!*" And we saw in an immense light that is God: "something similar to how people appear in a mirror when they pass in front of it" a Bishop dressed in White "we had the impression that it was the Holy Father." Other Bishops, Priests, men and women Religious going up a steep mountain, at the top of which there was a big Cross of rough-hewn trunks as of a cork-tree with the bark; before

reaching there the Holy Father passed through a big
city half in ruins and half trembling with halting step,
afflicted with pain and sorrow, he prayed for the souls
of the corpses he met on his way; having reached the
top of the mountain, on his knees at the foot of the
big Cross he was killed by a group of soldiers who
fired bullets and arrows at him, and in the same way
there died one after another the other Bishops, Priests,
men and women Religious, and various lay people of
different ranks and positions. Beneath the two arms
of the Cross there were two Angels each with a crys-
tal aspersorium in his hand, in which they gathered
up the blood of the Martyrs and with it sprinkled the
souls that were making their way to God.

Because of the symbolic and cryptic nature of the text,
John Paul directed Cardinal Angelo Sodano to explain to
the faithful:

The vision of Fatima concerns above all the war waged
by atheist systems against the Church and Christians,
and it describes the immense suffering endured by the
witnesses to the faith in the last century of the second
millennium. It is an interminable Way of the Cross
led by the Popes of the twentieth century . . . Even if
the events to which the third part of the Secret of Fatima refers now seem part of the past, Our Lady's call
to conversion and penance, issued at the beginning of
the twentieth century, remains timely and urgent today.

When reading the third part of the secret, one naturally
thinks of John Paul, as a bishop dressed in white, ascending
to the cross through a world in ruins, "half trembling with

halting step, afflicted with pain and sorrow," and praying for souls he meets on the way. After his death, one of the Pope's friends revealed another interesting association between the secret and John Paul's life: The Holy Father sometimes hiked and skied Mount Adamello, where many soldiers died during World War I. At the top of a nearby ridge, Cresta Croce, was an old wooden cross, "made with two slender trunks, still wrapped in a bark eroded by the wind until it had become like cork," as the secret mentioned. While they hiked, the Holy Father prayed for the deceased, many of whom were still buried under the perennial snows.

Despite the undeniable convergence between the "Bishop dressed in White" and John Paul, one discrepancy is obvious: the pope in the vision is murdered, whereas John Paul's life was spared. Cardinal Joseph Ratzinger, later Pope Benedict XVI, pointed out, "That here 'a mother's hand' that guided the bullet's path only shows once more that there is no immutable destiny, that faith and prayer are forces which can influence history and that in the end prayer is more powerful than bullets and faith more powerful than armies."

Shortly before becoming pope, Cardinal Wojtyła wrote in a poem, "If the word did not convert you, the blood will." Then, many years after the assassination attempt, his secretary said, "He often repeated that he considered it a grace that he could suffer. That this blood was necessary. This sickness and the suffering had something to do with the mystery of the saints' experience, given by God." In his final book, *Memory and Identity*, the Pope reflected again, "Perhaps there was a need for that blood to be spilled in Saint Peter's Square, on the site of the martyrdom of the early Christians."

Act Two Begins

After his assassination attempt and two surgeries, John Paul took a time of respite at Castel Gandolfo in order to recover. When he arrived for the period of convalescence, he told the crowd that greeted him with songs that their singing had improved in his absence! Then, he said, "And now Act Two begins."

It is difficult to imagine modern Catholicism had the Church not been blessed with twenty-four more years of his papacy. World Youth Days would not exist, less than half of the Theology of the Body would have been proclaimed, the *Catechism* would not have been issued, and hundreds of millions of souls would not have had the chance to encounter a living saint.

After healing, John Paul desired to express his thanks to the Virgin Mary for protecting his life. He took one of the bullets that struck him and gave it to the bishop of Fatima, who placed it among the gems in the crown of the statue of Our Lady of Fatima. Several biographers have noted that it was a perfect fit. Lino Zani explained, "To everyone's surprise, it was not even necessary to make a place for it, because there was already a hole in the crown into which the bullet fit perfectly, as if it had been designed that way." John Paul also took his sash, which had been pierced by the bullet, and offered it to Our Lady of Jasna Góra in Częstochowa, and offered his zucchetto to Our Lady of the Gate of Dawn in Vilnius, Lithuania. Then, during his 2000 visit to Fatima, he left the pastoral ring that had been given to him by Cardinal Wyszyński at the feet of the statue of our Lady.

In Saint Peter's Square, he installed a mosaic icon of the Virgin Mary with the Christ Child, overlooking the

Papal Apartments, with the words of his motto, *Totus Tuus*, inscribed beneath it. The image was installed in remembrance of the assassination attempt, but it also filled a need that the Pope realized before the attempt on his life occurred: of all the statues that surround Saint Peter's Square, there wasn't a single image of the Blessed Mother. A square marble stone was also placed among the cobblestones in Saint Peter's Square on the spot where the Holy Father was shot; it displays his coat of arms and the date of the failed assassination attempt. Every year, on the afternoon of the anniversary of the attack, he offered a private Mass of thanksgiving that his life had been spared. Instead of celebrating the Mass alone, every year he flew the two American women who had inadvertently been shot by Agça to Rome, so they could join him in giving thanks to God.

His first Wednesday audience back in Saint Peter's Square was on October 7, the feast of the Holy Rosary. Officials wanted to host the audience indoors for safety reasons, but John Paul refused and took his usual jaunt in the Popemobile as if nothing had happened five months earlier.

Although John Paul forgave his assailant in the ambulance moments after being shot, he wanted to meet with Agça in prison to forgive him. The Pope made the trip to Rome's Rebibbia Prison in December 1983 and spent more than three hours ministering to hundreds of prisoners. He did not learn much about Agça's motives during their private conversation, which lasted more than twenty minutes. John Paul believed the assassin did not act independently, but was commissioned to carry out the act. He later wrote, "I think it was one of the final convulsions of the arrogant ideologies unleashed during the twentieth century."

But the would-be killer's motive wasn't the topic of their discussion. Instead, Agça was astonished that the Pope survived, because he knew the shot was mortal. Agça never apologized, but wanted only to know about the third part of the secret of Fatima. He asked, "I know I was aiming right. I know that the bullet was a killer. So why aren't you dead?" John Paul knew the answer in his heart, which he had explained to others: "One hand shot, and another guided the bullet." Agça was bewildered by whatever powers preserved the life of the Pope, and expressed fear that the "goddess of Fatima" would seek vengeance to "get rid of him." John Paul allayed his fears and assured him that our Lady had forgiven him, too.

Decades later, it remains a mystery as to who was behind the assassination attempt. Agça's testimonies during various court appearances and interviews were inconsistent, to say the very least. At first, he named three Bulgarian accomplices. Then he claimed to be Jesus Christ and insisted that he acted alone. He said he never intended to kill the Pope, and added that he didn't know why he shot him. Then he suggested that a cardinal was behind the plot to kill the Pope, and even wrote to Dan Brown from prison, to see if he wanted to coauthor a book called *The Vatican Code*, followed by a movie. He also claimed that the Church offered him money to become Catholic and promised to make him a cardinal if only he'd convert. Italy granted him a pardon in 2000, at which point he was extradited to Turkey, where he began serving his sentence for the murder he had committed in 1979. When John Paul died in 2005, Agça requested that the Turkish government allow him to attend the funeral, but his request was denied. In 2010, he was released from prison.

Numerous theories have been postulated about who was behind the attacks and whether or not Ağça acted alone. Although some pointed the finger at Islamic radicals, the preponderance of evidence eventually showed that, however complicated the scheme, the ultimate responsibility for the assassination attempt lies with the Soviet Union. However, John Paul was disinterested in the details of the investigations into who may have plotted his demise. He said, "It doesn't interest me; because it was the devil who did this thing. And the devil can conspire in a thousand ways, none of which interest me."

During his visit to Fatima in 1982, on the eve of the one-year anniversary of his assassination attempt, another attempt was made on his life, which wasn't made public until after the Holy Father passed away in 2005. As he was walking toward the altar during a candlelight procession, a priest stabbed him with a bayonet. All papal biographies prior to 2005 state that the man "attempted" to stab the Holy Father, but none realized that he succeeded. John Paul didn't appear to be wounded, and even turned to bless the man who attacked him, as security forces pulled the assailant away. The Holy Father finished the prayer service without others noticing his wound. After returning to his room after the event, his aides noticed the blood on his cassock.

His attacker, Father Juan María Fernández Krohn of Spain, was an ultraconservative who opposed the reforms that were taking place within the Church after the Second Vatican Council and thought that John Paul was conspiring with communists to destroy the Church. He had been ordained in the Society of St. Pius X, but left the priesthood after the attack and was treated for mental illness. Despite this second attempt on the Pope's life, he continued for

more than two decades to walk among his people, refusing
to live in fear.

The Good Shepherd

The Holy Father had more brushes with death than most
Catholics realize. Perhaps his first close encounter was during his youth when his thirteen-year-old friend Bogusław
Banas jokingly picked up a revolver and aimed it at him,
saying, "Hands up, or I'll shoot!" Not knowing the firearm
was loaded, he pulled the trigger. He recalled, "It was
pointing straight at Karol, and it's a marvel I didn't kill
him. The bullet missed him by a hair's breadth and broke
a window." Following this incident, Wojtyła survived a
gauntlet of threats to his life under the Nazi and communist occupations of Poland.

Many years later, when he was told that Sarajevo was
unsafe for him to visit, he replied, "If missionaries, bishops,
and nuncios take risks, why shouldn't the Pope take them,
too?" His keepers wanted him at least to wear a bulletproof
vest, but he declined. He added, "the shepherd always has
to be in the middle of his flock, even at the cost of his own
life." When the Vatican security team encouraged him and
everyone in his entourage to wear them on their trip to
Nicaragua, he retorted, "If any in my entourage wish to
wear a bulletproof vest, they need not accompany me on
this visit. We are in the hands of God and we will be
protected by Him."

In Pakistan, before the Pope arrived to celebrate Mass in
1981, a terrorist died when his bomb exploded prematurely
at the entrance to the stadium. On two other occasions,
men with knives were arrested while lying in wait for the
Holy Father in crowds. Plots were also foiled in Venezuela,
Austria, Italy, the Ivory Coast, and even Poland.

One of the most significant papal assassination attempts was thwarted less than a week before the Pope landed in the Philippines to celebrate World Youth Day in 1995. On the evening of January 6, Manila police responded to a call to investigate a fire on the sixth floor of the Doña Josefa Apartments—less than a block from the papal nuncio's residence, where John Paul was scheduled to stay. Smoke was billowing from the window and the residents reported an unusual scent. By the time the authorities arrived, the two tenants from Unit 603 had fled and the fire had subsided. When the police entered the apartment, they discovered that one of the residents had accidentally ignited the fire while mixing chemicals in the kitchen.

The apartment was a live-in bomb factory in which investigators discovered sulfuric acid, nitroglycerin, and a host of other chemicals, along with wires, funnels, fuses, a pair of pipe bombs, and an Arabic manual for creating liquid bombs. They also found a Rosary, a crucifix, a Bible, a photo of John Paul, and maps of the routes on which he was soon to travel through the streets of Manila. A voicemail from a local tailor was left on the phone, saying that the cassock that was ordered was ready for a final fitting. However, the "intelligence gold mine" was the discovery of a laptop and four discs that were filled with elaborate terrorist plots and contact information. Altogether, the police confiscated enough evidence to fill three police vans.

Thanks to the accidental fire, international terrorist experts were alerted to a three-phase plot, code-named "Bojinka." It was reported that phase one was to have a bomber dressed in a priest's cassock slip into the papal entourage and murder the Pope with a bomb on his way to the San Carlos Seminary in Makati City. Phase two was to be launched less than two weeks after the Pope's assassination,

when terrorists were scheduled to plant bombs on eleven
flights from Asia to the United States. The devices were
timed to detonate almost simultaneously over the Pacific
Ocean, killing four thousand passengers. The final phase
of the operation was for a terrorist to crash an airplane
into CIA headquarters in Langley, Virginia. A former director of the CIA's Counterterrorism Division called the
plot, "Extraordinarily ambitious, very complicated to bring
off, and probably unparalleled by other terrorist operations
that we know of."

Unlike some of the other assassins who failed, those
behind this operation were not amateurs. One of the two
men who lived in the apartment was Abdul Hakim Murad,
who created the bomb that detonated under the World
Trade Center in 1993, injuring more than one thousand
people. The other man was Ramzi Ahmed Yousef, who
planned the World Trade Center bombing. At the time
of the 1995 papal assassination attempt, he was a fugitive
with a $2 million bounty on his head. His uncle, Khalid
Shaikh Mohammed, who masterminded the September 11
attacks, also lived in Manila at the time and helped plan
"Bojinka." Most of the money to fund the operation was
wired to a bank account owned by a man who worked for
an Islamic organization run by Osama bin Laden's brother-
in-law. Osama bin Laden said of the financier of the plot,
Wali Khan Amin Shah, "He was nicknamed 'The Lion.'
He is one of the best. We were good friends."

All the men were eventually captured and the terrorist plot to kill thousands was prevented. Nine days after
the providential apartment fire, John Paul peacefully celebrated Mass in Manila with between five and seven million
Filipinos.

It would not be long before the Pope's life would again be threatened. Two years later, as his plane was approaching the airport in Bosnia, NATO officials warned that it was dangerous to land. He insisted that the visit continue, and an F-16 fighter jet escorted him to the runway for protection. The Holy Father was informed that a bomb had been discovered under a bridge he was scheduled to drive over one hour later. The device had been assembled from more than fifty pounds of plastic explosive and twenty antitank mines. The Pope asked, "Are there people waiting for me?" "Yes." "Then I will go."

Four years later, when the Holy Father visited Syria in 2001, an Islamic terrorist group planned to have a female suicide bomber throw herself at the Popemobile in Damascus, then nearby snipers were to open fire after the detonation. On the eve of the trip, the CIA informed the Vatican, who provided the information to Syria's secret service to prevent the attack.

Not surprisingly, John Paul had a strong devotion to his guardian angel—although it is fair to speculate that he probably had a legion of them! He said, "My Guardian Angel knows what I am doing. My faith in him, in his protective presence, continues to grow deeper and deeper." Before deplaning in Turkey, a reporter asked him if he felt he was in danger. John Paul answered, "Love is stronger than danger."

He also spoke often of his absolute trust in the maternal protection of our Lady. Having read Saint Louis de Montfort's classic *True Devotion to Mary*, he would have known that the great Marian saint promised that, "This powerful Queen of heaven would sooner dispatch millions of angels to help one of her servants than have it said that a single faithful and trusting servant of hers had fallen victim to the malice, number and power of his enemies." Having the confidence of living under her mantle gave John Paul the courage to scold even the Sicilian Mafia, calling them to repent because God's judgment would come upon them one day. The Mafia responded by damaging two Roman churches with bombs, including the Pope's cathedral church, the Basilica of Saint John Lateran.

Considering the constant peril under which he lived, it is understandable why he considered himself to be an heir of Saint Paul, who described his own missionary work in his Second Letter to the Corinthians: ". . . on frequent journeys, in danger from rivers, danger from robbers, danger from my own people, danger from Gentiles, danger in the city, danger in the wilderness, danger at sea, danger from false brethren . . . And, apart from other things, there is the daily pressure upon me of my anxiety for all the churches" (2 Cor 11:26–29).

Love for the Mother

John Paul not only visited Mehmet Ali Agça in prison, he also received his mother, Mrs. Muzeyyen Agça, in a private audience after she showed up at the Vatican unannounced! During their exchange, he assured her of his forgiveness and presented her with a statue of the Madonna and Child. Those who knew the Holy Father noticed that he had a special place in his heart for mothers, perhaps because he had lost his own at such a young age.

Countless encounters that the Pope had with mothers testify to this. Upon being greeted by the mayor of Boston and his wife, the Holy Father turned his attention to the wife, saying, "Ah, Mrs. Your husband has a very important job. Like the Pope does. But don't believe it. Your job is more important. The future of the world is with the mothers. It is the mothers who raise the children. It is the mothers who will give us peace and make us free. Like Mary, the Mother of Jesus, we need you the most."

During a Wednesday audience in 1995, one of John Paul's assistants alerted him that there was an American mother in attendance who had recently lost her son in a car accident. John Paul signaled for her to be brought near the doors of Saint Peter's Basilica, where he could meet her afterward. Once the audience concluded, he walked to her and put one hand on the side of her face, while holding his papal cross with the other. He then leaned his forehead against hers and said, "Mothers are given much love but also much pain. Like Mary suffered when her son died. I know you have suffered, as Mary suffered. But like Mary, you will see your son again." An onlooker noticed, "The Holy Father's face seemed to reflect the pain that was in Charlene's heart. It was as if he was absorbing it, taking it from her. Charlene was sobbing, but you could almost feel her releasing some of the pain."

John Paul also had a deep love for those who were spiritual mothers, such as Mother Teresa. In 1982, while a battle was raging in West Beirut, Mother Teresa paid him an unexpected visit on her way to the war-torn nation of Lebanon. He gave her a candle with an image of our Lady on it, and she took it with her on her journey. Upon her arrival, she was unable to enter West Beirut because of the violence between the Israeli army and Palestinian guerrillas.

A film documentary on Mother Teresa recounted the tense situation:

Beirut was under siege. Mother Teresa felt that she wanted to get to West Beirut to see to the needs of the people there. She asked to see the American ambassador to see if he could help her to get across and he said, "Mother, you hear the shells?" And she said, "Yes, I hear them." He said, "You know, it is absolutely impossible for you to cross at this present time. We will have to have a cease-fire first." And she said, "Oh, but I have been praying to Our Lady and I have asked her to let us have a cease-fire here tomorrow, the day before her Feast Day." Ambassador Habib looked at Mother Teresa and said, "Mother, I am very glad you are on my side—that you are a woman of prayer." He said, "I believe in prayer and I believe that prayer is answered and I am a man of faith." But he said, "You are asking Our Lady to deal with Prime Minister Begin and don't you think the time limit is a little short—that you should extend it a little?" She quite seriously said, "Oh, no, Mr. Habib, I am certain we will have the cease-fire tomorrow." And he said, "If we have the cease-fire, I personally will make arrangements to see that you go to West Beirut tomorrow."

Sure enough, stillness and peace blanketed West Beirut the next morning as Mother Teresa traveled with Red Cross workers to a mental hospital for handicapped Muslim children, rescuing thirty-seven of them. John Paul's secretary noted that the cease-fire lasted for as long as the candle was lit.

Exceeding his affection for all earthly mothers was John Paul's love for the mother of Jesus. The rector of a local Catholic high school in Poland often observed Karol Wojtyła as a young teenager, visiting a secluded convent church, praying for hours at a time before an image of our Lady. During his college years, it was an annual tradition for university students to make a pilgrimage to the shrine of the Black Madonna in Jasna Góra. However, the devotional trip was banned under the Nazi occupation. Undeterred, Karol and two friends went to the monastery, even though Częstochowa was surrounded by Hitler's soldiers. Many years later as pope, he not only made it a point to visit Marian shrines in virtually every country he visited, he also entrusted every nation to Mary's maternal care.

Of all prayers, the Rosary was his favorite. He was never without his Rosary, and prayed it whenever he could, several times a day. Many of his associates noticed that he was "joyful and more radiant on Marian feast days." His driver in Poland recalled that while they were driving, "He was praying all the time and no matter what he was doing, he was always holding a Rosary in his hands. Sometimes I peeked in the rear mirror and when he saw that I was looking at him, he used to raise his eyes and smile warmly."

Upon arriving in Rome as a new Swiss Guard, Andreas Widmer admitted that he was curious about John Paul, and observed him closely one winter night, praying the Rosary:

As I watched him pray, softly speaking the words of the Rosary, be began radiating a sense of peacefulness and calm unlike anything I had ever encountered. The longer he prayed, the more absorbed in the prayer he became, until he seemed completely taken up in it, as if nothing and no one in the room could pull him back from the place where he'd gone. He was obviously still physically present, but his spirit seemed to be someplace else. I'd never seen anyone pray like that before. I didn't know it was possible. Up until that evening, I had always thought of prayer as an act of the imagination, a mental fantasy people cooked up to feel better about something, almost like a child talking to an imaginary friend. But there was nothing imaginary about what I saw that night. This man wasn't faking his immersion in God. What I saw was profoundly real and exceedingly desirable.

While in Fatima in 1991, John Paul spoke of the Rosary, saying, "It's our daily meeting which neither I nor Blessed Virgin Mary neglect." What is telling about this statement is that she didn't neglect her daily Rosary with him, either. To him, the prayer was not a monologue. When asked if the Virgin Mary ever appeared to him, he replied: No. But when asked if she has ever spoken to him, he answered: Yes. One can only wonder if the five new mysteries of the Rosary that he offered to the Church in 2002 were the fruit of such dialogues.

Those who knew him well said that he was often in conversation with Mary. On one such occasion, Monsignor George Tracy was concelebrating Mass with the Holy Father, and after Communion could hear him praying aloud. Monsignor Tracy noticed that he was extremely upset and seemed to be sobbing, "No, Maria, no, Madonna." After Mass was finished, a Vatican prelate asked the monsignor if he enjoyed his Mass with the Pope. He replied in the affirmative, but said that after Communion, the Holy Father was noticeably shaken, and it seemed that he was talking to the Virgin Mary. The prelate replied, "We know. He does that all the time, and she's the only one he listens to around here."

Totus Tuus!

As a young man in Poland, Karol Wojtyła often walked to and from work carrying Saint Louis de Montfort's *True Devotion to Mary*. Often during his break times, he paused to read the text. Many years later, as pope, he said, "I remember carrying it on me for a long time, even at the sodium factory, with the result that its handsome binding became spotted with lime. I continually went back to certain passages."

Through the writings of de Montfort, he discovered that it is not necessary to distance oneself from Marian piety in order to focus more on Jesus. Rather, authentic Marian devotion leads one closer to Christ. He recalled, "I was already convinced that *Mary leads us to Christ*, but at that time I began to realize also that *Christ leads us to his Mother*." He added, "One can even say that just as Christ on Calvary indicated his mother to the disciple John, so he points her out to anyone who strives to know and love him."

The foundation of Marian devotion is the understanding that Mary is the Mother of the Church. Vatican II explained, "In a wholly singular way she cooperated by her obedience, faith, hope, and burning charity in the Savior's work of restoring supernatural life to souls. For this reason she is a mother to us in the order of grace." Because of her role as Spiritual Mother, she is capable of distributing a torrent of graces from heaven to those in need of her prayers.

As a biblical foundation, the scriptures state that the fervent prayer of a righteous person is very powerful (Jas 5:16), that everyone in heaven is righteous (Rev 21:27), that people in heaven pray for those on earth (Rev 5:8), that the mother of Jesus could be seen in heaven (Rev

12:1–5), and that her offspring were "those who keep the commandments of God and bear testimony to Jesus" (Rev 12:17). Furthermore, if Saint Paul could claim to be a spiritual father and declare that he was in labor pains for others until Christ be formed in them, how much more would this be true of Mary! None suffered with Christ more intimately than Mary, who was, in the words of John Paul, "crucified spiritually with her crucified son."

Physical motherhood extends beyond birth pangs to the nourishment of children, and the same is true of Spiritual Motherhood. Because of the unique role she played in suffering with Christ as he acquired the graces of redemption, the Church believes Mary also plays a unique role in the distribution of those graces. Her Spiritual Motherhood is not a medieval Catholic invention, but rather, as John Paul said, "a gift which Christ himself makes personally to every individual." However, much depends on to what extent one accepts this gift, if at all.

Devotion to the mother of Jesus was an integral part of John Paul's spirituality, and it was from the pages of de Montfort's work that he took his papal motto: *Totus Tuus*. This is a shortened version of the phrase: *Totus tuus ego sum et omnia mea tua sunt* [I am all yours, and all that is mine is yours]. Whenever the Holy Father wrote a speech or book, he began by inscribing on the top of the first page "Totus Tuus," offering each of his works to Mary.

Total Consecration

Within the pages of *True Devotion to Mary*, John Paul discovered the practice of Marian consecration. One way to understand this devotion is to imagine that praying a Hail Mary is comparable to giving the Virgin Mary a rose. Praying an entire Rosary with love and devotion is like giving her an entire bouquet. However, Marian consecration is giving her one's own self. It is therefore the crowning of Marian devotion. It is a gift of self and a promise of love, whereby a person entrusts himself entirely to the Virgin Mary and invites her to unleash her full intercessory power to help him remain faithful to Christ.

In John Paul's Theology of the Body, he spoke about love as a gift of self that must be free, total, faithful, and life-giving. He declared that the highest expression of human freedom is to make a gift of one's self in love. It is this same concept of complete self-giving love that permeates John Paul's Marian spirituality. He considered his devotion to Mary not only as a total gift to her, but as a gift that is mutual—because she reciprocates her own gift of self. Saint Louis de Montfort explained that when Mary sees someone give himself entirely to her:

> . . . she gives herself completely in a wondrous manner to him. She engulfs him in the ocean of her graces, adorns him with her merits, supports him with her power, enlightens him with her light, and fills him with her love. She shares her virtues with him—her humility, faith, purity, etc. She makes up for his failings and becomes his representative with Jesus. Just as one who is consecrated belongs entirely to Mary, so Mary belongs entirely to him.

In the writings of de Montfort, the saint spoke about total consecration as a form of "Holy slavery." But because the idea of becoming a slave to Mary could easily confuse those who do not understand the firm Christological foundation of the devotion, he added, "it is better to speak of 'slavery of Jesus in Mary' and to call oneself 'slave of Jesus' rather

than 'slave of Mary.' We then avoid giving any pretext
for criticism. In this way, we name this devotion after its
ultimate end which is Jesus, rather than after the way and
the means to arrive there, which is Mary."

The goal of Marian devotion is simple. According to
Saint Maximilian Kolbe, it is to help people "love Jesus
with the Immaculata's heart." No human heart loved him
more than his own mother's, and now that she nourishes
the Church with her prayers from heaven, she is able to
communicate to her children a portion of her unparalleled
love for her Divine Son. This love can be exercised in very
simple ways, as de Montfort noted. He suggested that in
preparation for receiving Holy Communion, the faithful
should "Implore Mary to lend you her heart so that you
may receive her Son with her dispositions."

In de Montfort's work, he explained that many people
have a "devotion" to Mary, but it is imperfect because it
might be critical, scrupulous, superficial, presumptuous, in-
constant, hypocritical, or self-interested. On the other hand,
true devotion to her must be interior, trustful, holy, constant, and disinterested. In summary, he says that Marian
consecration is a smooth, short, perfect, and sure way to
Jesus. Although there are many forms and degrees of devotion to Mary, according to de Montfort, perfect devotion means "doing everything *through* Mary, *with* Mary,
in Mary, and *for* Mary, in order to do it more perfectly
through Jesus, *with* Jesus, *in* Jesus, and *for* Jesus."

When a person offers himself entirely to Mary, he is
disposed to receive "the greatest possible influx of grace,"
as Kolbe noted. This benefit is available because of the
unique relationship Mary has with the Holy Spirit, who
united himself with her at the moment of her Immaculate
Conception, and again in a unique manner through the

Annunciation. Saint Louis de Montfort remarked, "When the Holy Spirit, her spouse, finds Mary in a soul, he hastens there and enters fully into it. He gives himself generously to that soul according to the place it has given to his spouse." Saint Maximilian Kolbe echoed a similar sentiment, adding that Mary "will act through them in so far as they belong to her. Hence there must remain nothing in them that is theirs; they must be hers totally."

The idea of belonging totally to another human being strikes some people as problematic. Indeed, the language can sound jarring. But de Montfort insists upon it, asking, "Is it not reasonable to find that among so many slaves there should be some slaves of love, who freely choose Mary as their Queen? Should men and demons have willing slaves, and Mary have none?"

The practice of Marian consecration is nothing new. Popes have praised the devotion for centuries. John Paul reminded the faithful, "For it must be recognized that before anyone else it was God himself, the Eternal Father, who entrusted himself to the Virgin of Nazareth, giving her his own Son in the mystery of the Incarnation." Just as Jesus was formed in the womb of Mary, the idea of Marian consecration is that individuals entrust themselves to her in a similar way to be formed by her maternal love.

John Paul did not consider Marian consecration to be a peripheral devotion that might be helpful to pious individuals who appreciate sentimental language. Rather, he felt it was so essential to Catholic spirituality that he stated, "this 'perfect devotion' is indispensable to anyone who means to give himself without reserve to Christ and to the work of Redemption."

Despite such a strong papal endorsement, for many people the idea of Marian consecration is difficult to understand. Even John Paul admitted that he needed to reread *True Devotion to Mary* several times in order to understand it. However, he said:

> I found the answer to my perplexities due to the fear that the devotion to Mary, if excessive, might end by compromising the supremacy of the worship owed to Christ. Under the wise guidance of Saint Louis-Marie, I understood that, if one lives the mystery of Mary in Christ, such a risk does not exist.

As he discovered, authentic Marian devotion does not add to or take away from the finished work of Christ. However, it is a subject to be contemplated, not simply researched. A person might search for understanding through study, but he will only receive it through meditation. Saint Maximilian Kolbe points this out: "True knowledge of the Immaculata can only be acquired in prayer. The purer a soul is, the greater efforts it makes to avoid sin . . . the more and better will it get to know the Immaculata."

If one were to ask John Paul why his pontificate was so fruitful, he would have unhesitatingly affirmed that it was due to the entrustment of his papacy to the Virgin Mary. Through her maternal mediation, God chose to do marvelous things. In countless ways, she reciprocated John Paul's gift of self by giving herself to him.

A providential foreshadowing of this happened in Poland before he had been elected pope. During a celebration of the coronation of the statue of Our Lady of Ludźmierz, the scepter fell out of Mary's hands and was caught by Cardinal Wojtyła. The priest standing beside him said, "Karol, Mary shares her power with you." Years later, in *Crossing the Threshold of Hope*, John Paul said, "The victory, if it comes, will come through Mary. . . . *Christ will conquer through her, because He wants the Church's victories now and in the future to be linked to her.*"

John Paul's deep Marian piety is best expressed not by stories or theological reasoning, but the words of the following prayer he wrote, entitled "Totus Tuus":

Immaculate Conception, Mary my Mother,
Live in me, Act in me,
Speak in me and through me,
Think your thoughts in my mind,
Love through my heart,
Give me your dispositions and feelings,
Teach, lead me and guide me to Jesus,
Correct, enlighten and expand my thoughts and
     behavior,
Possess my soul,
Take over my entire personality and life, replace
     it with Yourself,
Incline me to constant adoration,
Pray in me and through me,
Let me live in you and keep me in this union always.
Amen.

11

THE CROSS

Three days before he was elected pope, Cardinal Wojtyła entered the Vatican and was assigned his cell for the conclave. Shortly thereafter, he heard the news that a close friend had been hospitalized in Rome after suffering a massive stroke. The patient, Bishop Andrzej Deskur, studied in the seminary with Wojtyła and was a longtime friend. The Cardinal immediately went to the hospital to pay him a visit, and returned again the next day on his way to the Sistine Chapel, arriving just in time to enter the conclave.

After being elected pope, countless new responsibilities demanded John Paul's attention. However, he knew which needed to come first. Despite the objections of his personal aides, the Holy Father's first trip out of the Vatican in 1978 was to the hospital, to visit Deskur. But his intention in going was not merely to comfort the sick.

Years later, he recalled the hospital visit he made on the day after his election, to see Bishop Deskur and the others who were ill:

I said to the patients that I counted greatly, very greatly indeed, on them: for their prayers and especially for the offering of their sufferings, which could provide me with a special strength, a strength that was and is necessary to me in order to perform in a less unworthy manner my serious duties in the bosom of the church of Christ.

John Paul's friend was confined to a wheelchair for the rest of his life, and the Holy Father saw providence at work behind this "sacrifice of Andrzej" in preparation for his election. A close observation of John Paul's life reveals that at nearly every major junction of his ascent to the papacy, someone appears to have suffered for him. Eleven years earlier, when he was summoned to Rome to become a cardinal, another friend of his lost his hand in a railroad accident. He said of both these priests, "I have become a debtor."

As a seminarian, several months before John Paul's ordination to the priesthood, his close friend and mentor, Jan Tyranowski, was hospitalized with an excruciating infection that eventually led to the amputation of his arm. Due to the illness, he was unable to attend the ordination. After John Paul left Poland to study in Rome, Tyranowski said to one of John Paul's fellow seminarians, "I am lying here doing nothing, but I still want to work for the salvation of the world, as you people are doing in the seminary—I don't want to remain idle. So I am offering up my pain for the benefit of all those in need—and for Karol as well."

Even before he became a priest, yet another victim soul seemed to be mysteriously offered for him. His close friend, Dr. Wanda Półtawska, had been tortured by the Nazis for five years in a concentration camp, and John Paul believed the suffering she endured was partly for him. He wrote to her husband, "And I thought, 'she suffered for me. God spared me this trial because she was there [the concentration camp].' It may be said that this belief was irrational, however it was still in me—and it stays inside me. The whole consciousness of 'sister' was built on that belief." John Paul believed that there are no coincidences in the plan of God, and therefore saw a deeper meaning behind this trail of crosses. The timeline of suffering in the lives of these four souls forged within John Paul a deep appreciation for the redemptive power of human suffering.

Redemptive Suffering

After concelebrating Mass with the Holy Father in his private chapel, a priest from Michigan had a brief opportunity to meet the Pope. The priest had a broken leg, and stood on crutches as John Paul approached him in the receiving line of guests. He said to the Pope with a twinge of humor and self-pity, "I broke my leg. Can I please have your blessing?" John Paul replied, "Don't waste your suffering." The Holy Father raised his hand, blessed the priest, and then with an open palm, thumped the priest on the head.

For John Paul, the Crucifixion was not merely an event that took place two thousand years ago. "In the cross lies Love's victory," John Paul explained. "In it, finally, lies the full truth about man, man's true stature, his wretchedness and his grandeur, his worth and the price paid for him." Not only is the cross the measure of man's worth, it is also the reminder of his calling.

Many who were raised in Catholic homes or educated in Catholic schools recall parents or nuns instructing them to "offer it up" if they didn't like something: "It's too cold? Offer it up." Unfortunately for most children and students, this sounds like a religious way of saying, "Stop complaining."

The idea of "offering it up" comes from the writings of

Saint Paul, who exclaimed, "Now I rejoice in my sufferings for your sake, and in my flesh I complete what is lacking in Christ's afflictions for the sake of his body, that is, the church" (Col 1:24). At first, it sounds at least presumptuous —and perhaps even blasphemous—that a mortal man would somehow make up what's "lacking" in the suffering of Christ. Did Jesus not suffer enough? What Paul is asserting is that Jesus did not die so that humans would never have to suffer, but so that they would know *how* to suffer. The Passion of Christ removed the threat of eternal suffering while revealing the power of temporal suffering.

In becoming man, Christ redeemed all things human: human labor, human love, human suffering, and so on. Each part of man's existence can take on a supernatural significance if only one has the eyes to see. In the case of suffering, through his Passion, death, and Resurrection, Jesus sufficiently merited all the graces necessary for the redemption of mankind. And if individuals suffer with him, they can participate in the distribution of these graces to mankind. It does not matter if the suffering is a bloody martyrdom, a toothache, unemployment, a rebellious child, or an alcoholic spouse. All things can be offered up as a prayer, and the intensity of suffering is not as important as the degree of love with which one embraces each cross.

Once a person discovers the meaning of suffering, it can be transformed into a powerful act of intercession. But the person who remains ignorant of its potential spiritual power could be compared to an illiterate person holding a winning lottery ticket. So much value, all gone to waste. What one person considers to be crushed grapes, another understands as a vintage glass of Dom Pérignon.

To help the Church understand this, John Paul published a letter on the Christian meaning of human suffering, entitled *Salvifici Doloris*, on the feast of Our Lady of Lourdes in 1984. In it, he explained how individuals can share in the suffering of Christ because he opened his suffering to all mankind:

> . . . the weaknesses of all human sufferings are capable of being infused with the same power of God manifested in Christ's Cross. . . . In him God has confirmed his desire to act especially through suffering . . . Christ achieved the Redemption completely and to the very limits but at the same time he did not bring it to a close. . . . every form of suffering, given fresh life by the power of this Cross, should become no longer the weakness of man but the power of God.

Throughout his pontificate, John Paul often made reference to a profound statement from the Second Vatican Council: that Christ *"fully reveals man to himself* and makes his supreme calling clear." This is perhaps most true in the realm of human suffering. John Paul explained that because Jesus understood the value of the cross, "Christ goes towards His own suffering, aware of its saving power." The goal is not merely for suffering to be accepted, but for it to become victorious! John Paul explains, "It is suffering, more than anything else, which clears the way for the grace which transforms human souls. Suffering, more than anything else, makes present in the history of humanity the powers of the Redemption."

By embracing the many crosses of daily life, a person not only sanctifies himself, but also releases a flood of graces for others. This is what Paul meant by completing what is lacking in Christ's afflictions for the sake of the Church. The body of Christ is not merely a collection of Christians. It is a living instrument of redemption—an extension of

Jesus Christ throughout time and space. He continues his salvific work through each member of his body. When a person understands this, he sees that the idea of "offering it up" is not just a theological reply to the question of human suffering, but rather a calling to participate in the salvation of the world.

Cardinal Wojtyła explained, "To meet with suffering, that is a specific type of harvest." He reminded the sick that they are not merely to be taken care of, but that they too can care for others through their suffering: "You can do very much by your prayer and your sacrifice, your suffering . . . you can obtain much from Jesus Christ for those who may not need physical help, but who often are in terrible need of spiritual help . . . Your role in the parish is not merely passive."

Through the example of Christ, one learns that not only should a person do good to those who suffer, but one can also do good *by* one's suffering. *Salvifici Dolores* declared, "In this double aspect he has completely revealed the meaning of suffering." When one understands the value of the cross and overcomes the sense that suffering is useless, the fruits of peace and joy are experienced. As John Paul explained, "The discovery of the salvific meaning of suffering in union with Christ *transforms* this depressing *feeling*." The Holy Father again referred to this joy in *Memory and Identity*:

It is this suffering which burns and consumes evil with the flame of love and draws forth even from sin a great flowering of good. All human suffering, all pain, all infirmity contains within itself a promise of salvation, a promise of joy: "I am now rejoicing in my suffering for your sake," writes Saint Paul (Col 1:24).

Besides the writings of the saints, the Polish poet Cyprian Norwid also shaped the Holy Father's appreciation for redemptive suffering. Commenting on Norwid, John Paul wrote, "It is significant that for Norwid crucifixes should not carry the figure of Christ, for in this way they could more clearly show the place where a Christian must be. Only those in whose interior Golgotha is lived each day can say: the Cross 'has become the door.'" Norwid believed Christians should live "Not with the Cross of the Savior behind you, but with your own cross behind the Savior."

Although the powerful ones of the world assume they wield the greatest influence, God's power is made perfect in weakness. In the Kingdom of God, the paraplegic is not less important than the business tycoon or celebrity, but in a certain sense, more so. As the archbishop of Kraków, Wojtyła said to the sick:

> Although I am young and strong, although I fly in air-planes, climb mountains, ski, I still turn to the weak-est, so that by the riches of their suffering they may bring down the strength and power of the Holy Spirit and the blessing of God upon my work in the Arch-diocese.

When human suffering is understood in its deepest meaning, it ceases to be something negative that is ex-perienced in a passive manner. Rather, one becomes free to meet suffering with courage, seeing it as an opportunity for active and positive collaboration in the work of human re-demption. Through God's grace, it can be transformed into an irreplaceable service for souls, and is no longer wasted. For this reason, John Paul exclaimed, "Prayer joined to sacrifice constitutes the most powerful force in human his-tory."

John Paul realized the tsunami of grace that was waiting to be unleashed by redemptive suffering and tapped into that source at every opportunity, drawing upon those graces to fulfill his mission. In his first *urbi et orbi* address on the day after his election as pope, he addressed the sick and told them he "is in great need of your help, your prayers, and your sacrifices, and this I most humbly beg of you." It was after delivering this message that he went to visit his friend Bishop Deskur. While at the hospital, he spoke to the patients, telling them that in spite of their ailments, they were "very powerful: powerful just like Jesus Christ crucified is powerful," and asked that they use that suffering for the good of the Pope's ministry. Then, on the World Day of the Sick, he again announced, "Dear brothers and sisters who experience suffering in a particular way, you are called to a special mission in the new evangelization and to find your inspiration in Mary, Mother of love and human pain."

Just as he always sought out young people when he visited different countries, he also exerted a special effort to connect with those who were ill. While at a basilica in Knock, Ireland, he visited with 3,000 disabled people, reminding them as well that because of the power of redemptive suffering, "there is something very special about your mission in the Church. . . . Your call to suffering requires strong faith and patience. Yes, it means that you are called to love with a special intensity." Even in its brokenness, the human body continues to be an icon of man's call to love through a total gift of self.

When the Pope needed special prayers to be answered, he turned to the sick. In his book *Rise, Let Us Be on Our Way*, he explained that he entrusted the needs of the Church to the prayers of the sick, "and the results were always positive." He remarked that "the weak are a source of strength," and he believed so firmly in this that before a friend underwent surgery, he gave him a rather significant intention: "I am entrusting the Church to you." In the eyes of the Lord, weakness affords those who are infirm with immense spiritual power.

Often, John Paul didn't merely ask for their prayers; he begged! To the sick in Poland, he said, "wherever you may be—I beg you to make use of *the cross* that has become part of each of you *for salvation*. . . ." Those who seemed to have no hope other than heaven became an inspiration to him. Speaking of the permanent invalids he has met, he remarked:

> Bereft of all strength, dying a slow death, how could these incurables, in human terms, accept their lot? Yet gradually some of them begin to realize that suffering, too, is a privileged vocation in the mystery of Christ and the Church. . . . More than once I have noted that this terrible irreversibility could be accepted not as a calamity, but as a sign of election and vocation, engendering that inner peace and even that joy which come to man when he discovers the meaning of his life and his identity, that is, the name by which God calls him. In my conversations with the most severely tested people, I have often been struck by a serenity, an unexpected happiness in which I could see only a tangible proof of the intervention of grace and the presence of the Holy Spirit in the heart of man.

To support those who were nearing the end of their earthly journey, he wrote a letter to the elderly in 1999, reminding them that God "always gives us the grace and strength to unite ourselves with greater love to the sacrifice of his Son and to share ever more fully in his plan of salvation." He added, "Physical condition or advancing of age are not obstacles to a perfect life. God does not look at external things but at the soul." He encouraged those who were nearing the end: "Death opens to souls a new horizon of life."

Com-passion

As a youth, John Paul admitted he was intimidated by human suffering and felt somewhat embarrassed in the presence of the sick, not knowing what he could offer them. In time, he grew to realize that by revealing to them their role within the drama of human redemption, he was reminding them of their importance—especially those who felt forgotten and insignificant. But in order to bring Christ to them, he knew it wasn't enough to explain their role in salvation history. They needed to encounter the love of God in a tangible way.

John Paul taught that one of the fruits of human suffering is that it awakens love in others. It reminds people to make a gift of themselves in order to serve those who live under the weight of the cross. In fact, the word "compassion" is derived from the Latin word *compati*, which means to "suffer with."

Caring for the sick is a standard facet of any priest's ministry, but even as a cardinal, Karol Wojtyła continued to seek out those who were ill. During a parish mission in Kraków, he asked the priest to bring him to those who were homebound, and spent two days visiting twenty sick people in basements, apartments, and attics. At each visit, he would talk, listen, and pray with those who were often unable to leave their own beds. When Wojtyła met a woman who was recovering from a brain tumor—while raising a disabled daughter and being married to an alcoholic—the priest recalled, "I noticed that his brow was covered with beads of sweat and his veins bulged. With his hand he wiped the tears from her face, and kissed her several times on the forehead." With each visit, he requested their prayers for the Church, and asked if they were satisfied with how their parish priest was caring for them.

As Pope, his apostolate to the suffering only widened. He visited numerous leper colonies around the world and even kissed some of the patients. Arturo Mari, a papal photographer, recalled, "I remember how the Pope behaved in the leprosarium . . . Many of us couldn't even look at some of these diseased people, at the deformed, without faces. He touched them, stroked them, kissed and blessed, helped them to eat."

While vising the poorest of the poor at Mother Teresa's home for the destitute and dying in Calcutta, he reminded them, "You are not God's abandoned children. Quite the opposite. God will find joy in your faith and courage." Journalists noticed that he not only greeted the sick with great affection, but even the dead: "he walked into the room where the day's corpses were laid out: two men, a woman, and a child. Even the cadavers received a gentle touch from him." He felt so at home with the poor that when visiting Mother Teresa in Calcutta, someone nearby heard him whisper to her, "If I could, I would make this my headquarters as Pope."

Early in his pontificate, he was saddened when he noticed homeless people sleeping by the colonnade of Saint Peter's Square, within view of his window in the Vatican. In order to care for them, he asked Mother Teresa to establish a homeless shelter within the Vatican and named it *Dono di Maria* [Gift of Mary]. Not only did he create the shelter, he often visited its residents—some of whom were the gypsies that so many Romans detested—in order to talk with them and share meals together. For the celebration of the Lord's Supper on Holy Thursday of 1980, he invited twelve of the homeless men to the Basilica of Saint John Lateran, where he washed and kissed their feet during the liturgy. In the summer of 2000, he hosted a meal for more than two hundred of them in the Vatican to celebrate the Jubilee. Rome's seminarians waited on them, serving ravioli, veal, sautéed potatoes, cheese, and fruit salad, with a pair of different wines.

Everywhere he went, he seemed to feel at home with the poor. While in Rio de Janeiro, he visited an impoverished favela where he encountered a destitute family. Because he had nothing of greater value to offer the mother, he took off the ring that Pope Paul VI had given to him when he became a cardinal, and gave it to her. For the rest of the papal visit, he borrowed another bishop's ring. The poor heard him say, "I did not come here out of curiosity, but because I love you."

He did the same in Africa, when he asked his motor-cade to stop beside a few poor huts by the roadside in a village in Chad. He entered one of the hovels, and spent time conversing with the residents. He habitually offered whatever he had, whether it was his time and attention or his financial help. In fact, he gave the majority of his royalties for one of his books to the children of Rwanda and other poor nations. When he learned that a friend of his needed to hospitalize his son to treat his severe depression, the Holy Father inquired, "Much bills? Very expensive? . . . Maybe the pope can help. The pope has some small money. Not church money, but the pope's small money. Maybe he can help."

The Holy Father didn't waste a moment of his papacy reaching out to those in need. His first action after his inaugural Mass was to break with custom and walk down to the pilgrims gathered in Saint Peter's Square to bless the handicapped people in wheelchairs—before greeting the heads of state and other official representatives. He expressed such compassion and reverence for those who were suffering that those who organized his Masses soon realized they shouldn't put more than thirty sick people near the altar because the Holy Father wanted to greet each of them individually, and this caused him to miss other scheduled appointments. On one such occasion, the organizers of his event failed to take this into consideration and seated more than three hundred sick people near the front. By the time John Paul was finished greeting each of them, the program was more than an hour late. He said, "with those who are suffering, you must never be in a hurry."

It was obvious that he loved the poor and sick, and it was obvious they loved him in return. While greeting disabled children at an event at Trinity College in Washington, D.C., a young girl asked, "Bless me, John Paul." Leaning over, he replied, "First you bless me." She did, and then he returned the favor and the two embraced.

However, John Paul seemed to lavish his greatest expressions of compassion upon those who seemed to deserve it the least. In one of the messages that Jesus gave to Saint Faustina, he said, "The greater the sinner, the greater the right he has to My mercy." This unfathomable mercy became visible when the Holy Father visited Missouri in 1999. While celebrating Mass in St. Louis, the Holy Father challenged Americans to become unconditionally pro-life, pointing out that the death penalty is unnecessary in a country that is able to protect itself with other means, and denies criminals the chance to reform.

Immediately after Mass, he asked to have a private meeting with the governor of Missouri, Mel Carnahan, who had previously approved the execution of more than two dozen criminals. On the day of their meeting, an inmate who had been convicted of murdering a married couple and their grandson was scheduled to die by lethal injection. John Paul petitioned him, "Have mercy on Darrell Mease." The next day, Governor Carnahan made national headlines when he announced that the sentence was commuted and the prisoner instead received life in prison without parole.

More than a decade earlier, John Paul was also success-ful in obtaining clemency for a sixteen-year-old girl who stabbed an elderly Bible study teacher to death in 1986. Some vilified the Pope for his interventions, but it is diffi-cult to argue against a man who forgave his own would-be assassin while still bleeding from his gunshot wounds. In his encyclical on God's mercy, he proclaimed, "Forgiveness demonstrates the presence in the world of the love which is more powerful than sin."

Misericordia

When John Paul met those who were suffering, he knew he was encountering Christ in a unique way. Therefore he did everything in his power to express God's mercy to them. As Father Michael Gaitley remarked, "Mercy is love when it meets suffering." The Latin word for mercy is *misericordia*, which literally means "miserable heart." Father George Kosicki offered another definition: "having a pain in your heart for the pains of another, and taking pains to do something about their pain." One of the most remarkable qualities of John Paul is that he sometimes had the ability to actually remove the pain.

While celebrating Mass at Saint Peter's Basilica on the day after John Paul's funeral, Cardinal Francesco Marchisano spoke of an extraordinary meeting that took place between himself and the late Holy Father. Five years earlier, Cardinal Marchisano underwent an operation on one of the main arteries in his neck that supplied blood to his brain. Due to a surgical error, his right vocal cord was paralyzed. His voice became almost imperceptible.

Because he was a longtime friend of Marchisano, John Paul was aware of his situation. Marchisano recounted, "As a father, he came out to meet me and, for two or three minutes, stroked the area where I had been operated. I was speechless. Meanwhile, he said to me: 'Don't be afraid, you'll see, you'll see. . . . The Lord will give you back your voice. You'll see. I will pray for you. You'll see . . .'" The Cardinal then "hugged him like one hugs one's own father." John Paul was also moved, and said to the Cardinal, "Thank you." Soon after, Cardinal Marchisano was cured.

In May 1990, John Paul walked off his plane in Zacatecas, Mexico, and began to greet the crowds. He spontaneously strayed from his designated route and approached a five-year-old boy named Heron who was stricken with leukemia. The mother, Maria del Refugio Mireles Badillo, had watched the child suffer through numerous rounds of chemotherapy and realized that he was dying before her eyes. Despite the reservations of her unbelieving husband, she convinced him to bring Heron to watch the Pope's plane land, two hours away from where they lived. When the Holy Father approached the family, he smiled and kissed the boy's bald head and moved on. The boy weighed only thirty-one pounds and had been unable to eat solid food for the previous two weeks. He said to his mother after the blessing, "I'm hungry. . . . I want some chicken." Within a few months, the child had no trace of leukemia in his body. Heron was permanently cured of his sickness—and his father was cured of his atheism!

Those who worked alongside the Holy Father testify that such miracles were not uncommon. After suffering three miscarriages, a married couple from Vancouver took a pilgrimage to Rome and briefly met the Holy Father. When they poured out to him their struggle with infertility, he informed them that they would have a son, and made a sign of the cross over the wife's head. What the couple didn't realize at the time was that they were already pregnant, and would give birth to a healthy boy who is now, not surprisingly, named "John Paul."

Cardinal Dziwisz did not keep a record of these miracles. He remarked, "I can only say that the Holy Father did not want to hear about it and always said, 'God performs miracles, I simply pray. Those are divine mysteries. Let's not dwell on it.'"

Entire books could be written—and in fact already have been—testifying to an "avalanche of miracles" that have been reported to the Vatican. Since the Pope's death, the postulator of his cause for canonization said that hundreds of reported miracles are flooding in. Like in the days of his earthly intercession, one of the most common themes of the letters is thanksgiving from couples who were previously unable to have children.

The most well-known of these posthumous miracles was the healing of a French nun, Sister Marie Simon-Pierre. For years, she suffered from Parkinson's disease or a neurological condition with similar symptoms. A month after the Pope's passing, her religious order, the Little

Sisters of Maternity, began praying to John Paul for her recovery. Her superior told her that she should not despair because "John Paul II has not said his last word." She was cured a few weeks later, and it was her miraculous healing that cleared the way for the Holy Father's canonization.

Such supernatural phenomena should not come as a surprise to the faithful. In the Bible, healings and exorcisms were performed through the mere shadow of Peter or the handkerchief of Saint Paul (Acts 5:12–16; 9: 11–12)! During a Wednesday audience, John Paul reminded believers that God's miracles are "linked to the order of salvation. They are the salvific signs which call to conversion and to faith." Such signs should draw the hearts and minds of the faithful toward the things of heaven. He added, "These miracles demonstrate the existence of the supernatural order, which is the object of faith."

Divine Mercy

Despite the miraculous work that God performed through the Pope's prayers for physical healings, the Holy Father knew that all such healings are temporary. Even Lazarus had to die again. What was more important to John Paul was that God might use him as an instrument of his Divine Mercy, bringing healing to souls.

In his encyclical *Dives in Misericordia*, he explained, "Conversion to God is always the fruit of the 'rediscovery' of the Father, who is rich in mercy." In many ways, the Pope became an icon of this unceasing mercy. During one of his Wednesday audiences, a group of former prostitutes were in attendance. One at a time, they came up with eyes full of tears to the Holy Father, who embraced and blessed them. He received criticism from some for his generous affection toward them. But he often stated that such meetings were as important to him as any meeting he might have with heads of states. His tenderness toward them was reminiscent of the affection of Christ himself. Like Jesus, he wedded objective moral truth and boundless mercy, liberating each of these women to be herself.

Each year on Good Friday, the Holy Father walked over to Saint Peter's Basilica and sat inside one of the confessionals. His assistants then randomly chose pilgrims from the other confession lines, asking them if they'd like to have him hear their confession. Some were ecstatic to accept the invitation, while others declined. He made a habit of doing this every Good Friday, except for the last, the week before his death.

His devotion to the sacrament began long before he ascended to the throne of Saint Peter. As a parish priest, Father Wojtyła sometimes spent up to an hour hearing a single confession. One of his penitents noted, "Time meant nothing to him." As a cardinal, he said, "sin is always a suffering of the human soul, a pain of the human conscience. That is why it is important that, at the moment of confessing our sins, there be on the other side of the confessional screen a man who is sensitive, who can sympathize." Then, as pope, he declared that every priest should "freely become a prisoner of the confessional," because "It is in the confessional that *his spiritual fatherhood* is realized in the fullest way." While speaking to the youth in America, he explained that in confession "you are freed from sin and from its ugly companion which is shame. Your burdens are lifted and you experience the joy of new life in Christ."

He even lifted the burden of sin from those who absolved others! While serving as a cardinal in Poland, he summoned a priest who had committed a "serious mis-demeanor." After a lengthy interview and a strong rep-rimand, the Cardinal took him to his chapel and prayed with him. Wojtyła knelt in prayer for so long that the priest became impatient because his train was scheduled to depart soon. Wojtyła finished his prayers, stood up, and asked the priest, "Will you hear my confession now?" The two walked to the confessional, and the priest absolved the Cardinal!

Many years later in Rome, a similar encounter took place. While walking a few blocks from the Vatican, a monsignor from the Archdiocese of New York recognized a beggar on the steps of a church. The two had been in the seminary together, but the poor man admitted he had "crashed and burned" in his vocation and left the priesthood. The priest managed to arrange for the poor man to meet with the Pope. When the two were alone, instead of probing for details about the poor man's fall from the priesthood, the Holy Father clasped his hands and asked him to hear his confession. The man objected, "I'm a beggar," to which John Paul replied, "So am I." With that, the fallen-away priest heard the Pope's confession and absolved him of his sins. The priest then dropped to his knees and asked the Holy Father to absolve him as well. After the confessions, John Paul remarked, "Do you see the grandeur of the priesthood? Don't besmirch it." The Pope then assigned the priest to a nearby parish, to minister to the homeless. As he wrote in *Veritatis Splendor*, "No human sin can erase the mercy of God, or prevent him from unleashing all his triumphant power, if we only call upon him."

Although not as miraculous or remarkable as the sacra-ment of reconciliation, God unleashed his triumphant power through the Pope during exorcisms on at least three occasions. During one of the cases, a husband brought his young wife, who was possessed, to the Vatican. Monsignor Dziwisz said the woman was writhing, screaming, and being tossed about by a demon: "Everyone ran away, but I stayed. They were all afraid what would happen. The Holy Father calmly said the exorcism, as it is in the liturgy. But nothing happened. It continued." Leaving, he said, "Tomorrow, I shall say Mass for you," and at that moment, everything stopped and the woman was delivered of the evil spirit.

Even after his death, John Paul still exercised his priestly authority over evil spirits. Father Gabriele Amorth, the chief exorcist in Rome, reported that since the Pope's passing, John Paul has been a particularly powerful intercessor during the exorcisms he has performed in recent years. He said, "I have asked the demon more than once, 'Why are you so scared of John Paul II?'" One response he has received is "because he pulled so many young people from my hands."

John Paul's Way of the Cross

In *True Devotion to Mary*, Saint Louis de Montfort wrote, "the most faithful servants of the Blessed Virgin, being her greatest favorites, receive from her the best graces and favors from heaven, which are crosses." If suffering is a sign of predilection, then John Paul must have been one of our Lady's favorites!

During his pontificate, he dislocated his shoulder, broke his femur, underwent surgeries for his hip and ankle and to remove his appendix, gallstones, and an orange-sized tumor from his colon. He suffered osteoarthritis in his right knee, an intestinal disorder, the loss of hearing in both ears,

Parkinson's disease, and underwent routine colonoscopies and was given a feeding tube—and this doesn't even include the injuries he sustained when he was struck by a Nazi truck in Poland, the mononucleosis he suffered as a bishop, or the two bullets he took during his assassination attempt! Because he spent no fewer than 164 days in the Gemelli Hospital, he started calling it Vatican III (after Saint Peter's and Castel Gandolfo)!

One of his assistants noticed him grimacing in pain, and asked, "Your Holiness, can I do anything to help? Is something causing you pain?" He replied, "By now, everything causes me pain, but that is how it must be." With each ailment, he sought God's plan behind it. He said, "I ask myself what God is trying to tell me with this disease." After one of his hospitalizations, he said, "I accept this trial too from the hands of God, who arranges everything in accordance with his providential plans, and I offer it for the good of the Church . . ." In his mind, there was no need to respond to suffering with anger and disbelief, but rather with mature love. When someone mentioned the impending suffering that would be required by one of his surgeries, he replied, "The Church needs suffering."

A prime example of intersection of John Paul's redemptive suffering and his apostolic fruitfulness occurred in 1994. The United States government was leading an effort to globalize abortion and contraception as a form of population control through the upcoming International Conference on Population and Development in Cairo. As one would imagine, the Holy Father would not sit by idly as world powers attempted to impose their agenda of normalizing abortion as a human right onto developing nations. John Paul knew that the directives being proposed at the conference would undermine families, not develop or strengthen them. Since the *"future of humanity passes by way of the family,"* he had to act.

John Paul declared 1994 to be the "Year of the Family," and wrote his *Letter to Families*, saying that the celebration gave him the "welcome opportunity to knock at the door of your home, eager to greet you with deep affection and to spend time with you. I do so by this letter . . ." But the Pope didn't reach out only to Catholics. He spent much of the year rallying leaders from all nations and religions against the antifamily agenda that was being promoted at the conference. He launched an unprecedented offensive, writing a letter to all the heads of state and meeting with many of them. He met with President Bill Clinton to share his thoughts on the matter, but without great results. According to a conversation John Paul had with the surgeon who operated on his hip, he was unable to make eye contact with the president. The Holy Father explained, "The only leader I never managed to have a proper conversation with was Clinton. While I was speaking he was always looking somewhere else, admiring the frescos and paintings. He was not listening to me. But patience, patience."

At eleven at night in April of the same year—the day before John Paul was scheduled to travel to Sicily and was expected to speak out against the Mafia—he fell in his bathroom and broke his femur. He was given an X-ray in the middle of the night, soon received a hip replacement, and remained hospitalized for a month. He said to one of his aides, "Maybe this was needed for the Year of the Family." In his mind, surely the worst news of all was that his days of skiing were over.

Upon returning to the Vatican, he offered a powerful testimony about the importance of human suffering:

Today I would like to express through Mary my gratitude for this gift of suffering, once more connected
with the Marian month. [The 1981 assassination attempt also occurred in May.] I have understood that
it is a necessary gift. The Pope had to be at the Gemelli
Hospital, had to be absent from this window for four
weeks, four Sundays, he had to suffer, as he had to suffer thirteen years ago, so again this year. I have med-
itated on all this and thought it through again during my stay in the hospital. . . . I realized that I must
lead the Church of Christ into the third millennium
with prayer and through various activities, but I have
also seen that it is not enough. It is also necessary to
lead by suffering with the shooting of thirteen years
ago, and with this new sacrifice. But why now? Why
in this Year of the Family? Precisely because the family is threatened, the family is being attacked. So the
Pope must be attacked. The Pope must suffer, so that
the world may see that there is a higher gospel, as it
were, the gospel of suffering, by which the future is
prepared, the third millennium of families . . . I am
indebted to the Blessed Virgin for this gift of suffering and I thank her for it. . . . I understand that it was
important to have this subject in front of the powerful
of this world. Again I have to meet with the powerful
of the world and I have to speak. With what topics? It
remains the subject of suffering. And I would like to
say to them: Understand it, understand why the Pope
was in the hospital again, suffering again. Understand
it, think it over!

He knew, as Father Jean C. J. d'Elbée wrote, "In the
apostolate, the money to buy souls is suffering, accepted

with love. . . . . What happiness it is to be able to suffer when
we cannot act! . . . The Lord has given us a field to work,
and we must irrigate it with tears falling from the winepress
of sorrow, in order that it may be fruitful." Thanks to
John Paul's work and suffering, the Cairo conference's final
program of action declared: "In no case should abortion
be promoted as a method of family planning." One day,
while at table at Castel Gandolfo, he remarked, "I don't
know whether history will remember this pope; I doubt
it. If so, I hope that he will be remembered as the pope of
the family."

Despite his countless physical trials, the greatest crosses
carried by the Pope were not visible to others. Like any
loving father, John Paul mourned deeply for the obvious
division and brokenness within the family of God. Year
after year, he bore the spiritual weight of dissenting theologians, wars, the scandal of priestly sexual abuse, the chilly
reception he received from the Orthodox despite his tireless
efforts of ecumenism, and countless other daily sorrows.
He noted that his office brought with it "thorns and crosses
that often remain hidden in the secrecy of the heart. But
. . . these sufferings are the guarantee of fruitfulness of an
apostolate that, with God's help, will produce abundant
results."

More than two centuries before the Holy Father was
born, Saint Louis de Montfort painted with his words a
worthy portrait of John Paul when he described the great
saints who were to come:

They will have the two-edged sword of the word of
God in their mouths and the blood-stained standard
of the Cross on their shoulders. They will carry the
crucifix in their right hand and the Rosary in their

left, and the holy names of Jesus and Mary on their heart. The simplicity and self-sacrifice of Jesus will be reflected in their whole behavior.

Preaching from the Cross

As John Paul's health worsened, some noticed that when his left hand was uncontrollably shaking, he sometimes struck the arm of his chair in a gesture of human frustration that he was unable to control his own body. In time, he grew to accept his new limitations and even displayed an irrepressible sense of humor about them. One of the nuns who assisted in the Papal Apartments noticed that he looked exhausted and remarked that she was "worried about Your Holiness." He cheerfully replied, "Oh, I'm worried about my holiness, too."

In order to stay healthy, he had a swimming pool installed at his summer residence in Castel Gandolfo, on his doctor's recommendation. Although the pool had been donated, some questioned him about the cost. He reminded them that the swimming pool would be cheaper than having another conclave.

When he fell in the Vatican and dislocated his right shoulder in 1993, he spent two days in the hospital and was forced to wear a sling for a month. He rhymed, "*Sono caduto ma non sono scaduto* [I've fallen but I haven't been demoted]," and joked that he could bless just as effectively with his left hand. Against doctor's orders, he was back on the slopes skiing less than three months later.

On another occasion, while slowly walking at a Synod meeting with bishops, he quoted Galileo's remark about the movement of the earth around the sun: "*Eppur' si muove* [Yet it moves!]." When asked how he was feeling, he sometimes joked, "I'm in good shape from the neck up! Not so good from the neck down." To him, his immobility wasn't an issue, and he reminded others, "The Church is governed with the head, not the legs!" He also mentioned that a person is as old as his soul, not his arteries!

Those who knew him well said that at first it was difficult for him to accept his deteriorating health. He didn't want to appear in public with his cane. But with time and abandonment came acceptance, and before long he was swinging it around at World Youth Day and pretending it was a hockey stick in St. Louis. When he met a cardinal who had suffered an injury and also needed a cane, he remarked, "My Dear Eminence, we've both been caned!" At times, he prodded his friends and visitors with the stick, or pretended it was a rifle or a pool cue. Eventually, he needed a walker to maneuver around the Papal Apartments. But he didn't appear to fret about his health, and even preferred not to know too much about it. He'd joke to journalists that he'd learn about his health from reading what the newspapers diagnosed him with. Toward the end, he became unable to walk, and handled this transition gracefully as well. From his wheelchair, he joked, "Everyone else has a mobile phone. I have a mobile chair!"

Even in his last days, he retained his lighthearted spirit. Two and a half months before his death, a Spanish bishop visited him and said that this would probably be the last time they would see each other. John Paul wisecracked, "Why, what's the matter? Are you sick?"

Although his body gradually refused to cooperate with his zeal, his output of work remained prodigious. When nearly 75 percent of Swiss citizens said that the Pope should abdicate his papacy because of his old age, he made a personal pilgrimage to Switzerland—and stayed in a senior citizen home! Seventy thousand people came to his Mass (twice as many as were expected). His assistants recommended that he sleep more, and pray and read less, but he wouldn't budge. In the last few years of his life, he slept thirty minutes later than usual in the morning, but prayed even more than before. As he once told his press secretary, Joaquín Navarro-Valls, "We shall have all eternity to rest."

In *Witness to Hope*, George Weigel summarized him well:

> He survives an assassination attempt, redefines the Catholic Church's relationship with Judaism, invites Orthodox and Protestant Christians to help imagine a papacy that could serve the needs of all Christians, preaches to Muslim teenagers in a packed stadium in Casablanca, and describes marital intimacy as an icon of the interior life of the triune God. After he faces a series of medical difficulties, the world media pronounce him a dying, if heroic, has-been. Within the next six months he publishes an international best-seller translated into forty languages, gathers the largest crowd in human history on the least Christian continent in the world, urges the Church to cleanse its conscience on the edge of the next millennium, and almost single-handedly changes the course of a major international meeting on population issues.

Regardless of his history of achievements, as his health deteriorated and rumors of his resignation swirled throughout the international media, people questioned if he was capable of fulfilling his task as the Vicar of Christ. Although the papacy involves a mountain of administrative responsibilities, the pope is not ultimately a spiritual executive. He represents Jesus Christ, who performed no task of greater importance than his Passion, death, and Resurrection. Now, the time had come for the Holy Father's final "hour" as well.

For his final international journey, he decided to go to Lourdes, to visit the grotto where the Virgin Mary appeared to Saint Bernadette. This time, he was not merely coming as a pontiff, but as a pilgrim. While at the apparition site, he said to the sick who were present with him, "I am here with you, dear brothers and sisters, as a pilgrim to Our Lady. . . . With you I share a time of life marked by physical suffering, yet not for that reason any less fruitful in God's wondrous plan. With you I pray for all those who trust in your prayers."

In the months that followed, his health continued to decline, and it became more difficult for him to travel or preach. He told his companions, "The Pope continues to speak, but now he speaks the language of the soul." Soon, even eating became difficult for him. The man who withstood the horrors of Nazism, toppled communism, and traveled the distance to the moon three times over needed others to cut his food and feed it to him.

Yet in the midst of his human limitations, he took a very different approach than many political leaders in history who didn't want people to hear of their illnesses or imperfections, let alone actually see them. Joseph Stalin was only five foot four, yet he adopted the moniker "Man of Steel" and ordered that his portraits make him look gargantuan and imposing. The North Korean dictator Kim Jong-il wasn't much of an athlete, standing at five foot three, but claimed to have scored eleven holes-in-one on his first round of golf, shooting a world record thirty-eight under par. John Paul had no time for such charades.

In the final months of his life, his face was swollen from cortisone. His aides stood at his side to wipe drool from his mouth as he attempted to address massive audiences. The man who for decades masterfully used inflections and dramatic intonations to stir the hearts of his listeners could now only slur his words. Many who witnessed him in such poor condition didn't know what to make of it: Shouldn't the Vatican public relations people avoid showing him like this? But John Paul didn't want anyone to look away in embarrassment. He wanted them to see him—for their own benefit. The man who taught the world how to live was now teaching all men how to die. He remarked, "I have written many encyclicals and many apostolic letters, but I realize that it is only with my suffering that I can best help mankind. Think of the value of pain, suffered and offered with love . . ." The time for his final sermon had come, and it was going to be preached silently from the cross.

His condition took a significant turn for the worse in February 2005, and his doctors decided that a tracheotomy was necessary due to his breathing difficulties. He asked if he could postpone the procedure until summer, but it wasn't an option. A doctor assured him, "Your Holiness, it will be a simple operation." John Paul responded, "Simple for whom?"

Because of the invasive nature of the procedure, John Paul wanted to know only one thing: Would he be able to speak again? The doctors attempted to alleviate his concerns, but when he awoke he was unable to talk. He signaled for a piece of paper and wrote, "What have they done to me?! But . . . *totus tuus*." It is possible that "totus tuus" are the last words he ever wrote.

Upon recovering from the operation he immediately began rehabilitation to learn to speak again. Those who were with him noticed how difficult it was for him to breathe through the tube that had been inserted in his trachea, and remarked that this was his own Way of the Cross.

Although he was too weak to leave the Vatican to make the Stations of the Cross on his last Good Friday, he was faithful to this devotion to the very end, watching the annual Roman procession from a television in his private chapel. Few will forget the iconic footage that was taken of him at this moment, embracing the cross with the corpus facing him. A week later, on the day before his death, he signaled to those with him that he wanted once again to pray the Way of the Cross.

On Easter Sunday, he stood at his window overlooking the crowds, who surely wondered if they would ever see him again. With great effort, he attempted to speak a blessing, but was unable. Instead, Cardinal Angelo Sodano read his address. When his handlers attempted to pull him away from the window, he refused to budge. Instead, he stood above the crowds and affectionately traced with his right hand a large sign of the cross over those gathered below. When he pulled away from the window, realizing his inability to speak, he whispered, "Maybe it would be better that I die if I cannot fulfill my mission. May your will be done. *Totus tuus*." Three days later, on Wednesday, March 30, the Holy Father made his last public appearance at the same window.

In the opinion of his assistant secretary, John Paul began dying the next day, during Mass on Thursday morning. He felt very weak and began to shiver, so Dziwisz suggested that he return to his room during Mass. However, John Paul insisted on finishing the Holy Sacrifice. By eleven, his temperature had spiked to more than 103 degrees, his blood pressure was dropping, and he had difficulty breathing. He had suffered severe septic shock and a collapse of his cardiovascular system as a result of a urinary tract infection. He was not rushed to the hospital, however, because there was nothing more to be done and he wanted to die at home, near the tomb of Saint Peter.

Lying in his bed, he asked that the Gospel of John be read aloud, and a priest was able to read into the ninth chapter before the Holy Father passed away. He also gestured that he wanted to speak to Sister Tobiana, and it was to her that he said his last words, in Polish: "*Pozwólcie mi odejść do domu Ojca* [Let me go to the house of the Father.]" Meanwhile, tens of thousands gathered in Saint Peter's Square, praying with Rosaries and candles in hand. His aides told him that crowds of young people had gathered outside his window and were singing. John Paul then began gesturing, as Dziwisz questioned him for clarification on what he was trying to communicate to the youth. According to Navarro-Valls, he was saying, "I have looked for you. Now you have come to me. And I thank you." Shortly before 7:00 P.M., he slipped into a coma, and approximately two hours later Dziwisz began to celebrate Mass with a few others at his bedside. A few drops of the Precious Blood were given to the Holy Father as Viaticum. Then, at 9:37 P.M., after the conclusion of the vigil Mass for the feast of Divine Mercy, on the first Saturday of the month, his great heart stopped beating. He died just as he was born eighty-four years earlier—with the sounds of people singing prayers outside his window.

Those by his bedside said his face was no longer wrinkled or pale, but appeared radiant. Instead of offering the prayer for the deceased, they sang an ancient hymn of thanksgiving, the *Te Deum*, just as the jubilant seminarians in Kraków had done twenty-six years earlier, at the dawn of his pontificate.

It fell upon Archbishop Leonardo Sandri to inform the world of the news, summing up everyone's emotions in one statement: "We all feel like orphans this evening." Cardinal Angelo Comastri, the archpriest of Saint Peter's Basilica, also spoke to the crowds, saying, "Now there is a special significance for the words that John Paul II pronounced in this square at the beginning of his pontificate on October 16 of 1978: at this moment, Christ is throwing wide open the doors of paradise, while Mary stands waiting, smiling at the door to embrace him and welcome him to the feast of the saints."

In the days to come, hundreds of thousands came to pay their respects. John Paul had gone out to the world, and now the world had come to see him. Pilgrims waited for more than a dozen hours in prayerful and silent lines that extended from Saint Peter's Square, down the Via della Conciliazione, and across the Tiber River. Monsignor Andrew Baker remarked that the silence from within the basilica could almost be heard outside, as if the nave of Saint Peter's extended down to the Tiber River and beyond. Alongside the main road, priests were sitting with their stolls draped over their shoulders, hearing confessions for hours.

Six days after his death, the world again gathered to witness his funeral. Tempestuous winds swirled around his cypress coffin, tossing the vestments of the cardinals as they clutched their miters and red zucchettos. Across the globe in Mexico City, tens of thousands gathered outside the Basilica of Our Lady of Guadalupe to watch the live television broadcast of the funeral from Rome. In front of the basilica, the organizers placed a throne that John Paul had sat upon during one of his Masses there, and a photograph of him was placed on it. As the winds whipped around Saint Peter's Square, a white dove landed upon the throne in Mexico City. Back in Rome, the winds closed the Book of the Gospels that rested on his coffin, as if to say: It is finished.

During the homily of the funeral Mass, Cardinal Ratzinger, who soon became Pope Benedict XVI, remarked:

> None of us can ever forget how in that last Easter Sunday of his life, the Holy Father, marked by suffering, came once more to the window of the Apostolic Palace and one last time gave his blessing *urbi et orbi*. We can be sure that our beloved Pope is standing today at the window of the Father's house, that he sees us and blesses us. Yes, bless us, Holy Father. We entrust your dear soul to the Mother of God, your Mother, who guided you each day and who will guide you now to the eternal glory of her Son, our Lord Jesus Christ.

During the liturgy, signs waved and chants ascended, "Santo Subito!" [Saint Now!]. The standard Vatican protocol is that a person's beatification process does not begin until five years after his or her death. However, because of John Paul's exceptional reputation for sanctity, Pope Benedict waived the waiting period and allowed the cause for his canonization to begin without delay.

When speaking in France nearly a decade earlier, John Paul had remarked, "Just when night engulfs us, we must think about dawn coming, we must believe that every morning the Church is revived through her saints." Each one of them has been raised to the altars not because they have conquered the world, but because they allowed Christ to conquer them. Every saint is a unique "victory of God in man."

EPILOGUE

In 1978, after Pope John Paul II learned of the death of his predecessor, John Paul I, he wrote a poem dedicated to Saint Stanisław, the heroic bishop from Kraków whose blood was spilled by a king while celebrating Mass. The wicked king assumed his sword would silence the words of the saint, but the death of Stanisław only served to invigorate the faithful.

As this book comes to a close, I invite you to slowly read —or better yet, meditate on—the poem below, reflecting how yet another bishop from Kraków, whose blood was poured out for the Church, has likewise ignited a new springtime in the hearts of the faithful, empowering us to pass through the trials to come:

I want to describe the Church, my Church,
born with me, not dying with me—
nor do I die with it,
which always grows beyond me—
the Church: the lowest depth of my existence and its
    peak,
the Church—the root which I thrust into the past
    and the future alike,
the sacrament of my being in God
who is the Father. . . .

There was a man; through him my land saw it
    was bound to heaven. . . .

I want to describe my Church in the man whose
    name was Stanislas.
And King Boleslas wrote this name with his sword
    in the ancient chronicles,
wrote this name with his sword on the
    cathedral's marble floor
as the streams of blood were flowing
over the marble floor.

I want to describe the Church in the name
which baptized the nation again
with the baptism of blood,
that it might later pass through the baptism of
    other trials. . . .

The King may have thought: the Church shall not yet
    be born from you.
the nation shall not be born of the word that castigates
    the body and the blood;
it will be born of the sword, my sword which severs
    your words in mid-flow,
born from the spilled blood—this the King may
    have thought. . . .

I want to describe my Church in which, for centuries,
the word and the blood go side by side,
united by the hidden breath
of the Spirit.

Stanislas may have thought: my word will hurt you
    and convert,
you will come as a penitent to the cathedral gate,
emaciated by fasting, enlightened by a voice within,
to join the Lord's table like a prodigal son.
If the word did not convert you, the blood will.

The bishop had perhaps no time to think:
let this cup pass from me.

A sword falls on the soil of our freedom.
Blood falls on the soil of our freedom,
And which weighs more? . . .

Whence rose this name which he received
   for his people?
for parents, for the clan, for the bishop's seat in
   Kraków,
for King Boleslas called the Brave and the
   Bountiful?
for the twentieth century?

This one name.

My prayer in writing this book is that the *one name* of
Pope Saint John Paul the Great, by means of his word and
his blood, will invigorate Catholics to be unafraid if the
Church needs to pass through the baptism of certain trials
that may come. Because there are no mere coincidences in
the plans of God, each member of the Church has been
chosen for such a time as this. There is no need to fear
Christ and his plan for each of us. We only need to trust
in Divine Mercy and love what Saint John Paul loved,
most especially young people, human love, the Most Blessed
Sacrament, our Lady, and the cross.

In one of his poems, John Paul wrote about the thoughts
of Saint Veronica after she wiped the wounded face of
Christ on his way to Calvary: "you have departed, but
through me you walk on." Perhaps the greatest legacy
that Saint John Paul will leave the Church is that he
will continue to walk on through those who loved him.

Therefore, let us heed the words he wrote in *Rise, Let Us Be on Our Way*: "Let us go forth full of trust in Christ. He will accompany us as we journey toward the goal that He alone knows."

~

Upon reading the remarkable life of Saint John Paul the Great, some might feel overwhelmed by his spiritual stature. Although his life is inspiring, it's not always easy to read about someone who spent hours at a time rapt in mystical prayer while the rest of us fumble to complete a decade of the Rosary without distraction. However, we would do well to remember the litany of humility, in which one prays to desire that "others may become holier than I, provided that I may become as holy as I should."

Everyone who reads this book can afford to pray more, including its author. Let's begin there. Instead of feeling intimidated by the imaginary chasm that seems to separate the saints from the sinners, let us follow their lead, and allow God to take care of the rest. To do this, turn to the back of this book, where you will find several pages that explain how you can learn more about Total Consecration, Divine Mercy, and the Theology of the Body. Immerse yourself in these resources, and you will discover why they were so dear to the heart of Saint John Paul the Great.

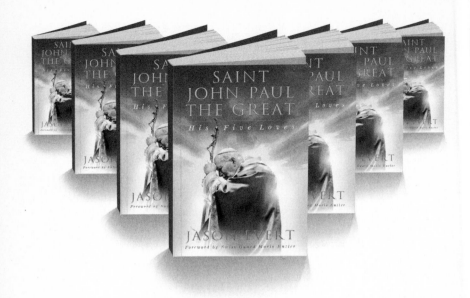

If this book strengthened your faith, share it with others for as little as
$2 per copy!

Think of those in your community who would benefit from reading it:

- Pass it out as a gift to parishioners after Sunday Mass at your church
- Share copies with your Confirmation or religious ed students
- Distribute it in your RCIA program
- Supply copies to your youth or young adult group
- Donate copies to a high school or college
- Give away copies on retreats
- Offer it as a gift for graduations or birthdays

ACKNOWLEDGMENTS

With deep gratitude, I acknowledge my debt to those who assisted me in compiling this work. Some offered vital counsel and corrections while others contributed generous amounts of time to share their personal experiences with the late Holy Father:

Msgr. Andrew R. Baker, Dr. Kazimierz Braun, Bishop Robert Brom, Msgr. Eduardo Chavez, Cardinal Stanisław Dziwisz, Mario Enzler, Fr. Franciszek Florczyk, Fr. Stan Fortuna, Fr. Michael Gaitley, Fr. Joseph Marcello, Cardinal Theodore McCarrick, Cardinal Justin Rigali, Fr. Thomas Rosica, Bishop Hugh Slattery, Fr. Andrew Swietochowski, Fr. Tomasz Szopa, Fr. George Tracy, Christopher West, Fr. Michael White, and Bishop Andrew Wypych.

I am also indebted to those who have blessed the Church with excellent books about Saint John Paul the Great, whose source materials were essential to the completion of this work. In particular, I wish to recommend to the reader the works of Boniecki, Dziwisz, Frossard, Mokrzycki, Oder, and Weigel.

I also wish to express my appreciation to George Weigel in particular for his invaluable contribution of fact-checking and helping me to extract any apocryphal papal stories from the text, and to Jane Cavolina for her superb editorial assistance. I must also thank my bride, Crystalina, for her patience with me during the writing of this book!

Finally, I give thanks and praise to God, for the gift of Pope Saint John Paul the Great!

BIBLIOGRAPHY

Works by Karol Wojtyła (Pope John Paul II)

Collected Plays and Writings on Theater, The, trans. by Bolesław Taborski. Berkeley: University of California Press, 1987.

Collected Poems, trans. by Jerzy Peterkiewicz. New York: Random House, 1982.

Eucharist and Man's Hunger for Freedom, The. International Eucharistic Conference, Philadelphia, 1976.

Faith According to St. John of the Cross. Eugene, Ore.: Wipf and Stock, 2009.

Love and Responsibility. Boston: Pauline Books and Media, 2013.

Love and Responsibility. San Francisco: Ignatius Press, 1993.

Man in the Field of Responsibility. South Bend, Ind.: St. Augustine's Press, 2011.

Person and Community: Selected Essays, trans. by Theresa Sandok, OSM. New York: Peter Lang, 2008.

Sign of Contradiction. New York: Seabury Press, 1979.

The Way to Christ. San Francisco: Harper, 1982.

Works by Pope John Paul II

Crossing the Threshold of Hope. New York: Alfred A. Knopf, 1994.

Dilecti Amici. 1985.

Dives in Misericordia. 1980.

Dominum et Vivificantem. 1986.

Ecclesia de Eucharistia. 2003.

Familiaris Consortio. 1981.

Gift and Mystery. New York: Doubleday, 1999.

Letter to Families from Pope John Paul II. 1994.

Letter to the Elderly. 1999.

Man and Woman He Created Them: A Theology of the Body, trans. by Michael Waldstein. Boston: Pauline Books and Media, 2006.

Memory and Identity. New York: Rizzoli, 2005.

Mulieris Dignitatem. 1988.

Redemptor Hominis. 1979.

Redemptoris Mater. 1987.

Novo Millennio Ineunte. 1979.
Rise, Let Us Be on Our Way. New York: Warner Books, 2004.
Roman Triptych. Washington, D.C.: USCCB, 2003.
Rosarium Virginis Mariae. 1980.
Salvifici Doloris. 1984.
Tertio Millennio Adveniente. 1994.
The Theology of the Body. Boston: Pauline Books and Media, 1997.
Veritatis Splendor. 1993.

Addresses by Pope John Paul II

Address at the Chapel of the Apparitions, Fatima, May 12, 1982.
Address at the Shrine of Divine Mercy, Kraków, June 7, 1997.
Address at the Shrine of Merciful Love, Collevalenza, November 22, 1981.
Address to High School Students, Madison Square Garden, October 3, 1979.
Address to the Sick, Knock, September 30, 1979.
Address to the Students of the University of Santo Tomas, Manila, February 18, 1981.
Address to the Young People at the Kiel Center, St. Louis, January 26, 1999.
Address to the Youth of Quebec at Olympic Stadium, Montreal, September 11, 1984.
Ad Limina Address to the Bishops of the Church in Washington, Oregon, Montana, Idaho, and Alaska, Vatican, October 9, 1998.
Homily, Camagüey, Cuba, January 23, 1998.
Homily for the Canonization of Sister Mary Faustina Kowalska, April 30, 2000.
Homily for the Canonization of Saint Maximilian Mary Kolbe, October 10, 1982.
Homily, Fatima, May 13, 1982.
Homily for the Inauguration of His Pontificate, October 22, 1978.
Homily, Mass for the Occasion of the Opening of the 10th National Eucharistic Congress. Fortaleza, July 9, 1980.
Homily, Mass for the Youth of Ireland, Galway, September 30, 1979.
Homily, Sanctuary of Alborada, Guayaquil, January 31, 1985.
Homily, St. Thomas Aquinas Parish, Rome, May 10, 1981.
Homily, Victory Square, Warsaw, June 2, 1979.
Homily for the XVII World Youth Day, Downsview Park, Toronto, July 28, 2002.

Meeting with the Young People of New Orleans, September 12, 1987.
Meeting with the Youth at Nakivubo Stadium, Kampala, Uganda, February 6, 1993.
Message for the XXVI Annual World Day of Prayer for Peace, January 1, 1993.
Message for the XXXIII World Day of Prayer for Vocations, August 15, 1995.
Message for the IV World Day of the Sick, October 11, 1995.
Message to Young People, Camagüey, Cuba, 1998.
Message to the Young People of Rome and Lazio Gathered for Eucharist Adoration in the Basilica of Saint John Lateran, Vatican, March 15, 2005.
Message to the Youth of the World on the Occasion of the XII World Youth Day, Castel Gandolfo, August 15, 1996.
Message to the Youth of the World on the Occasion of the XV World Youth Day, Vatican City, June 29, 1999.
Message to the Youth of the World on the Occasion of the XVII World Youth Day, Castel Gandolfo, July 25, 2001.
Prayer at the Grotto of Massabielle, Greeting of John Paul II to the Sick, Lourdes, France, August 14, 2004.

Books

Accattoli, Luigi. *Man of the Millennium: John Paul II*. Boston: Pauline Books and Media, 2000.

Allegri, Renzo. *John Paul II: A Life of Grace*. Cincinnati: Servant Books, 2005.

Andrew, Christopher and Vasili Mitrokhin. *The World Was Going Our Way: The KGB and the Battle for the Third World*. New York: Basic Books, 2005.

Bernstein, Carl and Marco Politi. *His Holiness*. New York: Doubleday, 1996.

Blazynski, George. *Pope John Paul II: A Richly Revealing Portrait*. New York: Dell Publishing, 1979.

Boniecki, Adam. *The Making of the Pope of the Millennium: Kalendarium of the Life of Karol Wojtyła*. Stockbridge, Mass.: Marian Press, 2000.

Braun, Kazimierz. "Norwid and John Paul II," *The Polish Review* Vol. LVI, No. 4, 2011.

————. "Norwidowa część w 'całości Jana Pawel II" [The Norwid part of the "entirety" of John Paul II], *Ethos*, 2004. As quoted in "Norwid and John Paul II," *The Polish Review* Vol. LVI, No. 4, 2011.

Burke, Greg, ed. *An Invitation to Joy*. New York: Simon and Schuster, 2000.

Buttiglione, Rocco. *Karol Wojtyła*. Grand Rapids, Mich.: William B. Eerdmans Publishing Company, 1997.

Chesterton, G. K. *Orthodoxy*. Nashville, Tenn.: Sam Torode Book Arts, 2008.

Climacus, Saint John. *The Ladder of Divine Ascent*, trans. by Archimandrite Lazarus Moore. New York: Harper & Brothers, 1959.

Craig, Mary. *Man from a Far Country*. London: Hodder and Stoughton, 1979.

Dziwisz, Stanisław. *A Life with Karol*. New York: Doubleday, 2008.

Dziwisz, Stanisław, et al. *Let Me Go to the Father's House*. Boston: Pauline Books and Media, 2006.

de Montfort, Saint Louis. *God Alone*. Bay Shore, N.Y.: Montfort Publications, 1987.

de Montfort, Saint Louis. *True Devotion to Mary*. Rockford, Ill.: TAN Publishers, 1985.

d'Elbée, Father Jean C. J. *I Believe in Love*. Manchester, N.H.: Sophia Institute Press, 2001.

Flynn, Ray. *John Paul II: A Personal Portrait of the Pope and the Man*. New York: St. Martin's Press, 2001.

Frossard, André. *Be Not Afraid*. New York: St. Martin's Press, 1982.

————. *Portrait of John Paul II*. San Francisco: Ignatius Press, 1990.

Gaeta, Saverio, ed. *John Paul II: The Story of My Life*. Boston: Pauline Books and Media, 2011.

Hebblethwaite, Peter. *Pope John Paul II and the Church*. Kansas City: Sheed & Ward, 1995.

Herman, Edward S. and Frank Brodhead. *The Rise and Fall of the Bulgarian Connection*. New York: Sheridan Square Publications, Inc., 1986.

Kowalska, Saint Maria Faustina. *Diary: Divine Mercy in My Soul*. Stockbridge, Mass.: Marian Press, 2011.

Kopciński, J., ed. "Jan Paweł II o Cyprianie Norwidzie w 180. Rocznice urodzin poetry" [John Paul on Cyprian Kamil Norwid on the occasion of the poet's 180th birthday], in *Norwid bezdomny. W 180 rocznicę urodzin poetry* [Norwid the Homeless. For the 180th anniversary of the poet's birth]. Warsaw: Instytut Dziedzictwa Narodowego, 2002.

Królak, Tomasz. *1001 Things You Should Know About the Blessed John Paul II*. Kraków: Wydawnictwo M, 2011.

Longford, Lord. *Pope John Paul II: An Authorized Biography*. New York: William Morrow and Company, Inc., 1982.

Malinski, Mieczyslaw. *Pope John Paul II: The Life of Karol Wojtyła*. New York: Seabury Press, 1979.

Manteau-Bonamy, OP, Father H. M. *Immaculate Conception and the Holy Spirit*. Libertyville, Ill.: Prow Books, 1977.

Mitchell, Father Peter. *John Paul II, We Love You!* Cincinnati: Servant Books, 2007.

Mokrzycki, Mieczysław. *He Liked Tuesdays Best*. Kraków: Wydawnictwo M, 2011.

Moody, John. *Pope John Paul II*. New York: Random House, 1997.

Mother Teresa. *Where There Is Love, There Is God*. New York: Doubleday Religion, 2010.

Murray, Barbara A. *John Paul II, We Love You*. Winona, Minn.: Saint Mary's Press, 2005.

Noonan, Peggy. *John Paul the Great*. New York: Viking, 2005.

O'Brien, Darcy. *The Hidden Pope*. New York: Daybreak Books, 1998.

O'Connor, Gary. *Universal Father*. London: Bloomsbury, 2005.

Oder, Sławomir with Gaeta, Saverio. *Why He Is a Saint*. New York: Rizzoli, 2010.

Oram, James. *The People's Pope: The Story of Karol Wojtyła of Poland*. San Francisco: Chronicle Books, 1979.

Paczkowski, Andrzej. *The Spring Will Be Ours*. University Park, Pa.: Pennsylvania State University Press, 2003.

Pigozzi, Caroline. *Pope John Paul II: The Pope I Knew So Well*. New York: Faith Words, 2000.

Royal, Robert. *The Catholic Martyrs of the Twentieth Century: A Comprehensive World History*. New York: Crossroad, 2000.

Scepter Publishers, *The Meaning of Vocation*. Princeton, N.J.: Scepter Publishers, 1997.

Sheed, Frank. *Saints Are Not Sad*. New York: Sheed & Ward, 1949.

Shirer, William L. *The Rise and Fall of the Third Reich*. New York: Simon & Schuster, 2011.

Szostak, John M. *In the Footsteps of Pope John Paul II*. Englewood Cliffs, N.J.: Prentice-Hall, Inc., 1980.

Svidercoschi, Gian Franco. *Stories of Karol*. Liguori, Mo.: Liguori / Triumph, 2001.

Szulc, Tad. *Pope John Paul II: The Biography*. New York: Simon & Schuster, Inc., 1995.

Vitek, John, ed. *My Dear Young Friends*. Winona, Minn.: Saint Mary's Press, 2001.

Walsh, Michael. *John Paul II*. London: Harper Collins, 1995.

Walsh, Sister Mary Ann, ed. *From Pope John Paul II to Benedict XVI: An Inside Look at the End of an Era*. Lanham, Md.: Rowman & Littlefield Publishers, Inc., 2005.

Weigel, George. *The End and the Beginning*. New York: Image Books, 2010.

————. *Witness to Hope*. New York: Harper, 2001.

Widmer, Andreas. *The Pope & the CEO*. Steubenville, Oh.: Emmaus Road, 2011.

Williams, George Huntston. *The Mind of John Paul II*. New York: Seabury Press, 1981.

Wuerl, Cardinal Donald. *The Gift of Blessed John Paul II*. Frederick, Md.: The Word Among Us Press, 2011.

Wynn, Wilton. *Keeper of the Keys*. New York: Random House, 1988.

Zani, Lino. *The Secret Life of John Paul II*. Charlotte, N.C.: Saint Benedict Press, 2012.

Zuchniewicz, Paweł. *Miracles of John Paul II*. Toronto: Catholic Youth Studio–KSM Inc., 2006.

Media

John Paul the Great: A Pope Who Made History. Rome Reports, 2005.

Mother Teresa. Video. Petrie Productions, 1986.

Nine Days That Changed the World. DVD. Directed by Kevin Knoblock. Citizens United and Citizens United Foundation, 2010.

Ocean of Mercy. DVD. Ignatius Press and Mercy Foundation Studios, 2013.

Pope John Paul II: Crusader for Human Dignity. DVD. AIM International Television.

Pope John Paul II: Statesman of Faith. DVD. A&E Television Networks, 2003.

Testimony: The Untold Story of Pope John Paul II. DVD. Directed by Pawel Pitera. TBA Group, 2007.

Lectures

Braun, Kazimierz. *Inaugural Lecture*, "John Paul II As I Remember Him." Anathan Theatre, Franciscan University of Steubenville, March 5, 2010.

Hahn, Scott. "The Healing Power of Confession." Lighthouse Catholic Media, 2012.

Gaitley, Father Michael. "The Message of Divine Mercy." Franciscan University of Steubenville, January 22, 2013.

Magee, Bishop John. "Untold Stories of the Last Three Popes." Lighthouse Catholic Media.

Pell, Cardinal George. "The meaning of religious freedom and the future of human rights." University of Notre Dame Australia School of Law, August 22, 2013.

Pope Paul VI. Address to the Members of the Consilium de Laicis. October 2, 1974. AAS 66, 1974.

Weigel, George. "The Legacy of John Paul II." Franciscan University of Steubenville, February 23, 2011.

Widmer, Andreas. "The Pope and the CEO: John Paul II's Leadership Lessons to a Young Swiss Guard." Franciscan University of Steubenville, November 10, 2011.

Articles and Commentaries

Abboud, Amin. "Searching for Papal Scapegoats Is Pointless." *British Medical Journal* 331, July 30, 2005.

"Anecdotes of a Papal Preacher, Father Raniero Cantalamessa Marks 25 Years in Post." Zenit.org, Vatican City, July 4, 2004.

Bertone, Tarcisio. "The Message of Fatima." Congregation for the Doctrine of the Faith, June 26, 2000.

"Bishop D'Arcy offers reflection to presbyterate." Warsaw, Indiana, October 22, 2009. Retrieved on November 3, 2009, from www.diocesefwsb .org.

Brzezinski, Matthew. "Operation Bojinka's bombshell." *Toronto Star*, January 2, 2002.

"Cardinal Marchisano Says Pope Healed Him." Zenit.org, Vatican City, April 10, 2005.

Connor, Tanya. "Nuns who experienced JPII miracle bring message of hope, victory." Catholic News Service, May 4, 2012.

Culture of Life Foundation. "New Research Shows Dangers of Condoms in HIV Prevention." *Culture & Cosmos* 1:23, January 13, 2004.

De Souza, Raymond J. "Moments—Private and Public—With the Pope." *National Catholic Register* Special Edition: John Paul II: A Life That Changed the World. April 10–16, 2005.

"Doubts About Condoms: Science Questioning Their Efficacy in Halting HIV/AIDS." Zenit.org, Nairobi, Kenya, June 26, 2004.

Follain, John. "Gunman Mehmet Ali Agca who shot Pope John Paul II seeks £3m in book deals." *The Sunday Times*, January 10, 2010.

Gray, Paul. "John Paul II: Empire of the Spirit." *Time*, December 26, 1994.

Gomez, Jim. "Police: Suspected Sept. 11 mastermind was uncle of 1993 World Trade Center plotter." Associated Press, June 25, 2002.

Jenkins, Brian. "Plane terror suspects convicted on all counts." CNN, September 5, 1996.

———. "Terrorism trial begins in New York: 3 men accused of plotting to bomb U.S. planes." CNN, May 13, 1996.

"John Paul II Fondly Recalls Louis de Montfort's Marian Doctrine in a Message on 160th Anniversary of 'True Devotion.'" Zenit.org, Vatican City, January 13, 2004.

"John Paul II Helps Possessed Woman in Vatican." Zenit.org, Vatican City, September 10, 2000.

Lattin, Don. "Pope John Paul II: 1920–2005 / Beloved, charismatic and controversial, John Paul II transformed the papacy." Accessed at sfgate.com.

Laugesen, Wayne. "Looking at the Good Fruit of World Youth Day Denver '93." *National Catholic Register*, August 23, 2013.

McDermott, Terry. "Early Scheme to Turn Jets into Weapons." *Los Angeles Times*, June 24, 2002.

———. "The Plot: How terrorists hatched a simple plan to use planes as bombs." *Los Angeles Times*, September 1, 2002.

Mintz, John. "Men in papal plot termed close to bin Laden." *Washington Post*, August 22, 1998.

Montalbano, William D. "It's 'Judgment' Day for Unveiled Sistine Chapel: Vatican: The Pope praises the restored Michelangelo masterpiece. Gone is centuries of grime—and modesty." *Los Angeles Times*, April 9, 1994.

Nottingham Walsh, Meg. "Out of the Darkness: Michelangelo's Last Judgment." *National Geographic*, May 1994, 118.

"Pope Meets Mother of Man Who Attempted to Assassinate Him." Associated Press, February 20, 1987.

Ratzinger, Cardinal Joseph. Homily for the Funeral Mass of the Roman Pontiff, John Paul II. Saint Peter's Square, April 8, 2005.

———. Theological Commentary, Vatican.va, June 26, 2000.

"Remembering the Old Lion," *Newsweek*, Special Report, April, 11, 2005.

"Rome's Exorcist Finding Bl. John Paul II Effective Against Satan." Catholic News Agency, Rome, Italy, May 17, 2011.

Ryder, R.E.J. "'Natural Family Planning' Effective Birth Control

Supported by the Catholic Church." *British Medical Journal* 307, September 18, 1993.

Sodano, Cardinal Angelo. Address Regarding the "Third Part" of the Secret of Fatima at the Conclusion of the Solemn Mass of John Paul II. Fatima, May 13, 2000.

Stackpole, Robert. "What Does 'Divine Mercy' Actually Mean?" DM 101: Week 1, September 1, 2005, www.thedivinemercy.org.

Struck, Doug, Howard Schneider, Karl Vick, and Peter Baker. "Bin Laden Followers Reach Across Globe." *Washington Post Foreign Service*, September 23, 2001.

"3 Plots Against John Paul II's Life Foiled Since 1995." Zenit.org, Rome, October 11, 2001.

NOTES

xviii   **"They try to understand** . . . Weigel, *Witness to Hope*, 7.

      "And Our Lord . . . Boniecki, *The Making of the Pope of the Millennium*, 836.

  xix   **"many a saint has** . . . Sheed, *Saints Are Not Sad*, Assembler's note.

   4   **"There was only one** . . . O'Brien, *The Hidden Pope*, 124.

      "After my mother's death . . . Pope John Paul II, *Gift and Mystery*, 20.

   5   **"The two of them could** . . . Bernstein and Politi, *His Holiness*, 26.

      "True prayer is waiting . . . Allegri, *John Paul II: A Life of Grace*, 50.

      "Thy will be done! . . . Oder, *Why He Is a Saint*, 12.

      "The violence of the . . . Frossard, *"Be Not Afraid!"*, 14.

   6   **"As I was praying** . . . Faustina, *Diary*, no. 1732.

   7   **"I would serve the** . . . John Paul II, *The Story of My Life*, 18.

      "at the altar of . . . Boniecki, *The Making of the Pope of the Millennium*, 62.

      "They hadn't gone half . . . Svidercoschi, *Stories of Karol*, 18.

   8   **"Suddenly, there was the** . . . O'Brien, *The Hidden Pope*, 167.

      "In Kraków, the Wojtyłas . . . Svidercoschi, *Stories of Karol*, 19.

   9   **"Young people see their** . . . Pope John Paul II, Annual World Day of Prayer for Peace.

      Entire families were murdered . . . O'Connor, *Universal Father*, 48.

      "hire young girls to . . . Bernstein and Politi, *His Holiness*, 58.

  10   **"The Poles are especially** . . . Shirer, *The Rise and Fall of the Third Reich*, 938.

      "The Slavs are to . . . Shirer, *The Rise and Fall of the Third Reich*, 939.

      At four o'clock . . . Svidercoschi, *Stories of Karol*, 24.

      Because the Nazis did . . . Boniecki, *The Making of the Pope of the Millennium*, 73.

  11   **"They laid him down** . . . Wojtyła, *Collected Poems*, 70–71.

  12   **"At times I feel** . . . Boniecki, *The Making of the Pope of the Millennium*, 65.

      "After a while, an . . . Oram, *The People's Pope*, 56.

      "Karol, you should be . . . Pope John Paul II, *Gift and Mystery*, 10.

  13   **"rather decisively rejected** . . . Szulc, *Pope John Paul II*, 77.

"Were you a good . . . Flynn, *John Paul II*, 160.

He was not a gifted . . . Williams, *The Mind of John Paul II*, 80.

"accomplish everything through . . . Boniecki, *The Making of the Pope of the Millennium*, 68.

"It's not difficult to . . . Weigel, *Witness to Hope*, 59.

14   "a decisive turning-point . . . Frossard, *"Be Not Afraid!"*, 125.

"martyr of love . . . Pope John Paul II, Homily for the Canonization of Saint Maximilian Mary Kolbe.

15   "I'm all alone . . . Svidercoschi, *Stories of Karol*, 38.

"He went to Mass . . . Boniecki, *The Making of the Pope of the Millennium*, 78.

"had opened up immense . . . Frossard, *"Be Not Afraid!"*, 14.

He enjoyed the night . . . Boniecki, *The Making of the Pope of the Millennium*, 83.

"In the boiler room . . . Boniecki, *The Making of the Pope of the Millennium*, 93.

"There were those who . . . Boniecki, *The Making of the Pope of the Millennium*, 84.

16   When a coworker's wife . . . Boniecki, *The Making of the Pope of the Millennium*, 102.

"I was a laborer . . . Accattoli, *Man of the Millennium*, 195.

"Right from the . . . Pope John Paul II, Address at the Shrine of Merciful Love.

17   "There is nothing that . . . Pope John Paul II, Address at the Shrine of Divine Mercy.

"How could I have . . . Pope John Paul II, *Rise, Let Us Be on Our Way*, 194.

"I just wanted to . . . Gaitley, "The Message of Divine Mercy."

"In fact, it was . . . Pope John Paul II, Homily for the Canonization of Sister Mary Faustina Kowalska.

18   "Before speaking these words . . . Pope John Paul II, Homily for the Canonization of Sister Mary Faustina Kowalska.

19   "The main idea is . . . Malinski, *Pope John Paul II*, 14.

John Paul later said . . . Kopciński, "Jan Paweł II o Cyprianie Norwidzie w 180. Rocznice urodzin poetry," 8.

20   "the Polish nation should . . . Szulc, *Pope John Paul II*, 103.

"A actor is not . . . Boniecki, *The Making of the Pope of the Millennium*, 71.

21   "The performers were like . . . Malinski, *Pope John Paul II*, 33.

"persistently reminds us . . . Braun, "Norwidowa część w 'całości Jana Pawel II," 416.

"His experiences from the . . . Królak, "Norwid and John Paul II," 181.

22 "Everything the Holy Father . . . Szulc, *Pope John Paul II*, 306.
23 "Towards the end of . . . Frossard, *"Be Not Afraid!"*, 15.
    "All I can say is . . . Pope John Paul II, *Gift and Mystery*, 34–35.
24 "Do you think you . . . Svidercoschi, *Stories of Karol*, 60.
    "What are you doing? . . . Pope John Paul II, *Rise, Let Us Be on Our Way*, 94.
    "He will study Polish . . . Pope John Paul II, *Gift and Mystery*, 5.
25 "One was beaten and . . . Weigel, *Witness to Hope*, 52.
    "became the largest monastery . . . Svidercoschi, *Stories of Karol*, 104; Weigel, *Witness to Hope*, 52.
    "The stench of Auschwitz . . . O'Brien, *The Hidden Pope*, 33.
26 "Lolek became a secret . . . O'Brien, *The Hidden Pope*, 216–17.
    "In spite of his . . . Królak, *1001 Things You Should Know About the Blessed John Paul II*, 18.
27 "Didn't you want to . . . Bernstein and Politi, *His Holiness*, 66.
    "Sometimes I would ask . . . Pope John Paul II, *Gift and Mystery*, 36.
28 "I have given permission . . . Bernstein and Politi, *His Holiness*, 70.
    "we have only a few . . . Bernstein and Politi, *His Holiness*, 70.
29 "The central heating had . . . Malinski, *Pope John Paul II*, 84–85.
    "hardly a symbolic way . . . O'Connor, *Universal Father*, 100.
30 By 1955, the number . . . Weigel, *The End and the Beginning*, 40.
    "The Germans will take . . . Paczkowski, *The Spring Will Be Ours*, 36.
    Birth control and abortion . . . Weigel, *Witness to Hope*, 97.
    "One day he did . . . Pope John Paul II, *Gift and Mystery*, 42–43.
32 "But snow will cling . . . O'Connor, *Universal Father*, 122.
    "Don't worry, Stanisław, they'll . . . Bernstein and Politi, *His Holiness*, 77.
33 "What! Did you convert . . . Svidercoschi, *Stories of Karol*, 128.
    "cutting man off from . . . Frossard, *"Be Not Afraid!"*, 97.
    "I did not destroy . . . Oder, *Why He Is a Saint*, 100.
    "Without this pope, it . . . Accattoli, *Man of the Millennium*, xi.
34 "It was the Providence . . . Oder, *Why He Is a Saint*, 102.
35 "translated first from Polish . . . Weigel, *Witness to Hope*, 174.
    "Everybody got a lot . . . Author's interview with Father Andrew Swietochowski, December 4, 2013.
36 "One thing struck me . . . Boniecki, *The Making of the Pope of the Millennium*, 151.
37 "So it was always . . . Braun, Inaugural Lecture.
    "We even had a . . . Braun, letter to author, December 14, 2013.
38 On one occasion as . . . Boniecki, *The Making of the Pope of the Millennium*, 479.

"The cardinal's shirt and . . . Braun, Inaugural Lecture.

"A campfire had always . . . Braun, letter to author, December 14, 2013.

"I have two responsibilities . . . Moody, *Pope John Paul II*, 48.

"Only the breviary did . . . Szulc, *Pope John Paul II*, 194.

39 "So I set off . . . Pope John Paul II, *Rise, Let Us Be on Our Way*, 8.

"That is a weakness which . . . Pope John Paul II, *Rise, Let Us Be on Our Way*, 9.

"Where do I sign . . . Svidercoschi, *Stories of Karol*, 144.

"When he did not . . . Boniecki, *The Making of the Pope of the Millennium*, 172.

40 Eight hours after his . . . Allegri, *John Paul II*, 136.

"Who will say Mass . . . Oder, *Why He Is a Saint*, 39.

"I'm waiting for Wojtyła . . . Weigel, *Witness to Hope*, 184.

41 "Wojtyła was the best . . . Szulc, *Pope John Paul II*, 245.

"an especially dangerous ideological . . . Oder, *Why He Is a Saint*, 61.

The government obsessed over . . . Weigel, *The End and the Beginning*, 102–3.

42 Although most of the . . . Bernstein and Politi, *His Holiness*, 321.

"The more deeply people . . . Szostak, *In the Footsteps of Pope John Paul II*, 110.

In fact, during the . . . Weigel, *The End and the Beginning*, 110.

"We don't want the . . . Weigel, *The End and the Beginning*, 160.

In The End and . . . Weigel, *The End and the Beginning*, 152–53.

43 "They were always there . . . Dziwisz, *A Life with Karol*, 43.

"came up with a . . . Dziwisz, *A Life with Karol*, 43.

Such maneuvers were necessary . . . Weigel, *Witness to Hope*, 216; Weigel, *The End and the Beginning*, 88–89.

44 "when he wrote to . . . Oder, *Why He Is a Saint*, 64.

"As a negotiator, he . . . Moody, *Pope John Paul II*, 62.

"I was aware that . . . Szulc, *Pope John Paul II*, 421.

"The career of every . . . Szostak, *In the Footsteps of Pope John Paul II*, 9.

"pay the penalty . . . Blazynski, *Pope John Paul II*, 161.

45 "impediments to transportation" . . . Boniecki, *The Making of the Pope of the Millennium*, 324–25.

46 When permission was granted . . . Boniecki, *The Making of the Pope of the Millennium*, 474–75.

However, Cardinal Wojtyła noted . . . Boniecki, *The Making of the Pope of the Millennium*, 678.

In the rain and . . . Flynn, *John Paul II*, 71.

48 **"Wojtyła made an excellent** . . . Królak, *1001 Things You Should Know About the Blessed John Paul II,* 44.

49 **"It is unbecoming for** . . . Blazynski, *Pope John Paul II,* 74.

"Oh yes, but in . . . Szostak, *In the Footsteps of Pope John Paul II,* 108.

Coworkers at the . . . Oder, *Why He Is a Saint,* 136.

50 **On one occasion, he** . . . Boniecki, *The Making of the Pope of the Millennium,* 83–84.

He passed it on . . . Svidercoschi, *Stories of Karol,* 124.

Within a week, it . . . Oder, *Why He Is a Saint,* 136.

His Polish housekeeper . . . Szostak, *In the Footsteps of Pope John Paul II,* 108.

"he refuses to wear . . . Oder, *Why He Is a Saint,* 140.

"Go into my bedroom . . . Oder, *Why He Is a Saint,* 140.

51 **"For a whole nursery** . . . Szostak, *In the Footsteps of Pope John Paul II,* 7–10.

52 **"He is not particularly.** . . Oder, *Why He Is a Saint,* 62.

A friend admitted that . . . O'Connor, *Universal Father,* 145.

When millions of copies . . . Weigel, *Witness to Hope,* 737.

"exalted mission which is . . . Williams, *The Mind of John Paul II,* 68.

53 **"Amid discord God strikes** . . . Szulc, *Pope John Paul II,* 44–45.

54 **"a waste of time** . . . Longford, *Pope John Paul II,* 75.

"I must say that . . . John Paul II, *The Story of My Life,* 84.

"If he wasn't praying . . . Pigozzi, *Pope John Paul II,* 177.

"One must arrange . . . Boniecki, *The Making of the Pope of the Millennium,* 113.

"Dedicate your time . . . Boniecki, *The Making of the Pope of the Millennium,* 741.

55 **"Every moment has to** . . . Bernstein and Politi, *His Holiness,* 51.

Wanda was instantly . . . Boniecki, *The Making of the Pope of the Millennium,* 211.

56 **"Angelino, keep those letters** . . . Allegri, *John Paul II,* 142–43.

"'How well he has . . . John Paul II, *The Story of My Life,* 66.

"My name is John . . . Magee, "Untold Stories of the Last Three Popes."

"Keep that . . . Magee, "Untold Stories of the Last Three Popes."

57 **"Another man better than** . . . Bernstein and Politi, *His Holiness,*152.

58 **He retreated to his** . . . Author's interview with Father Franciszek Florczyk, January 23, 2014.

Father Andrew Swietochowski, who . . . Author's interview with Father Andrew Swietochowski, December 4, 2013.

"One never knows . . . Oder, *Why He Is a Saint*, 70.

59 "When the number of . . . O'Connor, *Universal Father*, 191–92.
"I think that the . . . Frossard, *"Be Not Afraid!"*, 25.

60 Father Franciszek Florczyk, who . . . Author's interview with Father Franciszek Florczyk, January 23, 2014.
In a futile effort . . . Craig, *Man from a Far Country*, 17.

61 John Paul learned of . . . Weigel, *Witness to Hope*, 269.
"Amazing John Paul II . . . Craig, *Man from a Far Country*, 24.
"Be not afraid! Open . . . Pope John Paul II, Homily for the Inauguration of His Pontificate.

62 "It was there at . . . Author's interview with Cardinal Justin Rigali, January 14, 2014.

63 But his mind was . . . Author's interview with Monsignor Eduardo Chavez, August 19, 2011.
"Tell the Pope . . . Bernstein and Politi, *His Holiness*, 191.

64 "Christ cannot be kept . . . Pope John Paul II, Homily in Victory Square.

65 "call down from heaven . . . John Paul II, *The Story of My Life*, 77.
"someone said afterwards that . . . *Witness to Hope*, DVD.

66 "That was the turning . . . De Souza, "Moments—Private and Public —With the Pope."
"if I am not . . . Królak, *1001 Things You Should Know About the Blessed John Paul II*, 156.

67 "generous and tireless evangelizer . . . Pope John Paul II, *Gift and Mystery*, 91.
"he had travelled ten . . . Longford, *Pope John Paul II*, 130.

68 His longest trip was . . . Szulc, *Pope John Paul II*, 525.
"We can't wait for . . . Dziwisz, *A Life with Karol*, 97.
"What is the difference . . . Oder, *Why He Is a Saint*, 102.
"The more difficult the . . . Królak, *1001 Things You Should Know About the Blessed John Paul II*, 75.
"The more ready you . . . Pope John Paul II, Message for the XXXIII World Day of Prayer for Vocations.
"Italy two, Poland zero . . . Dziwisz, *A Life with Karol*, 111.

69 "Yes, I am convinced . . . *Pope John Paul II: Statesman of Faith*, DVD.
"There were a hundred . . . Widmer, "The Pope and the CEO: John Paul II's Leadership Lessons to a Young Swiss Guard."
"volcano of energy . . . Mokrzycki, *He Liked Tuesdays Best*, 46.
"Now we must decide . . . Weigel, *Witness to Hope*, 395.
Then during his brief . . . Wynn, *Keeper of the Keys*, 139.

70 In the first nine . . . Szulc, *Pope John Paul II*, 384.
John Paul averaged more . . . Accattoli, *Man of the Millennium*, 118; Weigel, *The End and the Beginning*, 434.

According to the postulator . . . Oder, *Why He Is a Saint*, 142.

He was such a . . . Szostak, *In the Footsteps of Pope John Paul II*, 212.

"On his holidays he . . . *Testimony: The Untold Story of Pope John Paul II.*

71 **Other times, he'd read** . . . Szulc, *Pope John Paul II*, 236.

"never stopped writing . . . Malinksi, *Pope John Paul II*, 42.

"the greatest intellect I . . . Longford, *Pope John Paul II*, 11.

"the division between physics . . . Boniecki, *The Making of the Pope of the Millennium*, 385.

72 **According to a special** . . . Pell, "The meaning of religious freedom and the future of human rights."

"for the weaknesses of . . . Pope John Paul II, *Tertio Millennio Adveniente*, 35.

"preparing for the Year . . . Pope John Paul II, *Tertio Millennio Adveniente*, 23.

73 **"a matter of choice** . . . Craig, *Man from a Far Country*, 181.

74 **"Oh, no** . . . O'Brien, *The Hidden Pope*, 292.

"He sort of reminded . . . Oram, *The People's Pope*, 137.

"This is an aspect . . . Cantalamessa, Zenit.org, Vatican City, July 4, 2004.

75 **"But by speaking slowly** . . . Cantalamessa, Zenit.org, Vatican City, July 4, 2004.

"is a man who . . . Szulc, *Pope John Paul II*, 424.

"He is such a . . . Frossard, *Portrait of John Paul II*, 32.

"To him the value . . . Oram, *The People's Pope*, 149.

76 **"The cardinal arrived for** . . . Oram, *The People's Pope*, 121.

"he spoke to me . . . Dziwisz, *A Life with Karol*, 63.

"Talking to him gave . . . O'Brien, *The Hidden Pope*, 78.

"Despite that killing schedule . . . Braun, *Inaugural Lecture*.

"had this incredible, mysterious . . . Braun, letter to author, December 14, 2013.

"a kind of geography . . . Pope John Paul II, *Crossing the Threshold of Hope*, 23.

77 **"Central Asia** . . . Author's interview with Cardinal Theodore McCarrick, December 16, 2013.

One year during Advent . . . Weigel, *Witness to Hope*, 273.

"You're new! What's your . . . Widmer, *The Pope & the CEO*, 74–75.

78 **John Paul had a** . . . Szulc, *Pope John Paul II*, 433.

"The Pope, the Pope! . . . Dziwisz, *A Life with Karol*, 83.

79 **"Are you the Pope** . . . Zani, *The Secret Life of John Paul II*, 98.

Early in his pontificate . . . O'Connor, *Universal Father*, 206.

"One bishop, who had . . . Weigel, *Witness to Hope*, 567.

"Holy Father, isn't it . . . Author's interview with Cardinal Theodore McCarrick, December 16, 2013.

80 **Some within the Vatican** . . . Weigel, *Witness to Hope*, 277.
"**The nuns were not** . . . Mokrzycki, *He Liked Tuesdays Best*, 44.
"**every man who seeks** . . . Wojtyła, *The Way to Christ*, 58.

83 "**I always explain [to]** . . . Królak, *1001 Things You Should Know About the Blessed John Paul II*, 187.

84 "**If you think of** . . . Frossard, *"Be Not Afraid!"*, 111.
"**I am an atheist** . . . Frossard, *"Be Not Afraid!"*, 45–46.

85 "**whether they have a** . . . Frossard, *Portrait of John Paul II*, 39.
He asserted that ministry . . . Oder, *Why He Is a Saint*, 43.
During his first parish . . . Bernstein and Politi, *His Holiness*, 77.
"**never happier than when** . . . Craig, *Man from a Far Country*, 80.

86 "**the eternal teenager** . . . Blazynski, *Pope John Paul II*, 62.
"**He lived and breathed** . . . Królak, *1001 Things You Should Know About the Blessed John Paul II*, 29–30.
Bishop Andrew Wypych assisted . . . Author's interview with Bishop Andrew Wypych, January 24, 2014.
Even after becoming the . . . Author's interview with Father Franciszek Florczyk, January 23, 2014.

87 "**I believe in youth** . . . Pope John Paul II, Homily, Mass for the Youth of Ireland.
"**young people are** . . . Pope John Paul II, *Crossing the Threshold of Hope*, 123.
"**You are the hope** . . . Pope John Paul II, *Crossing the Threshold of Hope*, 125.
"**the young are the** . . . John Paul II, *The Story of My Life*, 85.
"**the young people** . . . Craig, *Man from a Far Country*, 166.

88 "**If someone is interested** . . . Mokrzycki, *He Liked Tuesdays Best*, 144.
"**Take us with you** . . . Mokrzycki, *He Liked Tuesdays Best*, 142.
"**Don't you miss the** . . . Wynn, *Keeper of the Keys*, 72.
"**Then stay with us!** . . . Weigel, *Witness to Hope*, 317.

89 "**Young people of Ireland** . . . Pope John Paul II, Homily, Mass for the Youth of Ireland.
"**The applause, according to** . . . Author's interview with Cardinal Justin Rigali, January 14, 2014.

90 "**The turbulence created by** . . . Weigel, *Witness to Hope*, 680.
"**Young people were pointing** . . . Laugesen, "Looking at the Good Fruit of World Youth Day Denver '93."
"**Remember: Christ is calling** . . . Pope John Paul II, Address to the Young People at the Kiel Center.

91 "**still lives on in** . . . Weigel, *Witness to Hope*, 684.

"**Don't worry** . . . Zuchniewicz, *Miracles of John Paul II*, 165.

"**His appearances generate an** . . . Gray, *Time*, December 26, 1994.

92 "**As a young priest** . . . Pope John Paul II, *Crossing the Threshold of Hope*, 123–24.

93 "**Young people of every** . . . Pope John Paul II, Message to the Youth of the World on the Occasion of the XV World Youth Day.

"**Dear young people, do** . . . Pope John Paul II, Message to the Youth of the World on the Occasion of the XVII World Youth Day.

94 "**happy and demanding** . . . Mokrzycki, *He Liked Tuesdays Best*, 152.

"**Without the Gospel, man** . . . Pope John Paul II, *Memory and Identity*, 114.

"**approaching that stage in** . . . Pope John Paul II, Address to High School Students.

"**In times of darkness** . . . Pope John Paul II, Address to the Youth of Quebec at Olympic Stadium.

95 **One of John Paul's** . . . Frossard, *"Be Not Afraid!"*, 216.

"**Today, many priests try** . . . Weigel, *Witness to Hope*, 105.

"**Modern man listens more** . . . Pope Paul VI, Address to the Members of the Consilium de Laicis, AAS 66 (1974), 568.

"**In him the Gospel, the** . . . Frossard, *"Be Not Afraid!"*, 90.

96 "**For every person, an** . . . Mokrzycki, *He Liked Tuesdays Best*, 100.

"**so that God does** . . . Boniecki, *The Making of the Pope of the Millennium*, 169.

"**In his transcendence man** . . . Frossard, *"Be Not Afraid!"*, 73.

"*We are not the* . . . Pope John Paul II, Homily for the XVII World Youth Day.

"**And in the end** . . . Wojtya, *The Collected Plays and Writings on Theater*, 368.

97 "**It is no secret that** . . . Pope John Paul II, Address to the Students of the University of Santo Tomas.

"**fully reveals man to** . . . Pope John Paul II, *Redemptor Hominis*, 10.

"**It is not enough** . . . Weigel, *Witness to Hope*, 101.

But instead of . . . Pope John Paul II, Meeting with the Youth at Nakivubo Stadium.

98 "*Essential to preparing for* . . . Pope John Paul II, Meeting with the Youth at Nakivubo Stadium.

"**Genuine love** . . . Pope John Paul II, Message to Young People, Camagüey, Cuba.

"**These demands** . . . Pope John Paul II, *Dilecti Amici*, 10.

99 "**loveless object of use** . . . Karol Wojtyła, *Person and Community*, 290.

"*Happiness is achieved through* . . . Pope John Paul II, Homily, Camagüey, Cuba.

"Confronted with such demands . . . Frossard, *Be Not Afraid!"*, 112.
"The more you cling to . . . Pope John Paul II, Message to the Youth of the World on the Occasion of the XII World Youth Day.

100 "[Freedom] cannot simply be . . . Pope John Paul II, *Memory and Identity*, 74.
"Freedom cannot be understood . . . Pope John Paul II, *Letter to Families*, 14.
"Many would regard liberty . . . Frossard, *Be Not Afraid!"*, 98.
"Such a use of freedom . . . Frossard, *Be Not Afraid!"*, 113.

101 "their life *has meaning* . . . Pope John Paul II, *Crossing the Threshold of Hope*, 121.
When he became the . . . Oder, *Why He Is a Saint*, 165.

102 "to follow Christ on . . . Pope John Paul II, Homily for the XVII World Youth Day.
"The youth that I . . . John Paul II, *The Story of My Life*, 88.

103 "*As a young priest, I* . . . Pope John Paul II, *Crossing the Threshold of Hope*, 123.
In fact, according to . . . Bernstein and Politi, *His Holiness*, 83.
"we discussed [it] with . . . Szulc, *Pope John Paul II*, 209.

104 "One day, someone finally . . . Lattin, sfgate.com.
"confided the secrets of . . . John Paul II, *The Story of My Life*, 40.

105 "Sexual drive is a gift . . . Boniecki, *The Making of the Pope of the Millennium*, 140.
"The essential reason for . . . Wojtyła, *Love and Responsibility*, Ignatius Press, 134.

106 "When a man and . . . Burke, *An Invitation to Joy*, 49.
"only a chaste woman . . . Wojtyła, *Love and Responsibility*, Pauline Books and Media,156.

107 "it is a result of . . . Wojtyła, *Love and Responsibility*, Pauline Books and Media, 258
"Hence, there is a . . . Wojtyła, *Love and Responsibility*, Pauline Books and Media, 258.

108 "We must also constantly . . . D'Arcy, "Bishop D'Arcy offers reflection to presbyterate."
"What struck me then . . . D'Arcy, "Bishop D'Arcy offers reflection to presbyterate."

109 "he treated women with . . . Bernstein and Politi, *His Holiness*,116.
"Surely, this is the . . . Królak, *1001 Things You Should Know About the Blessed John Paul II*, 231.

110 "There must have been . . . Karol Wojtyła, *The Way to Christ*, 34, 35.
"Men must be taught . . . Karol Wojtyła, *The Way to Christ*, 38.

111 "Would you like to . . . Bernstein and Politi, *His Holiness*, 80.

"**each man must look** . . . Pope John Paul II, *Mulieris Dignitatem*, 14.

"*contemporary feminism* **finds its** . . . Pope John Paul II, *Crossing the Threshold of Hope*, 217.

"**a stew of nudes** . . . Montalbano. *Los Angeles Times*, April 9, 1994.

"**make it suitable** . . . Nottingham Walsh, *National Geographic*, May 1994, 118.

112 "*the sanctuary of the theology* . . . Pope John Paul II, Homily, April 8, 1994.

"**And while he is** . . . Frossard, *Portrait of John Paul II*, 79.

113 "**in a depth, simplicity** . . . Pope John Paul II, General audience of July 4, 1984.

"**the perspective of the** . . . Pope John Paul II, General audience of December 3, 1980.

"*God has a plan* . . . Pope John Paul II, Meeting with the Young People of New Orleans.

115 "**Only the nakedness that** . . . Pope John Paul II, General audience of February 20, 1980.

"**has the power to** . . . Pope John Paul II, General audience of July 23, 1980.

116 "**cannot fully find himself** . . . *Gaudium et Spes*, 24

117 "**opens the way toward** . . . Pope John Paul II, General audience of April 1, 1981.

"**creates precisely the** . . . Pope John Paul II, General audience of January 2, 1980.

"**Pope John Paul tells** . . . Wynn, *Keeper of the Keys*, 228.

"**all the peace of** . . . Pope John Paul II, General audience of January 2, 1980.

"**we acquire the virtue** . . . Pope John Paul II, *Memory and Identity*, 29.

118 "**we feel less and** . . . Pope John Paul II, *Memory and Identity*, 29.

119 "**We can find God** . . . Pope John Paul II, *Memory and Identity*, 30.

"**A certain man, on** . . . Saint John Climacus, *The Ladder of Divine Ascent*, 62.

120 "**theological time bomb** . . . Weigel, *Witness to Hope*, 343.

"**His harsh prohibitions, especially** . . . Bernstein and Politi, *His Holiness*, 404.

"**may chase even more** . . . Szulc, *Pope John Paul II*, 512.

"**violently opposed** . . . Szulc, *Pope John Paul II*, 537.

121 "**This is not my** . . . Wynn, *Keeper of the Keys*, 259.

"**The Pope is not** . . . O'Connor, *Universal Father*, 256.

"**There is nothing conservative** . . . Królak, *1001 Things You Should Know About the Blessed John Paul II*, 31.

"20 years into the . . . Culture of Life Foundation, *Culture & Cosmos*, January 13, 2004.

122   **"The greater the percentage** . . . Abboud, *British Medical Journal*, July 30, 2005, 294.

"Indeed, a study of . . . Ryder, *British Medical Journal*, 307, September 18, 1993, 723.

123   **"God who is Father** . . . Wojtyła, *The Way to Christ*, 55–56.

"from a profound analysis . . . "Doubts About Condoms," Zenit.org, June 26, 2004.

"All truth passes through . . . Commonly attributed to Arthur Schopenhauer.

124   **"Christ is found particularly** . . . Wojtyła, *The Way to Christ*, 55.

"Suppose we heard an . . . Chesterton, *Orthodoxy*, 86–87.

126   **keeping virtually the same** . . . Bernstein and Politi, *His Holiness*,125.

According to his press . . . Weigel, *Witness to Hope*, 807.

"in my consciousness, even . . . Królak, *1001 Things You Should Know About the Blessed John Paul II*, 129.

"There was a time . . . Frossard, *"Be Not Afraid!"*, 34.

127   **"he looked like he** . . . Dziwisz, *A Life with Karol*, 85.

"it seemed as if . . . Oder, *Why He Is a Saint*, 149.

"You could see that . . . Author's interview with Bishop Andrew Wypych, January 24, 2014.

"He lingered lovingly over . . . O'Brien, *The Hidden Pope*, 396.

128   **"For me, the Mass** . . . Królak, *1001 Things You Should Know About the Blessed John Paul II*, 26.

"nothing means more to . . . Oder, *Why He Is a Saint*, 31.

"This is why it . . . *Ad Limina* Address to the Bishops of the Church in Washington, Oregon, Montana, Idaho, and Alaska.

"very important, *very* important . . . Weigel, *The End and the Beginning*, 405.

"If the bishop doesn't . . . Blazynski, *Pope John Paul II*, 72.

129   **"the shepherd should walk** . . . Królak, *1001 Things You Should Know About the Blessed John Paul II*, 46.

One of his biographers . . . Szulc, *Pope John Paul II*, 532.

"he was immersed in . . . Mokrzycki, *He Liked Tuesdays Best*, 52.

"peppered with prayers, with . . . Dziwisz, *A Life with Karol*, 86.

130   **"No sooner does he pause** . . . Bernstein and Politi, *His Holiness*, 533.

"The Holy Father looked . . . Pigozzi, *Pope John Paul II*, 199.

"As soon as I meet . . . Pope John Paul II, *Rise, Let Us Be on Our Way*, 66.

"He prayed for everyone . . . Mokrzycki, *He Liked Tuesdays Best*, 52.

"the Holy Father wants . . . Zani, *The Secret Life of John Paul II*, 57.

131   **"It was then that** . . . Zani, *The Secret Life of John Paul II*, 57–59.

"It was my hope . . . Author's interview with Cardinal Theodore McCarrick, December 16, 2013.

132 "The Pope will now . . . Author's interview with Cardinal Justin Rigali, January 14, 2014.

"shaken to the core . . . Zani, *The Secret Life of John Paul II*, 99.

133 "When he prayed, it . . . Maciej Zięba, as quoted in *Newsweek*, Special Report, April, 11, 2005.

"In order to understand . . . Pope John Paul II, *Crossing the Threshold of Hope*, 16–17.

134 "You don't pray to . . . Frossard, *Portrait of John Paul II*, 74.

"Holy Spirit, I ask . . . Mokrzycki, *He Liked Tuesdays Best*, 57.

"the greatest things on . . . de Montfort, *God Alone*, 483.

135 "You would have to . . . Pope John Paul II, *Crossing the Threshold of Hope*, 19.

"not merely to speak . . . Oder, *Why He Is a Saint*, 35.

"we have two people . . . Wojtyła, *The Way to Christ*, 120.

"Man achieves the *fullness* . . . Pope John Paul II, *Crossing the Threshold of Hope*, 18.

"rapt in prayer . . . Oder, *Why He Is a Saint*, 152–53.

136 "I have always been . . . Pope John Paul II, *Rise, Let Us Be on Our Way*, 146–47.

"I remember that in . . . Królak, *1001 Things You Should Know About the Blessed John Paul II*, 135.

"love is ignited within . . . Boniecki, *The Making of the Pope of the Millennium*, 744.

137 "all activities should be . . . Frossard, *"Be Not Afraid!"*, 33.

"all of his major . . . Weigel, *Witness to Hope*, 276.

"In the absence of . . . Bernstein and Politi, *His Holiness*, 79.

"Help us, Jesus, to . . . Pope John Paul II, Message to the Young People of Rome and Lazio.

138 In 1995, Father Michael . . . Author's interview with Father Michael White, December 5, 2013.

139 "rekindle this Eucharistic . . . Pope John Paul II, *Ecclesia de Eucharistia*, 6.

139 "How many times in . . . Homily, Mass for the Occasion of the Opening of the 10th National Eucharistic Congress.

140 "an important daily practice . . . Pope John Paul II, *Ecclesia de Eucharistia*, 10.

"The Eucharist is the . . . Pope John Paul II, *L'Osservatore Romano*, 41, October 8, 1997, 7.

141 "And is not the . . . Pope John Paul II, *Ecclesia de Eucharistia*, 55.

"Were we to disregard . . . Pope John Paul II, *Ecclesia de Eucharistia*, 60.

142 **"The image of 'shepherd'**. . . Pope John Paul II, Homily, St. Thomas Aquinas Parish.

"I also bless the . . . Oder, *Why He Is a Saint*, 88.

143 **"I will without doubt** . . . Szulc, *Pope John Paul II*, 388.

"I have killed the . . . Moody, *Pope John Paul II*, 113.

144 **"May Our Lady protect** . . . Frossard, *"Be Not Afraid!"*, 223.

Thankfully, a surgical room . . . Pigozzi, *Pope John Paul II*, 194.

"I saw blood everywhere . . . Frossard, *"Be Not Afraid!"*, 236.

145 **"What did the Sanhedrin** . . . Frossard, *"Be Not Afraid!"*, 246.

146 **"As soon as I regained** . . . John Paul II, Address at the Chapel of the Apparitions.

"Will you offer yourselves . . . "Fatima: A Grace for Mankind," ewtn.com.

148 **"Consecrating the world to** . . . Pope John Paul II, Homily, Fatima, May 13, 1982.

"The Holy Father did . . . Allegri, *John Paul II*, 193.

"Hence any further discussion . . . Tarcisio Bertone, "The Message of Fatima."

150 **"The vision of Fatima** . . . Cardinal Sodano, Address Regarding the "Third Part" of the Secret of Fatima at the Conclusion of the Solemn Mass of John Paul II.

151 **"made with two slender** . . . Zani, *The Secret Life of John Paul II*, 69.

"That here 'a mother's . . . Cardinal Ratzinger, Theological Commentary.

"If the word did . . . Wojtyła, *Collected Poems*, 182.

"He often repeated that . . . *Testimony: The Untold Story of Pope John Paul II*.

"Perhaps there was a . . . Pope John Paul II, *Memory and Identity*, 164.

152 **"And now Act Two** . . . O'Connor, *Universal Father*, 255.

"To everyone's surprise, it . . . Zani, *The Secret Life of John Paul II*, 158.

153 **"I think it was** . . . Pope John Paul II, *Memory and Identity*, 166.

154 **"I know I was** . . . Dziwisz, *A Life with Karol*, 137.

"goddess of Fatima . . . Dziwisz, *A Life with Karol*, 138.

John Paul allayed his . . . Weigel, *The End and the Beginning*, 411.

Then he suggested that . . . Follain, "Gunman Mehmet Ali Agca who shot Pope John Paul II seeks ´£3m in book deals."

He even claimed that . . . Weigel, *Witness to Hope*, 883.

155 **"It doesn't interest me** . . . Allegri, *John Paul II*, 174–75.

156 **"It was pointing straight** . . . Malinski, *Pope John Paul II*, 274–75.

"If missionaries, bishops, and . . . Dziwisz, *A Life with Karol*, 102.

"the shepherd always has . . . Oder, *Why He Is a Saint*, 90.

"If any in my . . . Oder, *Why He Is a Saint*, 109.

In Pakistan, before . . . Andrew and Mitrokhin, *The World Was Going Our Way*, 358.

Other plots were also . . . Pigozzi, *Pope John Paul II*, 255; Weigel, *The End and the Beginning*, 128–29.

157 The apartment was a . . . Struck, *Washington Post Foreign Service*, September 23, 2001.

A voicemail from a . . . McDermott, *Los Angeles Times*, September 1, 2002.

158 "Extraordinarily ambitious, very . . . Jenkins, CNN, May 13, 1996.

At the time of . . . Brzezinski, *Toronto Star*, January 2, 2002.

His uncle, Khalid Shaik . . . Gomez, Associated Press, June 25, 2002; Jenkins, CNN, September 5, 1996; McDermott, *Los Angeles Times*, June 24, 2002.

"He was nicknamed . . . Mintz, *Washington Post*, August 22, 1998.

159 Two years later, as . . . Zuchniewicz, *Miracles of John Paul II*, 157; Mintz, *Washington Post*, August 22, 1998.

"Are there people waiting . . . O'Connor, *Universal Father*, 339.

when the Holy Father . . . "3 Plots Against John Paul II′·s Life Foiled Since 1995," Zenit.org, Rome, October 11, 2001.

"My Guardian Angel knows . . . Pope John Paul II, *Rise, Let Us Be on Our Way*, 26.

"Love is stronger than . . . Szostak, *In the Footsteps of Pope John Paul II*, 163.

"This powerful Queen of . . . de Montfort, *God Alone*, 357.

160 John Paul not only . . . "Pope Meets Mother of Man Who Attempted to Assassinate Him," Associated Press, February 20, 1987.

"Ah, Mrs. Your husband . . . Flynn, *John Paul II*, 26.

161 "Mothers are given much . . . Flynn, *John Paul II*, 132.

162 "Beirut was under siege . . . *Mother Teresa*, Video.

John Paul's secretary noted . . . Dziwisz, *A Life with Karol*, 175.

As a young teenager . . . Bernstein and Politi, *His Holiness*, 43.

163 "joyful and more radiant . . . Mokrzycki, *He Liked Tuesdays Best*, 85.

"He was praying all . . . Królak, *1001 Things You Should Know About the Blessed John Paul II*, 225.

"As I watched him . . . Widmer, *The Pope & the CEO*, 34.

164 "It's our daily meeting . . . Królak, *1001 Things You Should Know About the Blessed John Paul II*, 134.

When asked if the . . . Magee, "Untold Stories of the Last Three Popes."

"We know. He does . . . Author's interview with Monsignor George Tracy.

165 **"I remember carrying it** . . . Frossard, *"Be Not Afraid!"*, 125.
"I was already convinced . . . Pope John Paul II, *Gift and Mystery*, 28.
"One can even say . . . Frossard, *"Be Not Afraid!"*, 125.
"In a wholly singular . . . *Lumen Gentium*, 61.
if Saint Paul could . . . 1 Cor. 4:15; Gal. 4:19.
166 **"crucified spiritually with her** . . . Pope John Paul II, Homily, Sanctuary of Alborada.
"a gift which Christ . . . Pope John Paul II, *Redemptoris Mater*, 45.
167 **"she gives herself** . . . de Montfort, *God Alone*, 334.
"it is better to . . . de Montfort, *God Alone*, 367–68.
168 **"love Jesus with the** . . . Manteau-Bonamy, *Immaculate Conception and the Holy Spirit*, xxxii.
"Implore Mary to lend . . . de Montfort, *God Alone*, 375.
"doing everything through Mary . . . de Montfort, *God Alone*, 371.
"the greatest possible influx . . . Manteau-Bonamy, *Immaculate Conception and the Holy Spirit*, 108.
169 **"When the Holy Spirit** . . . de Montfort, *God Alone*, 299.
"will act through them . . . Manteau-Bonamy, *Immaculate Conception and the Holy Spirit*, 117.
"Is it not reasonable . . . de Montfort, *God Alone*, 313.
"For it must be recognized . . . Pope John Paul II, *Redemptoris Mater*, 39.
"this 'perfect devotion' is . . . Frossard, *"Be Not Afraid!"*, 126.
170 **"I found the answer** . . . "John Paul II Fondly Recalls Louis de Montfort's Marian Doctrine in a Message on 160th Anniversary of 'True Devotion.'"
"True knowledge of the . . . Manteau-Bonamy, *Immaculate Conception and the Holy Spirit*, 124.
"Karol, Mary shares her . . . Królak, *1001 Things You Should Know About the Blessed John Paul II*, 47.
171 **"The victory, if it** . . . Pope John Paul II, *Crossing the Threshold of Hope*, 220–21.
172 **"I said to the** . . . Oder, *Why He Is a Saint*, 78.
173 **"I have become a** . . . Oder, *Why He Is a Saint*, 79.
"I am lying here . . . Malinski, *Pope John Paul II*, 92.
"And I thought, 'she . . . Królak, *1001 Things You Should Know About the Blessed John Paul II*, 118; Oder, *Why He Is a Saint*, 80–81.
174 **"I broke my leg** . . . Author's interview with Father Stan Fortuna, December 23, 2013.
"In the cross lies . . . Karol Wojtyła, *Sign of Contradiction*, 89.
176 **"the weaknesses of all** . . . Pope John Paul II, *Salvifici Doloris*, 23, 24, 26.

"fully reveals man to . . . Pope Paul VI, *Gaudium et Spes*, 22.
"Christ goes towards His . . . Pope John Paul II, *Salvifici Doloris*, 16.
"It is suffering, more . . . Pope John Paul II, *Salvifici Doloris*, 27.
177 **"To meet with suffering** . . . Boniecki, *The Making of the Pope of the Millennium*, 304.
"You can do very . . . Boniecki, *The Making of the Pope of the Millennium*, 468.
"In this double aspect . . . Pope John Paul II, *Salvifici Doloris*, 30.
"The discovery of the . . . Pope John Paul II, *Salvifici Doloris*, 27.
"It is this suffering . . . Pope John Paul II, *Memory and Identity*, 167–68.
178 **"It is significant that** . . . Królak, *1001 Things You Should Know About the Blessed John Paul II*, 169.
"Not with the Cross . . . Pope John Paul II, *Crossing the Threshold of Hope*, 224.
"Although I am young . . . Boniecki, *The Making of the Pope of the Millennium*, 234.
"Prayer joined to sacrifice . . . Pope John Paul II, General audience, January 12, 1994.
"is in great need . . . Insegnamenti di Giovanni Paolo II, vol. I (1978), Vatican City: Libreria Editrice Vaticana, 1979, 19, as quoted in Dziwisz, *Let Me Go to the Father's House*, 11.
"very powerful: powerful just . . . *L'Osservatore Romano*, October 19, 1978, as quoted in Dziwisz, *Let Me Go to the Father's House*, 12.
"Dear brothers and . . . Pope John Paul II, Message for the IV World Day of the Sick.
179 **"there is something very** . . . Pope John Paul II, Address to the Sick, Knock.
"and the results were . . . Pope John Paul II, *Rise, Let Us Be on Our Way*, 75–76.
180 **"I am entrusting the Church** . . . Frossard, *Portrait of John Paul II*, 68.
"wherever you may be . . . Williams, *The Mind of John Paul II*, 296.
"Bereft of all strength . . . Frossard, *"Be Not Afraid!"*, 26.
"always gives us the . . . Pope John Paul II, *Letter to the Elderly*.
181 **"Physical condition or advancing** . . . Pope John Paul's message on his 83rd birthday, May 18, 2003.
"Death opens to souls . . . Angelus message, November 1, 1994.
182 **"I noticed that his** . . . Boniecki, *The Making of the Pope of the Millennium*, 355.
"I remember how the . . . Królak, *1001 Things You Should Know About the Blessed John Paul II*, 232.
"You are not God's . . . *Great Souls: Pope John Paul II*, DVD.

"he walked into the . . . Bernstein and Politi, *His Holiness*, 410.

"If I could, I . . . Dziwisz, *A Life with Karol*, 173.

183 For the celebration of . . . Szostak, *In the Footsteps of Pope John Paul II*, 219–20.

In the summer of . . . Pigozzi, *Pope John Paul II*, 81.

Because he had nothing . . . Oder, *Why He Is a Saint*, 142.

"I did not come . . . Mokrzycki, *He Liked Tuesdays Best*, 122.

"Much bills? Very expensive? . . . Flynn, *John Paul II*, 158.

His first action after . . . Blazynski, *Pope John Paul II*, 167.

"with those who are . . . Oder, *Why He Is a Saint*, 106.

184 "First you bless me . . . Szostak, *In the Footsteps of Pope John Paul II*, 170.

"The greater the sinner . . . Faustina, *Diary*, no. 723.

185 "Forgiveness demonstrates the . . . Pope John Paul II, *Dives in Misericordia*, 14.

"Mercy is love when . . . Gaitley, "The Message of Divine Mercy."

"having a pain in . . . Stackpole, "What Does 'Divine Mercy' Actually Mean?," www.thedivinemercy.org.

186 "As a father, he . . . "Cardinal Marchisano Says Pope Healed Him," Zenit.org, Vatican City, April 10, 2005.

"hugged him like one . . . Zuchniewicz, *Miracles of John Paul II*, 20.

"In May 1990 . . . Zuchniewicz, *Miracles of John Paul II*, 50–56.

187 After suffering three miscarriages . . . Zuchniewicz, *Miracles of John Paul II*, 17.

"I can only say . . . Zuchniewicz, *Miracles of John Paul II*, 21.

"avalanche of miracles . . . Zuchniewicz, *Miracles of John Paul II*, 15.

188 "John Paul II has . . . Connor, Catholic News Service, May 4, 2012.

"These miracles demonstrate . . . Pope John Paul II, General audience, January 13, 1988.

"Conversion to God is . . . Pope John Paul II, *Dives in Misericordia*, 13.

189 "Time meant nothing to . . . Bernstein and Politi, *His Holiness*, 78.

"sin is always a . . . Boniecki, *The Making of the Pope of the Millennium*, 763.

"freely become a prisoner . . . Królak, *1001 Things You Should Know About the Blessed John Paul II*, 26.

"It is in the confessional . . . Pope John Paul II, *Gift and Mystery*, 86.

"you are freed . . . Pope John Paul II, Address to the Young People at the Kiel Center.

190 "Will you hear my . . . Blazynski, *Pope John Paul II*, 161.

"I'm a beggar . . . Hahn, "The Healing Power of Confession."

"Do you see the . . . Oder, *Why He Is a Saint*, 32.

"No human sin can . . . Pope John Paul II, *Veritatis Splendor*, 118.

Although not as miraculous . . . "John Paul II Helps Possessed Woman in Vatican," Zenit.org, Vatican City, September 10, 2000.

191 **"Everyone ran away, but** . . . *Testimony: The Untold Story of Pope John Paul II.*

"because he pulled so . . . "Rome's Exorcist Finding Bl. John Paul II Effective Against Satan," Catholic News Agency, May 17, 2011.

"the most faithful servants . . . de Montfort, *God Alone*, 337.

192 **"Your Holiness, can I** . . . Oder, *Why He Is a Saint*, 172.

"I ask myself what . . . Oder, *Why He Is a Saint*, 171.

"I accept this trial . . . John Paul II, *The Story of My Life*, 170.

"The Church needs suffering . . . Dziwisz, *Let Me Go to the Father's House*, 28.

193 **"future of humanity passes** . . . Pope John Paul II, *Familiaris Consortio*, 86.

"welcome opportunity to knock . . . Pope John Paul II, *Letter to Families*, 1.

"The only leader I . . . O'Connor, *Universal Father*, 338.

"Maybe this was needed . . . Accattoli, *Man of the Millennium*, 217.

194 **"Today I would like** . . . Angelus message, May 29, 1994.

"In the apostolate, the . . . d'Elbée, *I Believe in Love*, 195, 203–04.

"In no case should . . . International Conference on Population and Development, Programme of Action, para 8.25.

195 **"I don't know whether** . . . Oder, *Why He Is a Saint*, 114.

"thorns and crosses that . . . John Paul II, *The Story of My Life*, 74–75.

196 **"They will have the** . . . de Montfort, *God Alone*, 307.

"worried about Your Holiness . . . Oder, *Why He Is a Saint*, 1.

"Sono caduto ma non . . . Weigel, *Witness to Hope*, 695; Szulc, *Pope John Paul II*, 457.

197 **"I'm in good shape** . . . Noonan, *John Paul the Great*, 10.

"The Church is governed . . . Pigozzi, *Pope John Paul II*, 242.

"My Dear Eminence . . . Oder, *Why He Is a Saint*, 125.

"Everyone else has a . . . Pigozzi, *Pope John Paul II*, 237.

"Why, what's the matter . . . Weigel, *The End and the Beginning*, 374.

198 **"We shall have all** . . . Accattoli, *Man of the Millennium*, 118.

"He survives an assassination . . . Weigel, *Witness to Hope*, 3.

199 **"I am here with** . . . Pope John Paul II, Prayer at the Grotto of Massabielle.

"The Pope continues to . . . Pigozzi, *Pope John Paul II*, 110.

200 **"I have written many** . . . Oder, *Why He Is a Saint*, 171–72.

"Your Holiness, it will . . . Dziwisz, *A Life with Karol*, 254.

"What have they done . . . Dziwisz, *A Life with Karol*, 254.

201 **"Maybe it would be** . . . Zuchniewicz, *Miracles of John Paul II*, 11.

202 **"Let me go to** . . . Dziwisz, *Let Me Go to the Father's House*, 37.
John Paul then began . . . Mokrzycki, *He Liked Tuesdays Best*, 177.
"I have looked for . . . Walsh, Sister Mary Ann, *Pope John Paul II to Benedict XVI*, 4.
Then, at 9:37 . . . Dziwisz, *A Life with Karol*, 258.

203 **"Now there is a** . . . Dziwisz, *Let Me Go to the Father's House*, 87–88.
Monsignor Andrew Baker remarked . . . Author's interview with Monsignor Andrew R. Baker, November 20, 2013.

204 **As the winds whipped** . . . Oder, *Why He Is a Saint*, 131.
"None of us can . . . Cardinal Ratzinger, Homily for the Funeral Mass of the Roman Pontiff, John Paul II.
"Just when night engulfs . . . Królak, *1001 Things You Should Know About the Blessed John Paul II*, 142.
"victory of God in . . . Boniecki, *The Making of the Pope of the Millennium*, 558.

206 **"I want to describe** . . . Wojtyła, *Collected Poems*, 169–73.

208 **"you have departed, but** . . . Wojtyła, *Collected Poems*, 165.

209 **"Let us go forth** . . . Pope John Paul II, *Rise, Let Us Be on Our Way*, 216.

Learn more about Marian Consecration!

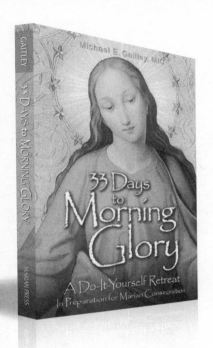

33 DAYS TO MORNING GLORY

FR. MICHAEL GAITLEY, M.I.C.

Fr. Gaitley masterfully summarizes the teaching of St. Louis de Montfort, St. Maximilian Kolbe, Blessed Teresa of Calcutta, and St. John Paul II, making it easy to grasp and simple enough to put into practice. He weaves their thoughts into a user friendly, do-it-yourself retreat that will bless even the busiest of people. If you've been thinking about entrusting yourself to Mary for the first time, or if you're simply looking to deepen and renew your devotion to her, *33 Days to Morning Glory* is the right book to read and the perfect retreat to make.

"The best hands-on book for Marian Consecration available today! It is excellent for anyone who does not have a lot of time, yet still desires to grow spiritually. Whatever the age of the reader, this retreat is a great place to grow closer to Jesus through his devoted mother Mary."

~Scott Foley

MARIAN CONSECRATION...
Now available as a group retreat!

Parish-based • Easy to implement • Short in length • Solidly Catholic
Affordable • Life-changing • Parish-transforming

How it works...

1. Gather a group.
Better yet, gather several groups of six to twelve people who want to consecrate themselves to Jesus through Mary.

2. Find a place to meet.
Ideally, this would be at a parish with the permission of the pastor, but your group can also meet at someone's home.

3. Read, Ponder, Meet *(RPM)*

Read...
Read the daily meditation in the retreat book, *33 Days to Morning Glory.*

Ponder...
Ponder the daily meditation with the help of the *Retreat Companion.*

Meet...
Meet with your group for weekly prayer, discussion, and to watch the accompanying talks on DVD.

Parish-based Programs from the
Marian Fathers of the Immaculate Conception

To learn more about how to organize and run a retreat and to order retreat materials, please call us or visit our website
(866) 767-3155 • LighthouseCatholicMedia.org

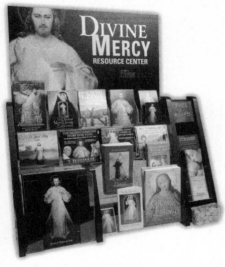
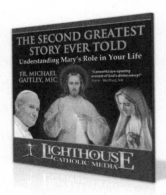